Tragedy in Paradise

Tragedy in Paradise

A COUNTRY DOCTOR
AT WAR IN LAOS

Charles Weldon M.D.

ASIA BOOKS

Published and Distributed by
Asia Books Co. Ltd.,
5 Sukhumvit Road Soi 61,
PO Box 40,
Bangkok 10110,
Thailand.
Tel: (662) 714 0740-2 ext. 221-223
Fax: (662) 381 1621, 391 2277
E-mail: customer_serv@asiabooks.co.th
Web site: www.asiasonline.com

Typeset by COMSET Limited Partnership.
Printed by Darnsutha Press Ltd.

ISBN 974-8237-38-9

Contents

Acknowledgements ix

Introduction xi

Air Support 1

A Step Into the Unknown 5

USAID Laos 15

The Land of a Million Elephants and the White Parasol 30

The Filipino Connection 42

Refugee Relief 51

Cholera Outbreak 57

To Stay or Not to Stay 75

The Problem 80

Partisan Warfare in Sam Neua Province 93

The Ambush 104

Epidemic 113

The Magnificent Seven 120

Coup Survival 131

Floods 140

Down But Not Out in Hong Non 144

On the Run From Houi Sa An 151

Must Try Harder 154

A Double Tragedy 156

Search and Rescue 158

New Kid on the Block 161

The Menagerie 170

A Gaudy Old Lady 172

Evacuation at Hua Muang 180

The Opium Proposal 184

Escape from Khang Khay 186

Back in the USA 196
Metrical 200
A Fishy Tale 206
Caravans at Nam Thoui, Chaos at Houi Thom 208
To School in Europe 217
A Close Call at Muang Heim 219
Pha Thi 228
Outstanding Woman of the Year 233
Love Story 234
Good Times, Bad Times 236
The Elephant 241
On the Hill 244
The Beginning of the End 246
Trouble with Uncle Oscar 251
The Ban Houi Sai Hospital Saga 257
Public Works Program 268
Disintegration 274
Epilogue 278

Glossary and Acronyms 281
About the Author 283

This book is dedicated to my three dear friends,
Edgar "Pop" Buell,
Father Lucien Bouchard, better known as "Father B",
and General "VP" Vang Pao.

Pop died in his sleep on New Year's Eve 1981, at the Manila home of our old buddy from Laos, Lyle Brown. Pop and Lyle had planned to visit me the next day at my temporary residence in Southern Luzon.

Father B continues his mission in the remote jungles of Kalimantan.

In 1975, after the Pathet Lao takeover, VP and his family and staff fled to the United States and settled in California. They would certainly have been murdered by the communists if they had remained in Laos.

The four of us worked, laughed, and cried together in our desperate efforts to help the Lao people. I shall forever be thankful for their kindness, devotion, and friendship.

Acknowledgements

I am particularly indebted to two of my friends and fellow workers from Laos—Edwin McKeithen and Fritz Benson—and to my editor, Richard Baker at Asia Books.

Win worked in Laos as a young IVS volunteer and USAID employee from 1959 until 1975, with the exception of two short breaks when he completed his masters degree in the United States. He very kindly read this manuscript and gave me the benefit of his wide experience and knowledge of Laos.

Fritz was also a young IVS volunteer in Laos who joined USAID. He was in the country from 1968 to 1974, and sweated and slaved in the refugee relief program with us. He was rewarded with a lovely Lao wife. Fritz's cooperation and assistance made it possible for me to publish this book in the US.

If Richard hadn't read and edited my manuscript, the book would never have seen the light of day.

My heartfelt thanks to the three of them.

Introduction

This is the story of a country doctor from Louisiana involved in the war in Indochina. It is an anecdotal description of some of the events that occurred during the eleven years from June 1963 to July 1974 when I lived and worked in the kingdom of Laos. It is a collection which is tied together by brief narrative sketches of my family and our daily lives.

Everything in the book is true to the best of my memory, although there could be small errors in the time-frame and minor details—as I have written largely without notes or references. The events are mostly chronological, although I have not considered a sequential time-frame as essential to the narrative as a whole. In two instances the correct names of minor characters were not used for the simple reason that I could not recall them. Another character has been given a fictitious name because my comments about him are unkind and demeaning.

Lao and Thai are similar—but separate—languages. Spellings of Lao words here should not be misconstrued as misspellings of commonly transliterated Thai words. All place names are spelled as they were at the time the events took place. After 1975, many place names may have changed, and in any case, different maps will provide different spelling variations of the same place.

My family and I love Laos and its people with a passion that is as strong now as it was the day we left the country in 1974. The domination and cruel revenge suffered by the Lao people for supporting the Royal Lao Government from their traditional enemy of many centuries—the Vietnamese (and their Pathet Lao collaborators)—is a horror that still haunts us. Their betrayal and abandonment by the United States government is heartbreaking and shameful to each of us. The harsh punishment and deaths of tens of thousands of innocent Lao in the post 1975 "re-education camps," and the terrified flight of hundreds of thousands of others to foreign lands rivals the horrors committed by Hitler and Stalin.

Originally, the anecdotes in this book were written as unrelated pieces over a period of several years for my children and grandchildren. They are stories of high adventure, tragedy, humor, human fortitude, suffering, love, and war—and the incentive for combining them into a book that covered our 11 years in Laos, was the hope that it might help to perpetuate our memories, happy and sad, of these dear and gentle people.

The unique circumstances of the medical program which I developed and supervised, provided a perfect opportunity to come to know the country and its people. We established our little bamboo-and-thatch dispensaries and hospitals in every province—often in small, insecure enclaves deep in communist-controlled territory. They varied in number between 150 and 250 at any given time, and I visited every one of them at least once each year—often two or three each day.

I traveled constantly—on foot, and by boat, horse, elephant, helicopter, STOL aircraft, and occasionally by Jeep—and in every year of the 11 I lived in Laos, more than 1,000 hours were spent in the air. I believe that I knew the country at that time as well as any living person.

An innocent victim of North Vietnam and the Vietnam War, as well as of US foreign policy, Laos was caught up in the turmoil and acrimony of the times. Many writers treat the country as a political joke, with little—if any—reason for existence. The fact that there are more people of Lao origin on the Korat Plateau in Thailand than in Laos itself, is cited as a reason for its political illegitimacy. Such logic is as foolish as saying Canada should not exist because most of the English-speaking people in North America live in the United States.

The lack of national identity is often referred to in political analyses—but in my experience, the Lao king and queen were as strong a unifying force for Lao people of all ethnic groups as any political institution in any other country. Unfortunately, during the war years, few writers dealt with Laos as a sovereign, independent entity with the rights and aspirations of any other country. Rather, it was usually considered as a pawn in the larger context of the Vietnam conflict.

Although the Royal Lao Government was generally ineffective, it was at least benign and benevolent within its limited means. People may have suffered because of the lack of action or attention, but seldom—if ever—because of some direct action on the part of the government. The many different ethnic groups lived together in peace and harmony. Each had its ecological niche, and there was plenty of land for everyone. No one coveted his neighbour's property, and they interacted in a pleasant and symbiotic way. The Hmong (called Meo when I worked in Laos) living in the mountains traded their unique products and skills for those of the Lao in the Mekong Valley. The pervasive tolerance of the Lao Buddhist ethic precluded friction with the animism and traditions of the other ethnic groups.

A mild climate, fertile land, and low population density made for a happy, contented people with a remarkable lack of want or privation. In peaceful times, with a minimum of effort, they were able to provide themselves with abundant food, comfortable housing, clothing, and other essentials of life. There was plenty of time for relaxation, games, singing, drinking, dancing, and making love. The rhythm of life with its festivals and celebrations followed the rhythm of the monsoon and the harvest. Life was easy. Life was good. The kingdom of Laos may have been the sole place on earth where Rousseau's paradise of "natural man" actually existed.

In my biased, professional view as a doctor, the only important problem these wonderful people had—if left alone—was the suffering and death which resulted from ignorance and lack of health care.

It was to this problem that I addressed myself for more than 11 years.

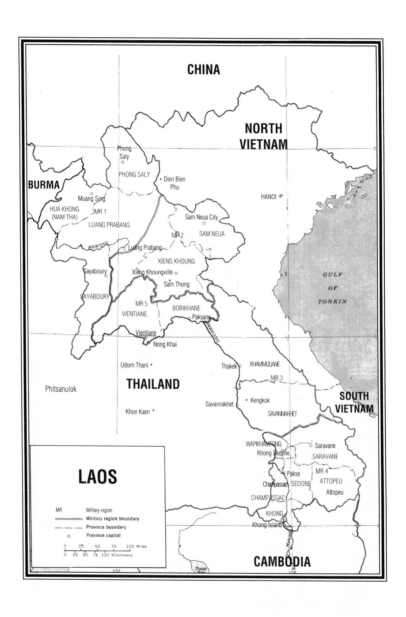

CHINA

NORTH
VIETNAM

BURMA

Phong
Saly
PHONG SALY
• Dien Bien
Phu

HANOI

Muang Sing
HUA KHONG
(NAM THA)
MR 1
LUANG PRABANG

Sam Neua City

MR 2
SAM NEUA

MEKONG
Luang Prabang

XIENG KHOUNG

Sayaboury
Xieng Khoungville

SAYABOURY
Sam Thong

MR 5
VIENTIANE
BORIKHANE
Paksane

Vientiane
Nong Khai

MEKONG

GULF
OF
TONKIN

Udorn Thani •
Thakek
KHAMMOUANE

MR 3

Phitsanulok
THAILAND

Savannakhet
• Kengkok
SAVANNAKHET

SOUTH
VIETNAM

Khon Kaen *

WAPIKHAMTONG
Khong Sedone
○ Saravane
SARAVANE

• Pakse
Champassac
SEDONE
MR 4
ATTOPEU
Attopeu
CHAMPASSAC

KHONG
Khong Island

MEKONG

LAOS

MR   Military region
                  Military region boundary
– – – – –   Province boundary
○   Province capital

0   25   50   75   100 Miles
0 25 50 75 100 Kilometers

102

Tonle
Sap

CAMBODIA

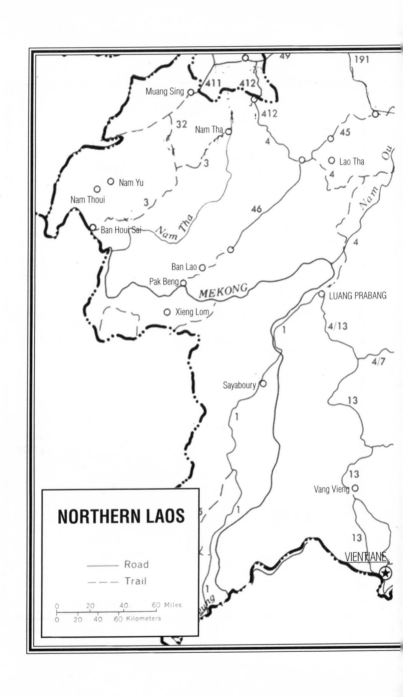

191

49

411   412

Muang Sing   412

32   Nam Tha   4   45

3   Lao Tha

Nam Yu   4

Nam Thoui

Ban Houi Sai   Nam Tha   46

Ban Lao

Pak Beng   MEKONG   LUANG PRABANG

Xieng Lom   1   4/13

4/7

Sayaboury   13

1

13

Vang Vieng

13

VIENTIANE

NORTHERN LAOS

—— Road
- - - Trail

0   20   40   60 Miles
0   20   40   60 Kilometers

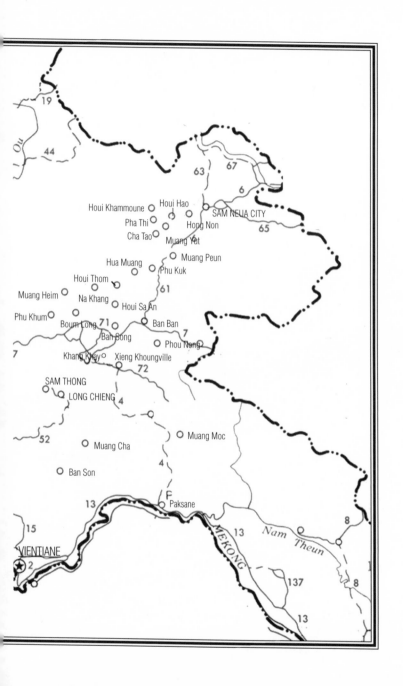

Air Support

Although I have mentioned pilots and planes throughout the context of the narrative, I should like to give the reader a clearer concept of the importance of air support in carrying out our programs in Laos.

There were few roads in the country at the time, and none of them were usable except in the immediate vicinity of the larger towns along the Mekong River. In most areas, roads were non-existent. Where they did exist, lack of maintenance and poor security often precluded their use—particularly in the hinterland, where most of the fighting and displacement of the civilian population occurred. Pack animals were used to a limited extent, but people usually moved on foot. The terrain was mountainous and rough, and narrow footpaths provided the only routes of communication.

Geographically, no distinct lines of demarcation separated the warring parties. Islands of communist influence existed in areas of rightist influence, and vice versa. Often, groups of people we were supporting were located hundreds of kilometers deep in unfriendly territory. The only means of supporting these isolated enclaves was by air. Without aircraft, no program was possible.

From the operational standpoint of people like myself, our support aircraft were of two types. First, those that moved people and cargo by landing them on the ground. These were the STOL aircraft—particularly the Helio Courier, Pilatus Porter, and De Havilland Caribou—and the helicopters such as the Sikorsky H34 and Bell Jet Ranger.

The second type of aircraft were those that dropped commodities such as food and ammunition. In this category were the C46 and C123B. There were a dozen or more other kinds of aircraft, and often their use for dropping or landing would alternate. Most of the fixed-wing pilots usually flew only one type of aircraft, but some of them were checked out in several different types. In emergencies they would fly any plane that needed a pilot.

Four different air contractors worked in Laos during the war years. The largest, and the only one present throughout my stay from 1963 to 1974, was Air America. Bird & Sons operated in Laos in the early sixties, but was purchased by Continental Air Services Inc.(CASI)—a subsidiary of Continental Airlines—which provided most of the air support for the health program in the late sixties and seventies. In the early seventies there was also a small chopper contractor, Arizona Helicopters.

Air America has its origin in (and with) various places, events, organizations, and people—including China, World War II, the CIA, Chiang Kai-Shek, General Claire Lee Chennault of the Flying Tigers, CAT— "the worlds most shot-at airline"—and who knows what else. In any event, all four of the air contractors were in some way related to Air America and the CIA. The history is well-known and far beyond the scope of this book.

For the type of work that we did out in the boondocks, most often we used the Helio Courier and, at a later date, the Pilatus Porter. If there were no strips, or the strips were unusable, we used the helicopters: an H34 or, later in the program, a Jet Ranger.

The Helio Courier was a small, four-place, piston-engined, high-wing tail dragger. Its special wing design and flaps gave it good STOL characteristics, but it was very difficult to fly. The Porter, first used for glacier landings in Switzerland, had room for six or eight passengers, and was a high-wing tail dragger powered by a turbo-prop. Its huge wing and reversible pitch prop give it outstanding STOL capability. It was a forgiving, easy plane to fly.

Those of us who worked in the insecure areas developed a close and enduring relationship with the pilots who flew our aircraft. *Our* lives often depended on them risking *their* lives to get us out of a dangerous situation. They never hesitated—no matter how bad the weather, how treacherous the strip, how erratic the winds, or how intense the ground fire. It must be remembered, too, that they rescued over 100 American pilots that were shot down over Laos and adjacent parts of North Vietnam. I have the same warm feeling and vivid memories of them as I have for my Marine buddies that hit the beach with me in World War II. It's an affection that time cannot kill or even dull.

The pilots became as dedicated to the program and as sympathetic to the plight of the refugees and irregular military as anyone else. We were all one team. As I write this story in the computer e-mail age, many of the pilots and I still keep in touch and continue a warm friendship. I correspond regularly with Rocky Neesom, Bill Andresevic, Joe Hazen, John Wiren, and Bob Moberg—all fabulous Helio pilots, and Wayne Knight and Dick Casterlin —great chopper pilots, who flew me around Laos 30-35 years ago.

The e-mails bring good news and bad. Recently, Dr. Patricia Walker was making arrangements for her father, Fred to visit his old friend Doc Weldon in Chiang Rai, Thailand. Fred was chief pilot for Air America for many years, and could fly anything with wings. The last time I saw him was in 1975. The Khmer Rouge were bombarding Phnom Penh with big rockets, and were paying special attention to the airport. Fred greased the old C46 in between the craters and picked up myself and some other grateful guys just before the Khmer Rouge took over the city. But that's another story

Before the trip, Dr. Walker informed me by e-mail that her father died peacefully in his sleep. He had to divert to his alternate and wouldn't now make it to Chiang Rai.

Another exotic air operation going on in Laos was that of the Forward Air Controllers (FACs). Gradually, as the war in Laos increased in intensity, more and more Vietnamese troops were committed to wiping out the resistance in Sam Neua and Xieng Khoung—and more and more US air power was committed to maintain the balance. At the inception, the US Air Force was bombing targets in close proximity to the troops in the field—without any radio contact or ground control. There were no radios on the ground that netted with the radios in the strike planes.

After General Vang Pao (VP) was blown off of a ridge in Sam Neua by the concussion of a bomb dropped by a US F105, a decision was made to remedy this unhealthy situation. General Harry "Hienie" Aderholt sent a small FAC team to Long Chieng to work with VP.

At first, the FACs worked on the ground with the troops—but they had radio contact with, and could control and direct, the strike aircraft. After a short time they took to the air with Air America pilots. For some reason we called these FACs "Butterflies." Why? I never knew. Finally, the US Air Force sent specially-trained FAC teams with their own aircraft to Laos. These were called the "Ravens." The word Raven is like the word Hmong: I never heard either word during my stay in Laos.

The Ravens flew the Cessna O1 Bird Dog, and—later—an improved model, the O2. This was a small, two-seat, piston-engined, unarmed and unarmored plane that flew at very slow speed. The American pilot usually had a local guide in the back seat. They located the targets, marked them with smoke, and directed the strike aircraft.

Most of the FACs worked out of Long Chieng, but a few were also stationed in Luang Prabang, Vientiane, Savannakhet, and Pakse. They performed a very critical, extremely dangerous job, with a high attrition rate.

The Ravens were highly motivated, skilled, and brave men. Most of them were also arrogant, egotistical, and boisterous. I never got to know any of them well, except Captain Tom Shera who married my secretary Mary Miller. They were in the air and we were on the ground, and we had very little contact. Usually their tour of duty lasted only six months, so there wasn't much time to get to know them.

Christopher Robbins has written an excellent book of their work in Laos entitled simply, *The Ravens.* I strongly recommend it.

A Step Into the Unknown

Ed Dyke kept repeating, "A real live goddamned American doctor! I can't believe it! A real live goddamned American doctor!"

Ed had a high velocity round through his right leg. Fortunately, the bullet hadn't hit the bone or any major vessel or nerve. His back-seat man wasn't so lucky. He was in a critical condition. When he ejected, the force produced a compression fracture of a thoracic vertebra. There seemed to be damage to the spinal cord, and he was paralysed from the waist down.

At times it seemed incredible how poor the liaison and exchange of information was between the various agencies of our government. There we were in the middle of a nasty, unpopular war that was tearing the United States apart, American planes were flying over us and bombing areas near where we were working—yet the pilots weren't aware there were any Americans within hundreds of miles, much less on the ground below them.

I had just transferred the two airmen from a helicopter to a Caribou, and we were on the way to the hospital at the Korat Air Force base in Thailand.

Lieutenant-Colonel Edward Dyke had flown into Dien Bien Phu in Northwest Vietnam at 35,000 feet in an F4 Phantom, indicating an airspeed of 1,250 knots. He reduced to 450 knots and dropped down on the deck to make a photo recon run. The plane was over a jungle area thought to be free of anti-aircraft weapons. Suddenly there was vibration, and warning lights lit up the panel like a Christmas tree. He'd been hit.

At that speed, the plane could tear itself to pieces in a fraction of a second, so he set the F4 on its tail to kill airspeed, and gave a "mayday" with his location on the emergency frequency, 121.5mhz. At 10,000 feet, the plane was disintegrating. Although the airspeed was still far too fast, they could wait no longer. Ed gave the word to his buddy, and the two ejected.

By good fortune, we were working in a tight but friendly little enclave in Southeast Phong Saly province—just across the border in Laos, only a few kilometers away. Our chopper pilot heard the "mayday" and headed for the downed plane immediately. Ed's parachute was quickly spotted, and he was on the chopper within minutes. He wasn't injured, and he'd seen where his crewman fell. He directed the chopper to the spot.

The crewman was hung up in a tree by his parachute, and was obviously badly hurt—but he was quickly cut loose and put aboard the chopper. Just as the aircraft was airborne, however, the enemy arrived. The chopper was hit by a hail of small-arms fire, and Ed took a round in the right leg.

Fate couldn't decide what to do with him that day, but all things considered, Ed felt she had smiled. Here he was on a Caribou headed for the US Air Force hospital in Korat, Thailand with a "real live goddamned American doctor," when, by all odds, he should be dead, or—at best—a prisoner of the Vietnamese.

After the two airmen were stable and comfortable, I sat next to Ed's stretcher and tried to talk to him above the 100-decibel roar of the De Havilland. His first question was, "Doc, how in the hell did you get way up here, and what are you doing?"

It was indeed a good question—and one I'd often asked myself. However, it wasn't possible to give a complete answer on the flight to Korat.

Now, I suppose, the answer is what this book is all about, and in this prologue, I shall explain how and why the Weldon family came to be in Laos during the war in Indochina.

✪ ✪ ✪

Patricia McCreedy and I graduated from medical school together in 1951, and were married shortly after. Nine years later, we were both doing general practice in rural Southern Louisiana. My father was over ninety years old and I wanted to be nearby to care for him, so we settled in the small town of Maringouin near my home. We had three lovely, healthy children—Becky, Ray, and Walter—a comfortable home, and a financially successful business. But we were frustrated by increasing boredom.

Although we made many friends whom we cherish to this day, the small town in which we lived offered little in the way of entertainment or intellectual stimulation. Being the only doctors in the area, it was seldom that we could leave for a change of scene to relax and refresh ourselves. We had grown stale and tired. Soon after the death of my father in 1960, through many evenings of long discussion, misgivings, and equivocation, we decided that we would try to find something challenging overseas.

Pat had recently read Margaret Mead's *Coming of Age in Samoa*, and while we idly chatted about the book, I coincidentally happened to see—in a medical journal I was thumbing through—a notice for medical positions in American Samoa. They needed a public health officer and a pediatrician. We immediately felt that something was telling us to go there, and I sent a letter to the medical director of the Territory of American Samoa the next day. If we were accepted, Pat would be the public health officer and I would be the pediatrician. We would go to Samoa for one or two years, and then return to the US and establish ourselves in practice in a more compatible and stimulating environment.

Within a few weeks, we were indeed accepted—and were soon embroiled in the turmoil of getting ready to leave for Samoa.

Our most difficult problem was finding someone to take over our practice. We felt a strong obligation to choose exactly the right doctors to take care of the people we had served for the previous few years, but this turned out to be more difficult than we anticipated. There were several doctors interested in buying the practice, but the only two whom we felt were suitable happened to be just out of school. They frankly admitted that they not only had no money, but were substantially in debt. Our better sense of responsibility overcame our avarice, and we lent them the money to get started.

About two weeks later we landed at Pago Pago in American Samoa.

Since this book concerns Laos, and not that idyllic Polynesian island, I shall cover the two wonderful years we spent there as quickly as possible. Briefly, I want only to point out how the Samoan experience influenced our decision to continue working overseas, instead of returning to the US as we originally intended.

❂ ❂ ❂

The territory of American Samoa comprises a group of small islands that lie lost in the vast Pacific some 2,500 miles southwest of Hawaii. Tutuila is the largest island, and Pago Pago, the capital and administrative center, is located there. The total land area is only 76 square miles, and at the time we were there, the population was about 35,000. The other Samoan Islands, located about sixty miles north and west of Tutuila, make up the tiny, independent state of Western Samoa, previously a United Nations mandate to New Zealand.

The islands are lush, fertile, and beautiful. The climate is ideal, with temperatures varying from the upper seventies to the lower eighties, and with cool, gentle trade winds blowing throughout the year. In Pago Pago, late each afternoon, a towering cumulus cloud builds up over Rainmaker—an imposing, jungle-covered peak that overlooks the harbor. A torrent of rain falls for a half hour or so, and then quickly dissipates—leaving the atmosphere delightfully fresh, and the sky clear and bright.

Most of the population is centered at Pago Pago. The interiors of the islands—mostly rugged outcroppings of volcanic rock covered with heavy jungle—are not inhabited. Outside the capital, the people live in the few villages that dot the coastline where small alluvial areas occur that are suitable for agriculture and the raising of pigs and chickens. The reef and the ocean teem with a never-ending feast of seafood, and the land provides an abundance of fruit and vegetables with minimal human effort.

Samoans are huge people by any standard. Men are usually over six feet tall and weigh well over 200 pounds. They are lean and muscular with superb bodies. Women are almost as tall, and since obesity is a mark of status and affluence, they often exceed 300 pounds in weight. The image of a beautiful, willowy Polynesian siren is a nothing more than a myth. Nevertheless, the women have a gracious, witty, and uninhibited relationship with the men that makes them very attractive and delightful companions.

A benign environment, an abundance of nutritious food, and a form of eugenic infanticide—only recently abandoned—have produced a healthy vigorous people when compared with other developing cultures.

At the time of our arrival, in early 1961, it was soon apparent to us that there were three significant health problems in Samoa. These were tuberculosis, filariasis, and excessive infant mortality. However, by third world standards, their incidence was moderate in magnitude, with the possible exception of filariasis.

This latter disease is caused by a filarial worm that is transmitted from person to person by a mosquito when the worm is in the larval, microscopic stage. The adult worm grows, causes inflammation, and blocks the lymphatic system—causing swelling of the tissues, and producing the disease that is usually called elephantiasis. The classic picture is the huge, swollen leg, scrotum, or breast. It is seldom fatal, but is terribly disabling and disfiguring.

Pat had been hired to head the public health services, while I was to be the head of the pediatrics department in the hospital. It just so happened that Rex Lee, the governor of the territory, had a confrontation with the doctor who was director of medical services soon after our arrival. The director left on the first available plane, so by default—and against my protestations—I became director of medical services. The governor didn't want any of the doctors who were present at the recent disagreement to assume the job, and being a new arrival, I was untainted—although he assured me that he would recruit a new medical director in a short time. I was soon buried in program planning, budgets, and other administrative matters—instead of tending to sick children.

Governor Lee was a career bureaucrat in the Department of the Interior, and was an intelligent, capable, experienced, and tough administrator. He had been sent to Samoa as a trouble-shooter to correct years of neglect and inefficiency in the administration of the island territory that was beginning to have wide and critical coverage in the media. His promise that he would recruit a new medical director never happened, but we nevertheless became close friends and worked well together. Fortunately, the governor placed high priority on health, and we had his complete support in attacking the problems mentioned above.

Tuberculosis was the easiest to bring under control, as new drugs were just being released that were highly effective. There was no drug resistance at that time, and these medications, in conjunction with thorough case finding, enabled us to close the TB ward in the hospital at the end of our first year in the islands.

The excessively high infant mortality rate was caused, in large part, by ignorance—on the part of the mothers—of infant care and nutrition. There was certainly no lack of food or other resources; Samoa had a strongly matriarchal society with a unique infrastructure of traditional women's committees in each village. These committees were soon re-organized by Pat and her Samoan counterpart, Arieta Mulitauopele, to focus on health and solve this problem.

Arieta was a huge, dynamic woman—a high-talking chief in her own right—and a fine public health nurse. She and Pat quickly became close friends and made a formidable team. They traveled constantly, meeting with the women in the committees, and imparting the knowledge and know-how that, after two years, resulted in a drop in infant mortality from 80 to 18 per 1,000 live births.

The situation with filariasis was more complex—and Pat and I had little knowledge or expertise in this field. We badly needed outside assistance, and—through Governor Lee—we were able to prevail on Dr. John Kessel to come to Samoa and guide us.

John Kessel was professor emeritus, and previously head of the Department of Parasitology at UCLA School of Medicine—and he was the world's foremost authority on filariasis. A vigorous seventy years of age, the old patriarch was a delightful gentleman, a scholar, and a joy to know. Under his supervision, and with a great deal of hard work by Arieta and the women's health committees, we were able to eradicate filariasis from American Samoa during the two years we were there.

Our children thrived and loved Samoa—and the Samoans loved them as they did all children. In that benign and protective environment, they wandered at will and played from land to sea, unaware of whether they were swimming or running. There was plenty of time for family picnics, snorkelling on the reef, and TV-free evenings of story-telling and games. These were wonderful, happy hours that brought our family closer together than we ever had been in the States.

In the euphoria of what we considered our great success in combating the evil forces of disease and pestilence, and the happy family adjustment to our new lifestyle, we decided to seek other fields to conquer in the suffering third world. Our arrogance was only exceeded by our naivety. Little did we know that the tiny, isolated microcosm of American Samoa had scant resemblance to the rest of the third world—and to the realities of life and war in Southeast Asia. The success we had in Samoa was, in large part, due to Arieta and Rex Lee.

I dropped by for a chat with the governor.

"Pat and I want to leave, Rex. We've been here for over two years and it's time to move on to other things. We're getting a bit 'rock happy.' You know, small islands close in on you after a while."

"Oh for Christ's sake," he shot back. "What are you talking about? You and Pat are doing a great job. You can't leave now. I was just fixing to call you. I got a cable this morning. The budget for the new hospital's approved."

"You don't need us to build the new hospital, Rex. The things we wanted to do have pretty well been accomplished. This is a good time for us to leave."

We argued for a while, but Rex soon realized that we had definitely decided to go. I asked him if he had any suggestions how we might find employment overseas, doing the same sort of work we'd done in Samoa.

"If you want to stay in government service, you might check out the Agency for International Development [USAID] in the Department of State," he told us. "They've got a terrible reputation for inefficiency at Washington level, but they have plenty of technical assistance programs in developing countries that are well administered and productive.

"It's possible they might have something that would interest Pat and you. I'm telling you though, the personnel department can be difficult to deal with—or even talk to—if you don't have some sort of connection. Do you know anyone in Washington that has any influence? Drop a few names?"

"No. Never even thought of it."

"Okay, go to Washington and contact USAID anyway. I'll give you the phone number of Dick Allen, a friend of mine—one of the secretaries in the White House. If you hit a snag—and you probably will—call Dick. I'll contact him in the meantime and tell him to expect a call. Hope everything works out."

Rex wrote down the name and number for me, and a few weeks later we departed Samoa.

On arrival in Los Angeles, I rented a car. We told the kids this was strictly a pleasure trip—that we'd go anywhere they wanted, stop as often as they wanted, and there'd be no restriction on cokes, hamburgers, or other necessities. It took over two weeks to get past Disney Land, Marine World, and the San Diego zoo. Six weeks later, we arrived in Washington and contacted USAID.

Just as Rex Lee had warned us, we went from office to office in the Department of State for three or four days without being able to ascertain if there were any positions open in the health field overseas, or if USAID would be interested in hiring us.

Completely frustrated, I phoned Dick Allen in the White House and gave him my name.

Before I could explain the purpose of my call he said, "Oh yeah, Rex told me you'd be here and might need some help with AID. I'll give them a call for you."

He took the name of our hotel, told me to remain there, and said he'd have someone in USAID contact us shortly.

Before the day was over, we were having cordial discussions with the health and personnel people in USAID, and it was obvious they were trying to find a spot for us.

However, it soon became apparent that the only place with positions open for two doctors with our background was Laos. The personnel officer asked us if we'd be interested. Pat looked at me and I looked at her, and almost in chorus we said, "Absolutely. We've always wanted to go to Laos."

As soon as we were alone in the hall, I grabbed Pat by the arm and asked, "Where in the hell is Laos?"

She burst out laughing. "I think it's in Africa . . . uh . . . maybe Asia."

We went to the library, found out where Laos was, and the next day started processing to go there.

When we got to the point of detailed discussions about the positions Pat and I would occupy in the Lao mission, we found that there was only a job for me that could be allocated in Washington. However, they assured us that Pat would be hired after our arrival in Laos. This caused us some concern, but we decided to go ahead. We devoted the next two days to physical examinations for all the family, and when we completed these successfully, I signed the necessary documents. We departed Washington with relief—the five of us in an excited, happy mood.

From Washington we drove to Biloxi, Mississippi, where Pat's parents lived, and then went to New Orleans. Our household effects from Louisiana and Samoa were stored there, so we planned to make that our point of departure. It took three or four days to sort out the things we would take to Laos, and to make the necessary shipping and storage arrangements. We had many old friends in New Orleans from medical school days, and there was a constant party going on in our two adjoining hotel rooms.

Finally—when everything was packed, shipped, or placed in storage, and when tickets, travelers checks, and passports were in order—we took off for Laos. After a change of planes in Los Angeles, and brief stops in Honolulu and Tokyo, we landed in Manila. The USAID Laos desk in Washington wanted us to stop there to meet Oscar Orellano—director of Operation Brotherhood (OB)—and his staff.

Operation Brotherhood was a non-profit organization which ran small hospitals in Laos through a contract financed and administered by USAID. As chief of the public health division of USAID Laos, I would be responsible for the contract. I shall describe the organization in more detail later.

Oscar Orellano met us at the airport and took us to the hotel. It was late in the afternoon and the children were tired after the long trip from New Orleans. Our host wanted to take the family to dinner that evening, but—with apologies—we declined and agreed to meet the next morning.

After a good night's sleep, everyone was eager to get out and see some of Manila. Oscar arrived early with a very pretty, personable young lady from his office who would take the children to breakfast and then show them around the city—while he introduced Pat and myself to the OB headquarters staff.

Oscar Orellano was a large, slightly obese man with smooth, olive skin. He radiated charm and good manners; was pleasant-looking, smiling, and self-assured; and was impeccably dressed in a seersucker suit, white shirt, and black string tie. He reminded me more of a Southern Louisiana French-Creole gentleman than a Filipino administrator. Although at least fifty years old, his appearance was much younger, and there was no doubt that he was accustomed to considerable affluence.

We spent two delightful days being briefed, wined, and dined by Oscar and his staff, and were very impressed with the efficient operation of their office and their air of dedication and altruism. Most of their activities in Manila concerned daycare centers and nutrition programs in slum neighborhoods—and we visited some of these projects and found them highly innovative and apparently successful.

The time passed rapidly, and soon Oscar was putting us on a plane for Bangkok. We thanked him for all his kindness and hospitality, and hoped to see him soon in Vientiane. When we were airborne, I reflected on the past two days. Despite my overall favorable impression, I couldn't shake off a vague, uneasy feeling that there'd be problems with Mr. Orellano in the future.

Three hours later, we landed at Don Muang Airport in Bangkok, and took a cab into town for the hotel, before flying to Vientiane the next afternoon. We all immediately fell in love with Bangkok and the Thais. At that time there was no city in the world that was more hospitable and friendly to the traveler. Although Bangkok has changed in the 36 years since that time, our romance with the now sprawling, polluted, and smelly city still endures.

The next afternoon, we went out to Don Muang again, and boarded a DC3 for Vientiane. The old "gooney bird" flew at about 5,000 feet, and the kids were delighted to be in a plane from which they could see the ground. It was a bright, clear day, and as the plane climbed out of Bangkok over the central plain—one of the richest rice-growing areas in the world—the geometric pattern of green, brown, and chartreuse paddy fields, cut by long, straight canals, was a magnificent sight.

13

In about a half hour the paddy fields were behind us, and we continued over the low, scrub-covered hills of the Korat Plateau—the least productive and least attractive region of the country. An hour-and-a-half after leaving Don Muang, the plane began its descent and crossed the huge, muddy Mekong River—leaving Thailand and entering Laos.

We could see Vientiane, the capital, strung out along the east bank of the river—but the city was almost lost in a jungle of coconut palms and brilliant, flamboyant trees. The plane made a smooth landing, taxied up to a small wooden building with fading green paint, and came to a stop.

The forty passengers were guided toward a door of the small building, and formed a line outside—as there wasn't enough space inside for everyone. This was Wattay Airport, the Lao international air terminal, which handled the one flight each day to and from the outside world. We slowly filed by a counter attended by one representative each from health, customs, and immigration as they checked our passports and declarations. On leaving the building on the opposite side, we immediately found ourselves on the street.

A tall, greyhaired man who was obviously an American, walked up, introduced himself, and asked if we were the Weldon family. He was Mr. Berryhill, the assistant director for technical services of USAID Laos, who would show us to our temporary housing and see that we got settled in. I was a little surprised that the doctor I was to replace hadn't met us. I'd been told in Washington that a Dr. Herman Platt was the present chief of the public health division of USAID, and that we would overlap for about three weeks.

The drive into town gave us an exotic view of lush, tropical gardens filled with a mass of brilliant flame trees and bougainvillea; several beautiful Buddhist temples; and thick-walled, masonry houses in need of paint and repairs.

We arrived at a house in the middle of town, in a small compound with the unlikely name of "Leeville." The place was furnished and ready for occupancy, with linens, and food and drink in the refrigerator. It was late in the afternoon, so Mr. Berryhill said he would send a car in the morning to take me to the office. We thanked him for meeting us, and he departed.

Our sojourn in Laos had begun.

USAID Laos

A car duly picked me up at seven the next morning and took me to the USAID offices. It took about 15 minutes over a narrow, crumbling blacktop street filled with huge pot-holes. There were few cars on the street, but it was seething with pedestrians, bicycles, and pedicabs.

USAID was housed in a large, two-story building that appeared to be an old residence. The walls were painted an unattractive yellowish-brown, and it had a general air of neglect and disrepair. I entered the building and found the public health office, which consisted of a tiny room, two desks, and four or five chairs. There was a petite, pleasant-looking lady at one of the desks. I introduced myself, and found that she was Esther Cardova from the Philippines, the public health secretary. She told me that Dr. Platt had just called to say he'd be late, and for me to make myself comfortable. About then, Mr. Berryhill walked in and suggested that he show me around since Dr. Platt hadn't arrived.

At that time there were only about thirty Americans in USAID Laos, and over half of them were stationed in the field. Because there were so few Lao with English-language ability or office skills, most of the non-American employees were Filipinos—hired through a contract with a Manila recruiting organization.

Mr. Berryhill and I walked around to the various offices making introductions and chatting briefly with everyone. We then ended up at the office of Charles Mann, the director of USAID.

Charles Mann was about fifty years old. He was born in Germany, but fled to the United States with his parents in the thirties, thus escaping the Holocaust. Since he was fluent in German, French, and Italian—as well as English—he had worked for the government as an interpreter during World War II, and continued in government service after the war. Although he had no formal education above high school level, he was a knowledgeable, astute man.

When we were introduced, he was abrupt almost to the point of rudeness—and certainly didn't seem particularly pleased to see me. Rather, he dismissed us as quickly as possible, with the excuse that he was extremely busy. I could see that Mann's discourtesy embarrassed Mr. Berryhill, but neither of us said anything.

Dr. Platt had still not arrived, so Mr. Berryhill took me to his office. Over coffee, he gave me a briefing on the structure of the American mission in Laos and the USAID projects. It soon became evident that there was no assistance program in health whatever.

I cannot recall exactly the amount of the annual budget for US assistance to Laos at that time, but it was about thirty million dollars. This was spread over currency stabilization, refugee relief, agriculture, education, and community development—but not one cent for health other than the funding of the OB contract.

My dismay and perplexity was obvious to Mr. Berryhill, and he was quite frank with me. There was considerable animosity between the director, Charles Mann and Herman Platt, the USAID chief of public health. Mann considered Platt completely incompetent, and wouldn't approve funding for any of the projects that Platt had tried to put together.

Eventually there was a knock on the door and a man walked into the room. Mr. Berryhill introduced me to Dr. Herman Platt, the man I was to replace.

Dr. Platt was a small, trim, swarthy individual in his early forties, balding with a circle of jet-black hair and full sideburns. A narrow face with a long, thin nose and pointed chin was accentuated by dark, penetrating eyes. He wore a beautiful white shirt with full billowing sleeves that was open almost to the waist, revealing a hairy, muscular chest. A pair of sleek, tight black pants contrasted with the white shirt. This macho figure was reminiscent of Rudolph Valentino, or possibly a Spanish matador—and I felt I'd never be able to match such splendor.

Dr. Platt and I went to the public health office, and I quickly found out that he was a well-known cardiologist from Hollywood who had many famous movie stars for patients. He claimed to be a black belt karate expert, loved to tango and practice yoga, and said that he "practically lived out in the jungle" and always carried a long stick to flip the many venomous snakes out of his path. I could hardly believe my eyes and ears, but soon began to realize why there was no health programming, and why Charles Mann— after tolerating Platt for two years—hadn't been overjoyed at seeing me, his new public health officer. He imagined, no doubt, that I would be equally as incompetent as Platt.

During the three weeks that Platt and I overlapped, we planned several field trips, but there was always—at the last minute—some crisis which caused postponement. I discovered later that he had only been out of Vientiane possibly three times during his two-year tour.

At the Ministry of Health, Platt introduced me to the minister and his staff. Our reception was polite but cool, and it was clear that a good working relationship had not been established. I decided to mark time until Platt got out of the way, and busied myself getting acquainted with the USAID staff and administration.

There was, however, one USAID health activity in Vientiane that was of some interest. A rented, Lao-style house near the center of town was used as a medical warehouse and supply facility—with a fairly large stock of medications and a few pieces of medical equipment that had been turned over to USAID by the American Military Assistance Group when they left the previous year, 1962, under the implementation of the Geneva Accords. It was run by a Filipino, Epiphano "Pop" Handog, and an assistant, Deriquito. Handog was an experienced medical warehouseman, and could be a valuable asset if things started moving. I was surprised that USAID maintained the facility as there was no real need for it under the present circumstances.

I also spent a lot of time getting acquainted with Jovito "Vitoy" Naranjo—the head of OB, and nephew of Oscar Orellano, whom we met in Manila. Vitoy was a charming young man, and we quickly became friends. There was one large OB hospital in Vientiane at that time, and three smaller ones in Sayaboury, Paksong, and Attopeu. The Vientiane facility also included the central administrative offices and a nursing school. It was agreed that as soon as I could get away, Vitoy and I would make a trip to the Paksong and Attopeu hospitals in the South, and then the Sayaboury hospital in the Northwest.

At the USAID offices I tried to gauge what was expected of me—and what might be possible in the way of developing a health program. My subsequent meetings with Charles Mann were more satisfactory than the first, but I still didn't receive much encouragement from him. However, he did indicate that he would consider any proposals I wanted to make, but it would be most difficult to fund anything before the next fiscal year. The general attitude seemed to be that after Platt, if I did nothing, everyone would be just as happy.

Esther Cardova, the secretary, had been very kind in helping Pat get the house straightened out, hiring a maid and cook, and getting the kids started in school. Fortunately, Pat was occupied at home, as it was becoming increasingly apparent that there was no position for her in USAID, as had been indicated in Washington—at least not immediately. We hoped something would be worked out before too long.

Becky, Ray, and Walter were fascinated with Vientiane, its friendly people, pedicabs, the huge central market, and life in general. The small American elementary school was well run, and they liked it and adjusted quickly.

The first three weeks soon passed, and one afternoon I had just returned to the office after going to the airport to see Dr. Platt off to the US. I was sitting at my desk when a man walked in. He was short and thin—almost emaciated—and appeared to be in his early fifties. Thick, black, horn-rimmed glasses accentuated a round, wrinkled face and a bald head. He was dressed in plain, unpressed black trousers, and a rumpled, white short-sleeve sport shirt.

Before I could get up, he stuck out his hand and introduced himself. "Doc, my name's Pop Buell."

We shook hands. "Glad to know you Mr. Buell. Charles Weldon."

"Don't call me *Mister* Buell, son. Everyone calls me Pop—and I sure as hell ain't gonna call you Charles. How's about I just call you Doc and you call me Pop?

"Okay Pop," I replied with a slight laugh.

"I heard we had a new doctor and I wanted to meet you right away. Last 'un we had wuzn't much, and we sure could use a good 'un."

"Well, Pop, I hope I can live up to your standards." He ignored the slight hint of sarcasm in my reply. "What can I do for you. . . ?"

Despite his nondescript appearance, brusque manner, and atrocious grammar, it was clear—as soon as he spoke—that he was a man of consequence and intelligence. Now, as I write this 36 years later, I remember that day as if it was yesterday—because it certainly marked a fateful point in my life.

Though we had only just met, Pop insisted that I take a plane to Sam Thong the next morning and spend a few days with him. I had other plans, but he was so insistent that I finally agreed. I didn't know where Sam Thong was, or how to get there, but Pop told me just go to the Air America office at the airport about seven o'clock and he'd have a plane waiting for me.

The next morning, the plane was indeed waiting when I arrived at the airport, and we were soon heading north from Vientiane to some unknown place called Sam Thong—my first trip out of the capital city.

Forty-five minutes later, the small Helio Courier droned away at 6,000 feet over a sea of white cloud, broken only by the summit of a mountain— Phu Bia, the highest peak in Laos—shining in the sun far to the north.

Sam Thong, as I discovered later, was the center of Pop Buell's refugee operations in the mountains of Xieng Khoung province. With nothing to look at but the white clouds and the tip of Phu Bia, my mind wandered over the events of the previous few months that had brought me to this exotic and lovely land. Of course, I didn't realize at the time that it would become my home for the next 11 years; 11 years of exhilarating excitement and happiness, mixed with soul-rending agony, and ending in bitter disappointment and frustration.

The pilot, Al Rich nudged me in the side and shouted in my ear above the noise of the engine, "Hold on Doc, we're going down."

I was suddenly jerked back to reality as he sent the little plane spiralling down through a tiny hole in the overcast. We seemed to be headed for a crash in the midst of thick, green jungle, but at the last second he pulled up the nose, and a minute later we landed on a dusty, dirt strip in what appeared to be a bowl-shaped depression surrounded by mountains.

On one side of the strip was a long building with bamboo siding and a thatched roof, and scattered around the little valley were a few other bamboo-and-thatch houses among huge pine trees almost as tall as California redwoods. We taxied over to the long building, Al cut the engine, and we got out.

It was a cold foggy morning. A few men stood around—dressed in baggy, black pants, and black shirts with red and green waist sashes that held large knives—but no one took much interest in the plane until one man came over and retrieved some burlap sacks out of the back, which I later found out were filled with bread.

This was Sam Thong.

Just as we were walking up to the building by the strip, Pop walked out, unshaven and dressed in military fatigues. We shook hands and he invited me inside. A crude sign on the door welcomed the visitor to VILLA POP.

The building had a dirt floor and was divided into two rooms—the smaller one we had just entered through being a combination office, communications center, conference room, and living quarters. A radio transceiver sat on an old, military, folding field desk; there was a crude bamboo bed covered with a stack of green GI blankets without any mattress or pillows; and a couple of rough, wooden benches completed the furnishings.

The other, much larger part of the building was used as a storage area, and had a wide door opening onto the airstrip through which supplies could be loaded onto the aircraft. The place was piled full of rice, butter oil, powdered milk, sacks of salt, hoes, shovels, machetes, buckets, blankets, rolls of black cloth and black plastic, iron bars, and all sorts of other assorted items. In one corner were shelves stacked with bottles and cans of medicines, boxes of bandages, and other medical supplies. Next to the office, in a large, open space, were several canvas folding cots with GI green blankets where the local workers slept. An open fire on the dirt floor provided the only facility for preparing food.

A short time after we arrived, more STOL aircraft and helicopters began to land. They were quickly loaded with supplies from the warehouse, and took off again, often without cutting their engines. Soon, the place was a bedlam of noise, dust, and scurrying people. It looked completely chaotic, but was actually an orderly and carefully-planned supply operation in support of the various refugee groups. The aircraft contracts were paid on an hourly basis, and Pop didn't let them sit idle—yet there never seemed to be enough planes to get all the work done.

Pop introduced me to the staff that happened to be in the office at the time. The only other American was Tom Ward—a tall, spectacled young man in his late twenties; ex-associate professor of history from the University of Texas; affluent, cultured, and an intellectual. He was Pop's alter ego. More than thirty years later, I still don't understand how he ended up in the mountains of Northern Laos—but he turned out to be the perfect complement to Pop.

Nai kong Bleu Vu was a short, stocky Meo tribal leader assigned by General Vang Pao (VP)—the Meo armed forces commander-in-chief—as Pop's counterpart. Even on first meeting, one felt that he was a man of competence and authority. *Nai kong* is an honorific title given to tribal males who demonstrate outstanding leadership qualities.

Tong Sar was a dynamic, husky little guy with a pockmarked face, about thirty years old. He was referred to as Pop's son, and although he claimed to be Lao, he was probably Cambodian. A polyglot who spoke colorful

English—as well as ten or more other languages (he claimed 22)—he was Pop's right-hand man.

Joe Baccam, a young Tai Dam refugee from North Vietnam, supervised the loading and dispatching of the aircraft.

Ly Choi, a young Meo boy, operated the radio and maintained a log of all take-offs and landings. He knew the flight times for all the aircraft to the sites, and if any plane was twenty minutes late and hadn't reported in, he initiated a radio check to find it. If it couldn't be located by radio, a search was immediately started using the other aircraft in the area. Over the years, this simple procedure saved many lives—from planes that crashed due to mechanical failure, or were shot down.

There were also two young boys, Noi and Ut, about eight or ten years old, who had no family and lived with Pop and Tom. They ran errands, helped keep the place straight, and made coffee for the staff, visitors, and pilots.

The last person introduced to me was a smiling and pleasant, gangling young Lao named Chan.

Pop told me that the main reason he wanted me to visit Sam Thong was to have Chan show me the hospital and some of the dispensaries in the refugee villages. Chan and I would go ahead and look around, and Pop and I would talk that night.

Chan—who claimed to have gone through the *medcin assistant* school in Phnom Penh, Cambodia—was in charge of the hospital at Sam Thong, and also supervised and supported a few peripheral dispensaries in the refugee villages. The medics in these dispensaries had been trained by the American Special Forces' White Star teams working in Xieng Khoung before the 1962 Geneva Accords—which required that all foreign troops be withdrawn from Laos.

Chan also had twenty medics in training at Sam Thong. These trainees acted as hospital staff but were later assigned to operate dispensaries when Chan felt they were competent to do so. He kept three or four of the best at Sam Thong to help him in the hospital and assist with the training. A new group of students would be brought in, and the cycle would be repeated until the hospital was adequately staffed and all the refugee villages were served by dispensaries.

The hospital, students quarters, classroom, and kitchen were located about 100 meters from the airstrip, and were constructed of bamboo and thatch with dirt floors. The hospital had one large ward of about fifty bamboo beds—each with three or four blankets for the patient to sleep on, and one used as a pillow. Most of the beds were filled with wounded soldiers, but there were some civilian men, women, and children. No attempt was made to close or repair any of the wounds. They were cleansed and dressed each day, and the more seriously wounded were given antibiotics. All were given multi-vitamins and food. Those that couldn't walk were carried out to the latrine by family members—if they were fortunate enough to have family with them—but if the patient was unaccompanied, the medics carried them. This was the only medical care available to the several hundreds of thousands of people in Northern Laos harassed and displaced from their homes and lands by the North Vietnamese and Pathet Lao.

It was obvious that most of the sick and wounded were dying out in the jungle without any care. If they were fortunate enough to get to Sam Thong, the chances of survival were considerably better—but still marginal. Nevertheless, it was a clean and well-organized operation that was impressive when one considered the resources available.

Chan spoke fairly good English so we had no great problem in communication. I was deeply impressed at what he was trying to do against such an overwhelming problem, and admired his courage and dedication. However, it became evident, the more we talked, that he knew little about medicine, and that his training was minimal. I found out later that he hadn't been to any sort of medical school; was not Lao, but a Thai from Udorn; and his only training had been as an orderly in a Thai hospital.

After looking at the hospital, we took a Helio Courier to two of the refugee dispensaries. The rugged limestone mountains were covered with dense, emerald green forest, except where patches had been cleared to plant corn, dry rice, and vegetables. In the deep valleys, one could catch glimpses of clear, sparkling streams as they ran through towering trees and occasionally dropped off into rainbow-tinted waterfalls. These rainforested valleys were extremely malarious, and thus uninhabited. All the villages were located on the high ridges—which were relatively free of the disease. It was wild and breathtakingly beautiful countryside.

Chan and I landed at two of the refugee villages and checked the little bamboo dispensaries. They were orderly and neat—but poorly-supplied and without much of a patient load. Using Chan as an interpreter, I talked to some of the villagers as we walked around, and received the impression that there was a high incidence of sickness—especially diarrhea among the children. Malnutrition was evident, and even through casual observation it was a major problem.

In both villages we visited, the water supplies were no more than small, grossly contaminated streams flowing immediately adjacent to the houses. Food, clean water, and environmental sanitation would probably make a greater impact on health than medicines.

We returned to Sam Thong late in the afternoon, just as the last of the aircraft was taking off for Vientiane. Unless there was a very special reason, no aircraft remained overnight (RON) upcountry, as there was no adequate security. All had quietened down as Pop, Tom Ward, and I sat outside the office on a wooden bench, talking and enjoying the cool evening.

On the opposite side of the airstrip, across a small depression, a group of thatched huts sprawled up the steep slope of the mountain. Smoke rose through the roofs as the fires were lit to cook the evening meal, and people walked back and forth across the strip from the village to where we were sitting.

The men wore black baggy trousers and shirts; and the women—short, heavily-embroidered black skirts with black leggings, black blouses, and embroidered caps. Around their necks were heavy, decorative silver collars, and their waists were bound with colorful, pink and green sashes. Everyone was barefoot.

Frequently, one of the Meo men would walk up and talk to Pop for a few minutes, or some little child would jump onto his lap and try to find the piece of candy or balloon that he always carried in his pocket. Occasionally, a whole family would arrive, and although I couldn't understand what was said—it was evident that Pop was being consulted on some problem or being asked to arbitrate some dispute.

About dark, we walked over to one of the houses in the little village across the strip, where dinner had been prepared for us. After a couple of shots of fiery local corn whisky, Pop, Tom, and I sat with the Meo man who was our host around a crude table made from a rice drop palette. The hot meal of glutinous rice, fried chicken, and vegetable soup was delicious. There were no plates, and everyone ate with their hands and with two big spoons directly from the bowls of food by the light of a flickering candle.

When the men finished eating and left the table, the women and children sat down for their meal. We chatted for a short time and had one more round of the corn whisky. After thanking our hosts, we walked back across the strip to Pop's office to spend the night.

The office crew had already gone to bed on the folding cots in the warehouse, and the building was in darkness. Tom lit a couple of candles, and Pop got out a bottle of the same whisky we'd drunk over dinner. I could see it was going to be a long, hard night.

During the evening we covered a wide variety of subjects and passed the bottle around frequently. Toward the last we argued about who'd had the hardest life during the Great Depression in the thirties. Was it worse on Pop's farm in Indiana, or our farm in Southern Louisiana? Whether I'd squeezed as much cow shit between my toes as he had when we were boys, and what was the best way to castrate a calf? I was trying to establish my credentials as a farm boy, but Pop would have none of it. He was convinced I was a phoney. Tom acted as judge and moderator, and—to provoke Pop—decided in my favor that I was in fact a *bona fide* Cajun "coon ass."

The old man raged that we were a couple of "ed'cated fools" and he didn't need us tellin' him what was what. Late in the cold, damp night, we finally pulled off our boots and all crawled up on the big bamboo bed, wrapped up in blankets, and immediately fell asleep.

Before the alcohol had destroyed all reason, however, Pop recounted some of his background and his experience in Northern Laos.

Born on a farm in Steuben County, Indiana, in 1913, his parents were very poor, and the work on the farm prevented him from having much formal education. He didn't go to high school, and struggled for survival through the Depression. Despite being exempt from military service, Pop volunteered for the army toward the end of World War II. He didn't go overseas, but became skilled as a demolition expert.

By the late fifties he was a successful, affluent farmer; had made a very happy marriage; and had two children—Howard and Harriet—whom he adored. Although he never ran for office, Pop was active in local and state politics. He was well respected in the community, and was able to influence his farmer friends and neighbors. His political support was cultivated and valued.

At the height of a fulfilling and satisfying life, disaster struck. His wife, Malorene died of cancer after a relatively short illness. Life lost all its joy and meaning for Pop, and his grief was overwhelming. He could no longer exist in an environment which reminded him of his beloved wife continuously each day. He turned the farm over to Howard and saw that Harriet and her school-teacher husband were financially secure. He then joined the International Voluntary Services (IVS).

As the name implies, IVS is a worldwide organization made up of volunteers—involved in community development at the village level—who work without pay in third world countries. Although the membership and funding are largely American, the headquarters is in Geneva, Switzerland, and volunteers come from many different countries. Pop was assigned to Laos as an agricultural advisor in 1959, and was stationed at Lat Houang on the Plain of Jars in Xieng Khoung province.

In 1960, Pop worked with the Meo in the villages on the southern perimeter of the Plain of Jars, and formed a close rapport with them. As he got to know them and began to learn their language, he soon realized that they weren't greatly different from himself or his farmer friends in Indiana. Conservative, independent, shrewd, and with strong family ties, they thought like he did, and experienced the same problems he had on his own farm.

Around this time he also got to know (the then) Lieutenant-Colonel Vang Pao—VP—and they formed a close and enduring friendship. VP was 28 and Pop was 47 when they first met, and Pop became not just a friend to VP, but a councillor and father figure as well. When the communist Pathet Lao (PL) forces and neutralists attacked the rightist forces at the end of 1960 and into 1961, 70,000 Meo were displaced from their villages. They were in desperate need of assistance. Pop continued to work with them, and he mobilized the resources they needed to survive—particularly rice and medicines. By merely being the man on the spot, he became the American representative. The refugee supplies came from the USAID mission in Vientiane, and were delivered by Air America and Bird & Sons contract aircraft, which were controlled by Pop.

By the end of 1961, and after several moves, the refugees—with Pop's help—settled in the mountains surrounding the Plain of Jars. VP established the Meo military headquarters at Long Chieng, and Pop set up and ran the refugee relief operation out of Sam Thong. When he completed his two-year volunteer agreement with IVS, Pop accepted a position with USAID—but his job was essentially unchanged. He continued to work with the refugees from his headquarters at Sam Thong.

✪✪✪

When I woke in the morning, the sun was over the horizon, and Pop and Tom were already up and about. Much to my surprise, my head was clear and I felt good. Ut, one of Pop's houseboys, gave me a cup of coffee and a small bun. Pop and I sat outside in the rising sun and drank our coffee. The mountain air was chilly, and the warmth of the sun and the hot coffee really hit the spot. Pop said that after the aircraft arrived, he wanted to take me to Long Chieng to meet VP.

Around nine o'clock we climbed aboard a Helio and flew over to Long Chieng. Although only about five kilometers apart, the two places are separated by a deep valley between two high ridges covered with dense, almost impenetrable jungle. It would take most of a day to walk from one place to the other. In later years, a dirt road was built to connect the two, but it was so winding and difficult, that it took about an hour or more to drive. In one of the STOL aircraft or a chopper, the trip took around ten minutes.

Around 1970, a treacherous, almost impassable road was completed from Vientiane to Long Chieng, but access to the place was rigorously controlled. There was no safe or practical way to get to either Long Chieng or Sam Thong from the outside world except by air. The two places were connected by field telephone and radio, but the only outside communication was through the USAID, CIA, or military radio nets.

At the time of my arrival in 1963, all civilian activities were centered at Sam Thong, and all the military activities at Long Chieng. No aircraft were permitted in the Northern region—above the 1962 Geneva Accord cease-fire line just north of Vientiane—without the clearance of Pop or VP, and no aircraft landed at Long Chieng with any person who wasn't previously cleared by either of them. Because of these security measures, Long Chieng became known as the "secret CIA base"—a rather euphemistic title for such a squalid collection of ramshackle bamboo-and-thatch buildings. It was one of the most unattractive places in Laos.

In reality, there was nothing much of a secret nature going on at Long Chieng except the presence of two CIA operations officers and a handful of Thai Police Aerial Re-supply Unit (PARU) military advisers. By no stretch of the imagination was there any clandestine activity at Sam Thong other than the USAID support to the dependants of VP's irregular troops—who, in large part, were refugees.

The main reason for the limited access to the area was simply that VP and Pop didn't want to be bothered with uncontrolled visiting. There was too much work to do.

We landed on a short, dirt strip in a cloud of red dust, and walked over to VP's house about 100 meters away. The residence was an unpainted, one-story structure with a corrugated-tin roof. Four people were sitting talking on the wide front porch, and they got up and greeted us very cordially. Pop introduced me to VP, Vint Lawrence, Tony Poe, and Captain Macorm, the Thai PARU commander.

Vang Pao, the Meo leader, was born in a small village in the Nong Het area, located in the mountains of Xieng Khoung on the east side of the Plain of Jars, on Route 7 just before it enters Vietnam. When Vang Pao was a child, Chao Saykham, the hereditary prince of the old principality of Xieng Khoung was the primary school inspector for the province—and the first Lao official in the colonial administration to take an interest in providing education for the ethnic minorities. He knew Vang Pao's father, and encouraged him to send his bright, high-spirited son to the new school he had established.

The first day Vang Pao went to school, he was so filthy that Chao Saykham made him go home and bathe before he would allow him in the classroom. Nevertheless, it was the beginning of a close and warm relationship that continued when Chao Saykham became the governor of Xieng Khoung and VP became the regional military commander.

Vang Pao was a good student and did well in school. In his early teens he acted as an interpreter for the French force that had parachuted into the Plain of Jars to organize the resistance against the Japanese. At that early age he was already fluent in Meo, Lao, and French, and also spoke some Vietnamese and English. Later, he became a lieutenant in the Forces Armee du Royaume (FAR) when the Lao national army was formed. Through most of the first Indochina War, he served with the Meo irregular troops on the Plain of Jars under the tribal leader, Touby Lyfoung.

In 1954, the young Lieutenant Vang Pao led 850 of the hilltribe irregulars (one unit of the 8,000 men in Operation Condor) through the rugged mountains of Sam Neua in an unsuccessful attempt to relieve the French garrison at Dien Bien Phu. He established a reputation as an aggressive and effective field commander.

After the fall of Dien Bien Phu and the signing of the Geneva Accords of 1954, Vang Pao returned to regular duty with the FAR. By 1959, he'd advanced to the rank of lieutenant-colonel, and in 1964 Major-General Vang Pao was made commander of the Military Region 2. This area included Xieng Khoung, Sam Neua, and Borikhane provinces; the area of Laos that the North Vietnamese placed the highest priority on occupying and controlling.

After the US Military Advisory Group (MAG) was pulled out of the country under the 1962 Geneva Accords, the CIA stationed three field operations officers at Long Chieng, but one was transferred very shortly after he arrived. They acted as advisers to Colonel (later General) Vang Pao, and controlled the military support being supplied to the Meo, as well as intelligence gathering.

Vint Lawrence was a tall, handsome young man in his late twenties; charming, personable, and intelligent. He was as fluent in French and Lao as he was in English, and his quiet self-assurance reflected a background of affluence and good schooling. He and VP became close friends, and had great respect and affection for each other. They worked together effectively and harmoniously.

Anthony Poshepny—Tony Poe—contrasted sharply with Vint Lawrence. Tony was a tough Pole in his mid-thirties, built like an Olympic wrestler, crude, shrewd, and hard drinking. When he was 19, he'd hit the beach at Iwo Jima as a US Marine in World War II—and had never stopped fighting since. A man of great personal courage and determination, Tony completed many long and dangerous missions behind enemy lines, and was as good a guerrilla tactician as anyone that ever fought in small, irregular wars. I know of at least five times that he was wounded, and it's a miracle—or just sheer luck—that he's still alive.

Captain Macorm, the PARU commander was a quiet, pleasant, and rather handsome young man. A highly competent, professional soldier, "Mac" was in charge of the forty original Thai military advisors that were assigned to Laos to carry out what the Thai government considered an extremely important and sensitive mission—criteria that could be applied to all PARUs.

Although all the men were tough combat soldiers, the PARU name had been carefully chosen for its non-specificity and ambiguity as part of their cover. The PARUs were fighting men of whom any country would be extremely proud. Of the original group, 27 lost their lives fighting in Laos.

After 1966, the number of CIA operations officers and Thai advisors and technicians were increased at Long Chieng. The total population reached over 40,000, and by the late sixties it was possibly the second-largest town in Laos. Despite this, it was still hardly more than a collection of crude huts that provided shelter and some security for 5,000 or more families whose men were in a desperate struggle for survival against the North Vietnamese invaders.

After chatting for an hour or so, Pop and I took off in a Helio. Over the next two days, we visited several of the Meo refugee villages on the southern edge of the Plain of Jars, sleeping wherever night found us.

Pop seldom slept at Sam Thong. Even when he was very busy, he would work all day at the center, and then—late in the afternoon—fly to some refugee village to spend the night. In the evenings, the people wouldn't be working, and he could sit and discuss their problems. Early the next morning he would fly back to Sam Thong to continue the work that had to be done.

After three exciting, fascinating days and nights, I returned to Vientiane. The trip had been a revelation—and my mind was filled with ideas of how to make a contribution to the work VP and Pop were doing. I could hardly contain my excitement. I wanted to get started immediately.

The Land of a Million Elephants and the White Parasol

> *"This a privileged corner of the world, where the people's mores have retained an exquisite simplicity. My affection quite naturally went toward the Laotians who are so gentle and so peaceful and who remain gay even in the worst of misfortunes."*

Auguste Pavie, the French consular officer stationed at Luang Prabang in 1885, made the above statement—and the effect that Laos has on the Westerner who knows the country and its people has never been better stated. The natural beauty of its misty mountains; its towering, emerald forests; its wild, turbulent rivers; together with its charming, friendly people, has a profound impact on the visitor.

A landlocked country with an area of 150,000 square kilometers, Laos extends 1,200 kilometers north and south, and 400 kilometers from east to west in a long, narrow strip (see map). Vietnam borders it to the east, Thailand to the west, and Cambodia to the south. There is a short border with China in the North, and an even shorter frontier with Burma in the Northwest. The mighty Mekong River separates Laos from Thailand for several hundred kilometers, but the Lao provinces of Sayaboury in the Northwest, and Champassac in the South, are on the river's west bank. Rugged, calcareous ridges—with peaks rising to 3,000 meters—run north and south, enclosing narrow valleys used for wet rice agriculture. Most of the country is heavily forested—despite centuries of slash and burn farming.

In May or June, monsoon winds from the southwest bring warm, moisture-laden air from the Indian Ocean. In the lowland areas, the rains—averaging 150-200 centimeters per year—usually produce a bountiful crop, although both drought and flood destroy the harvest on infrequent occasion.

In the mountains, orographic cooling—the sudden uplifting of air by the rising slope—causes much heavier rainfall, often exceeding 400 centimeters. The rainy season is cool and pleasant. The mornings are sunny, but not unduly hot; most rain falls for only an hour or two in the late afternoon; sunsets are truly magnificent; and the evening sky is clear and bright. Less than one third of the rain comes from heavy, overcast skies that are usually thought of as characteristic of the monsoon.

The monsoon subsides by October, and very little rain falls in the dry season from that time until the following May. The first part of the dry season from November through February is cool with occasional thunderstorms. Fog often persists until mid-morning and interferes with air operations.

March, April, and May are humid, hot, and dusty, and there isn't a cloud in the sky. However, the sun is often obscured during the hot season by a heavy pall of smoke—as the swidden farmers burn trees and brush felled to clear the new rice fields; and lowland paddy farmers burn off rice stubble in preparation for plowing. The whole northern part of the Southeast Asian peninsula is afire from the Bay of Bengal to the South China Sea, and this is the most unpleasant time of year.

In Laos, as in most of Southeast Asia, the rhythm of life is determined by the southwest monsoon—and this is true in war or peace. The preparation of the land, planting, cultivation, and harvest of the rice is governed by the onset and cessation of the rains. Festivals, religious ceremonies, marriages, and other social activities accommodate to the agricultural cycle.

During the years of war in Laos, the enemy began preparations for the perennial military operations when the roads and trails dried out in October. By the end of January or beginning of February, men and munitions were in place, and the "dry season offensive" commenced. Military activity was brought to a halt by the onset of the heavy rains in June.

In the sixties and seventies, there was no effective road system in Laos. Routes were built during the French colonial period—from the royal capital of Luang Prabang to Saigon (Route 13), and from Savannakhet to Vinh (Route 9) in Central Vietnam—but after the defeat of the French, lack of security and maintenance precluded their use except at rare, short intervals. The Vietnamese-controlled roads from Hanoi (Route 6) and Vinh (Route7) into the Plain of Jars in Xieng Khoung were exclusively used by the invaders for military purposes. A few unimproved roads near the Mekong towns served only their immediate areas.

31

The Mekong—navigable from the Chinese border in the North to the Khong Falls on the Cambodian border in the South—has always been an important transportation and communication link, but did little to relieve the isolation in the hinterland, even a few kilometers away from its banks. Travel and transportation through the countryside was entirely by foot—or with pack animals—on narrow trails.

☉

The population of Laos in 1963 was estimated at 3,500,000—with about 60% Lao-Tai, and 40% hilltribes. It was, in large part, a country of 10,000 small, economically self-sufficient villages—each with a population seldom exceeding 300. Once or twice a year, a few people would go to the nearest market town to sell some handicrafts, agricultural or forest products, and buy salt, iron bars, or metal tools in return. Any money left over was spent on clothing, and—possibly—silver or gold bars or jewelry. The precious metal was a joy for a wife, a source of prestige for her husband, and a resource in time of need.

The people of Laos can be divided into three poorly-defined ethnic and linguistic groups. Mon-Khmer tribes—the aboriginal people—are scattered throughout the country, and are usually called Lao Theung, or middle Lao, as they occupy land between the mountains and the river valley. In the southern part of the country, they are also called Kha—a pejorative term meaning slave. They are the least cohesive group, and the least developed. There were about a million Lao Theung during my time in the country.

The Sinitic Meo—also called Hmong by some writers and young refugees—and Yao are the most recent arrivals; pushed out of Southern China into Laos over the last 90-150 years. They fled repressive military action by the Han Chinese—which is often an explanation for their rebellious and independent behavior. In the literature of Laos, they are sometimes referred to as the Lao Soung, or high Lao, as they live at the highest levels in the mountains.

During the 11 years I lived and worked with these people, I never heard them use either the term Lao Soung or Hmong to describe themselves. The Yao most often refer to themselves as Mien. Both the Meo and Yao have strong clan organization and a highly structured leadership. They are tough, independent, and make good soldiers. There were about 350,000 Meo, and fewer than 30,000 Yao in the country during the war years.

The largest ethnic group are the Lao-Tai, including the lowland Lao wet rice farmers, as well as the mountain-dwelling Tai dry rice farmers. The Tai are found in the Northern provinces that border China, Burma, and Vietnam, while the Lao are found throughout the country in the river valleys that have flat alluvial areas suitable for wet rice farming—particularly along the Mekong.

The Lao and Tai are the same people ethnically and linguistically, and their dialects are usually—but not always—mutually understandable. There is some cultural divergence due to their adaptation to different physical environments. In addition, the Tai are more vigorous and assertive, but these characteristics could also be environmental in origin. All are Buddhist, and use derivations of the Pali-Sanskrit orthography, that—with some effort—are usually mutually legible. The Lao are sometimes called Lao Loum, or Lowland Lao, as opposed to the Lao Theung and Lao Soung. There were about two million ethnic Lao, and 100,000 Tai in the country at the time I worked in Laos.

The Lao-Tai people were thought to have originated in Southern China, or possibly farther north in the region of the Altai Mountains. Over a period of 5,000 years they were gradually pushed south by the Han Chinese, and occupied much of Burma, Southern China, Northwestern Vietnam and what is present-day Laos and Thailand. In the southern extent of their migration, they displaced the Mon-Khmer, and established themselves in the river valleys that were suitable for growing wet rice.

More recent research suggests that their origin may have been centered in Northeast Thailand—with expansion to the north, and then displacement back to the south. By the twelfth century—under strong Buddhist and Indian religious and cultural influence—they had developed stable agrarian communities. These grew into small principalities that became somewhat feudal in nature if strong leadership manifested itself. Under these leaders they alternately coalesced and fragmented—both from internal strife, and from the external pressure exerted by the Burmese to the west, and the Khmers to the southeast.

✪

Laos as a historical and political entity appears in the fourteenth century. The kingdom of Lan Xang (The Land of the Million Elephants and the White Parasol) was established in 1353 by Prince Fa Ngum, who had defeated Chiang Mai and the smaller Thai states along the Mekong. Fa Ngum—a Lao raised in Cambodia—married a daughter of the Khmer king, and under his dynasty, Lan Xang developed into a prosperous realm—with a unified administration; a strong, well-disciplined army; a regular population census; and active trade with all its neighbors.

During the fourteenth and early fifteenth centuries, Lang Xang controlled most of what is present day Laos, Northern Thailand, and the 12 Tai Cantons in Northern Laos and Northwest Vietnam. It was an area comparable in size to California.

In the seventeenth century, internal strife divided Lang Xang into two kingdoms: Luang Prabang in the North, and Vientiane in the South. Greatly weakened by the split, the two kingdoms eventually fell easy prey to their stronger neighbors—the Siamese (Thai), Burmese, and Vietnamese. Vientiane was completely destroyed by Siam in 1828, and the kingdom of Luang Prabang was reduced to vassalage and forced to pay tribute to both China and Vietnam.

The French arrived on the scene in 1885 when Auguste Pavie was appointed consul general at Luang Prabang. Over the next seven years, Pavie explored much of Laos on three separate expeditions. During the course of his explorations, he had several confrontations with Siamese troops—which caused France to take forceful diplomatic action against Siam. As a result, Siam renounced all claims of suzerainty over Laos, but France agreed that all territory on the west bank of the Mekong belonged to Siam. This was partially rectified in 1902 and 1907, but large Lao-populated areas remained under Siamese control—particularly on the Korat Plateau, in what is Northeast Thailand today.

Although the kingdom of Luang Prabang continued to exist, the French colonial government directed most of its affairs, and exerted complete control over the rest of Laos. They were able to administer the country, with a minimal number of French personnel, by adopting the traditional village and district administrative system—which was elective, democratic, and efficient. At the middle administrative level—where literacy and dependability were essential—large numbers of Vietnamese were brought in by the French. As a consequence, the administrative centers along the Mekong gained large Vietnamese populations which may have outnumbered the Lao in some instances.

The French colonials did little to develop the country, and were content merely to collect the head tax, corvee labor, and exploit the opium trade. There appeared to be no substantive economic potential in Laos, and a significant investment of money or personnel could not be justified— although minor efforts were made in education and medical care.

In some cases the French favored a small, ethnic Lao elite with education in Hanoi, Saigon, Phnom Penh, and—in a few instances—France. This group, although greatly outnumbered by the Vietnamese was able to control high positions in the civil service because of their ability to interface with the Lao population. In other words, the Lao elite were able to continue their traditional patronage relationships and control large segments of the rural population—to their advantage and that of the French.

The tribal people were more or less ignored by the French, except in such specific instances as their involvement in the opium trade. Whereas the Lao admired the French and their culture, the tribal groups despised them because of their discrimination and brutal treatment. The French solution to a tribal problem was simply to murder the local leader. This resulted in several bloody rebellions during the colonial administration, and created a Francophobia which continues even to this day.

During World War II, the Japanese abolished the French administration and a "National Independence Movement" arose in Vientiane. On September 2nd, 1945, members of this movement formed a provisional government. During the war, both French guerrillas and Lao independence fighters—the Lao Seri—had operated against the Japanese, and against each other. The French were working toward re-establishing their control, and the Lao Seri were striving to establish an independent state.

As the war ended, there was much maneuvering by the French, and Prince Phetsarath—the king's half-brother, and head of the provisional government in Vientiane—was unable to get the support of the king in Luang Prabang. The king and the royal family preferred the security of French protection rather than to expose themselves to the aims of their powerful neighbors. As a consequence, the various Lao nationalist groups created another provisional government in Vientiane called the Lao Issara (Free Lao) on October 12th, 1945.

In this confused situation, the communist Viet Minh's overriding interest was to prevent the French from regaining control of Indochina. They supported the Lao nationalist movement—as represented by Phetsarath and the Lao Issara—and called on the Vietnamese and Chinese in Laos to obey Lao authority and help unite the country. To facilitate this policy, Ho Chi Minh sent Prince Souphanouvong—Pethsarath's half-brother—back to Laos to help organize the resistance to the French.

Souphanouvong had been working in Vietnam in the engineering corps. A brilliant, dynamic man who had spent most of his life in France and Vietnam, he hated French colonialism, and had strong emotional ties to the Vietnamese—as well as a Vietnamese wife. Like many other future communist leaders in Vietnam and Cambodia, he had been strongly influenced by socialist philosophy while a student in France.

The Vietnamese communists hadn't wanted the large Vietnamese population in the Lao towns to take too overt a role in resisting the French efforts to re-establish their control. This might frighten the Lao, and motivate their nationalist leaders to accept the French if there was a threat of Vietnamese domination. Souphanouvong was the ideal person to represent their interest because he could direct events toward their goals without it appearing to be a Vietnamese intervention.

In October 1945, Souphanouvong arrived in Savannakhet in Central Laos with about a dozen Viet Minh officers and enlisted men dressed in Lao uniforms. He was met by thousands of armed Vietnamese and communist cadre who had been instructed by Ho Chi Minh of the necessity "to keep Laos out of the hands of the imperialists, otherwise Vietnam will never be able to remain independent."

However, all did not go as Souphanouvong had anticipated. Oun Sananikone—one of the more capable Lao Issara leaders—had already arrived in Savannakhet from Thailand, and had assumed leadership of the area. Oun was cooperating with Phetsarath, but eventually, at Souphanouvong's insistence, agreed to the formation of a new liberation front—the Committee for an Independent Laos. Souphanouvong was chairman, Oun vice chairman, Phoumi Nosovan was named chief of staff, and Phetsarath was made honorary chairman. Souphanouvong informed Phetsarath that he was willing to merge their organization with the Vientiane Lao Issara movement, and also notified the provincial governors that they should form regional independence committees.

A few days later, Souphanouvong arrived in Vientiane by riverboat and confronted the Lao Issara government. Khammao Vilay had replaced Phetsarath as prime minister, and Souphanouvong was able to force Khammao to appoint him to both the post of minister of foreign affairs, and commander-in-chief of the armed forces.

It appeared that the Lao resistance forces might prevail against the king and the French, but they were out-maneuvered. Ho Chi Minh accepted a ceasefire with France in return for French recognition of his republic as a "free state" in Vietnam within the Indochina Federation and the French Union.

By May 1946, the French army had re-established its protectorate. The Lao Issara leaders fled to Thailand, as did Souphanouvong. Thousands of Vietnamese who had compromised themselves escaped to Northeast

Thailand, leaving only 20-25% of the previous Vietnamese residents in the Lao towns. Communist cadre who had come from Vietnam, quietly slipped back to the east.

In 1946, Laos and France signed a "*modus vivendi.*" A National Constituent Assembly convened in March 1947, and two months later it promulgated the Lao Constitution. On July 19th, 1949, France formally recognized the independence of the kingdom of Laos within the French Union. Parliamentary elections were held, and the structure of the Royal Lao Government (RLG) resembled that of other limited constitutional monarchies. The legislative branch in the administrative capital of Vientiane had an upper house appointed by the king, which was a deliberative body with little power. The lower house was elected by popular vote. The king and the royal family resided in the royal capital at Luang Prabang, filling only a ceremonial role.

Although the French presence was less oppressive, and most of the Vietnamese functionaries were removed, Laos was far from independent in a true sense. The French and their troops still had control of the country. Independence forces operating out of Thailand continued the resistance, but with decreasing success and increasing problems with the Thai. Within two or three years, most of the leaders had become discouraged and joined the Vientiane government.

On the Vietnamese side, the Viet Minh had taken the lead in organizing the Lao leaders and men who had fled in that direction. For a time there was liaison and cooperation between the resistance forces in Thailand and those supported by the Viet Minh. However, Katay Don Sasorith, who headed the Lao government in exile in Bangkok, and Prince Souphanouvong, who headed the Viet Minh-supported forces, had a complete breakdown of relationship, and the two groups went their separate ways.

With the triumph of the Chinese People's Liberation Army in 1949, there was substantial Chinese support to the Viet Minh. Operations against the French greatly increased, both in Vietnam and Laos. In 1953, Viet Minh forces with a few hundred Lao People's Liberation Army soldiers occupied Northeastern Sam Neua and Phong Saly, and penetrated into Xieng Khoung and Luang Prabang. On April 19th, 1953, Souphanouvong announced the establishment of a resistance government in Sam Neua City—and this continued to be the headquarters of the Lao independence movement—later the Pathet Lao—until they took over the government in 1975.

After the Vietnamese triumph at Dien Bien Phu in 1954—and the subsequent accords that resulted from the Geneva Conference on Indochina—the political situation was left in an ambiguous state in all three Indochinese countries. This was particularly true as far as the communists were concerned. Vietnam was divided north and south, but the Viet Minh believed they would be able to unite the country by controlling the elections that were supposedly to take place within two years.

In Laos, the communist Pathet Lao forces were not permitted to hold on to the territory they had occupied, but would hold "re-groupment areas" whose future would be decided by elections organized by the royal government.

In Cambodia, the Khmer Issarak resistance forces were not even considered. Although the Geneva Accords were claimed as a great victory by the Indochinese communists, it was—in reality—a disappointment to them. They had expected to keep their territorial gains, and keep their military forces in place. In any event, Laos had finally regained its independence.

At this point I shall not go into the details of the complex political events which occurred in Laos between 1954 and 1963 when I arrived. It would be tedious for the reader and is not within the province of an anecdotal and non-scholarly book such as this. Nevertheless, a few comments might provide a better understanding of what followed.

The US, the Soviet Union, France, Canada, China, India, Great Britain, Poland, Thailand, Burma, Cambodia, North Vietnam, South Vietnam, and Laos participated in the Geneva Conventions which dealt with the political problems that arose from the defeat and withdrawal of the French from Indochina. The Geneva Accords on Indochina in 1954, and on Laos in 1962, guaranteed the neutrality of Laos, and called for the withdrawal of all foreign troops from the country except those specified to help the Lao in preparing for their security. The accords were to be implemented under the supervision of an International Control Commission (ICC), composed of members from India, Canada, and Poland.

China and the Soviet Union wanted to see communist governments in all the Indochinese states, but would prefer that Cambodia and Laos be independent of Vietnam. North Vietnam, of course, wanted to take over South Vietnam and establish communist governments in Laos and Cambodia under their control. The US wanted to contain the communists in North Vietnam, and keep South Vietnam, Cambodia, and Laos from domination by North Vietnam; simply an extension of the broader US foreign policy of containing communism worldwide. A sense of urgency was added by proponents of the "domino theory"—that if one Southeast Asian state fell to the communists, all the others would fall one after the other.

The ICC was rendered ineffective by the Vietnamese and Pathet Lao refusing access to the areas they controlled. Also, the Polish delegation deliberately obstructed the work of the commission and supported the communists. The Indians, who headed the three delegations, assumed a passive and neutral role. The Canadians made a sincere effort to carry out the terms of the accords, but were frustrated by this combination of adverse factors.

By 1963, Laos was divided into rightist, neutralist, and communist factions—both politically and geographically. The communists controlled Northern Nam Tha, Phong Saly (except for a small area bordering on Luang Prabang) Eastern Sam Neua, and the Tchepone area in Eastern Savannakhet. They also had small enclaves on the eastern edge of the Plain of Jars in Xieng Khoung; in Luang Prabang; Vientiane; and in Borikhane. A narrow strip of Laos that bordered on North and South Vietnam throughout its entire extent was an integral part of the Ho Chi Minh Trail. This deliberate annexation of Lao territory by the North Vietnamese to supply the insurgency in South Vietnam was considered a *fait accompli,* even by the RLG.

The neutralists had established themselves on the western edge of the Plain of Jars, and in the immediate vicinity of Vang Vieng—a small but important town on Route 13, 100 kilometers north of Vientiane.

Less than a third of the countryside, and an even smaller proportion of the population, was under the control of the communist and neutralist forces. The RLG was firmly established in all the Mekong River towns from the Chinese border in the North, to Cambodia in the South. Through the tribal leaders—particularly Vang Pao with the Meo in Xieng Khoung and Sam Neua; Chao Mai with the Yao in Nam Tha; and Vuk with the Kha in the Bolovens Plateau-Saravane area—the RLG had strong support among the ethnic minorities. However, if one counted all the populace committed to all the combined antagonists—communists, neutralists, and rightists—the total would have been fewer than a million people. Over 70% of the Lao population had absolutely no commitment to any faction.

The typical Lao village was a self-sufficient economic, social, and political institution. Rare contact with the government usually left the villager without benefit or deprivation. The people gave little to the government, and received little in return. This limited horizon precluded the development of a strong sense of nationalism, except through the institution of the monarchy. The king and queen were revered by all ethnic groups. The average villager had an enviable, free, and contented life—mostly without the need of outside assistance. Fertile land and a mild climate provided adequate food and shelter. They wanted only to be left alone.

In 1950, the leftists formed a new Lao independence movement, headed by Prince Souphanouvong, called the Neo Lao Issara (Free Lao Front). It was part of the communist plan to organize the resistance to the French on separate, national fronts—and it included Kaysone Phomvihan as minister of defense; Nouhak Phoumsavan, minister of economy and finance; Suk Vongsak, minister of education; and Phoumi Vongvichit, minister of the interior. In addition, Sithon Kommadan, Kha chieftain from the South; Faydang Lobliayao, Meo chieftain from Xieng Khoung; Ma Khaykamphithoun; and Khamthay Siphandone, were all on the resistance council, but not designated as cabinet members. All the members of the Neo Lao Issara had strong ties to the Vietnamese—by parentage, marriage, or long association.

After independence in 1955, the Lao communist party was secretly established, and the following year, the front organization was publicly proclaimed. They called the party the Phak Pasason Lao (the Lao People's Party) and named the front, the Neo Lao Hak Sat (the Lao Patriotic Front).

Early on, the term Pathet Lao distinguished the Neo Lao Issara from the rightist Lao Issara and the RLG. However, this distinction was soon lost, and Pathet Lao eventually came into general usage—in a non-specific sense—to designate any indigenous Lao communist organization; troops or adherents.

Several attempts to form a viable coalition government with representation from the three factions all failed. By the end of 1963, all the communist cabinet members had left Vientiane, and their positions had been filled by rightists, or by neutralists who did not deviate too far to the left. Although the government in Vientiane was nominally neutral and headed by the neutralist prime minister, Prince Souvanna Phouma, it was strongly influenced by the Western countries, particularly the United States.

A civil war was tearing the country apart, with each faction fighting the other two. The North Vietnamese had invaded the country in sufficient strength to protect their political and territorial interests, and to control the Lao communists. Although they had signed the Geneva Accords, they had no intention of withdrawing their troops from Laos. The Western countries had withdrawn all their military assets except those allowed under the accords. The feeble economy was kept alive by foreign exchange supplied by the "Western" donor nations—the United States, Great Britain, Japan, and France. The problems were overwhelming and the future was not promising.

However, the worst aspect of the situation was that whatever happened in Laos would result from events that would take place in Vietnam. The country's legitimate interests would never be considered on their own merit, but only within the context of the political aspirations of the powers involved in the Vietnamese conflict.

This beautiful country and its sweet and gentle people would never be given the chance to reach its separate and legitimate destiny.

The Filipino Connection

Since the OB contract was the only health project of any significance funded by USAID Laos, I wanted to take a look at their hospital operations as quickly as possible. The total budget for the project amounted to 1.5 million dollars per year, and this included the operation of the four hospitals; the running of the nursing school; and administration and procurement of drugs and supplies. The cost per patient per hospital day was about five dollars, and the average cost per outpatient visit was fifty cents. These figures were so low they were hard to believe—and led me to think that the quality of care must certainly reflect such a low expenditure.

I spent two days with Vitoy Naranjo looking at the Vientiane facility, and—much to my relief—the quality of care was much higher than one would assume from the level of funding. The buildings were cheaply and poorly constructed, but well maintained; the large, open wards were clean and bright with a cheerful atmosphere; the dietary service was good; and the nursing care was excellent. The nursing supervisor, "Joji"—Vitoy's wife—was a quiet, attractive young lady who gave an impression of efficiency and professionalism. Obviously, she ran a top-notch program.

There was also Vincenta "Toots" Calderon, who directed the nursing school as well as a public health program in some of the outlying villages. She had a masters degree in nursing education from Columbia University in New York. The doctors seemed qualified for this type of activity, but I reserved my evaluation until I could observe them in greater depth. However, considering what I had seen so far, I was well pleased.

The Filipino staff was young, enthusiastic, and dedicated. Vitoy, Joji, and Toots provided strong leadership and discipline, while maintaining a pleasant, relaxed relationship with both their fellow Filipinos and the Lao. Above all, they were training the Lao—who had only a basic education—to a high level of proficiency in nursing and other hospital skills.

The American mission had two "milk run" flights each day from Vientiane to Northern and Southern Laos. The aircraft were Air America C47s or occasionally C46s. Heading north they landed at Luang Prabang, Sayaboury, and Ban Houi Sai. Going south they stopped at Savannakhet, Pakse, and Attopeu. On the return trip they made the same stops.

The week after I visited Pop at Sam Thong, Vitoy, Toots, and I took the milk run south to visit the OB installations at Paksong and Attopeu. The following week we planned to go to Sayaboury. The old C47 was hot and uncomfortable, and wallowed through the bumpy air. About half of the forty passengers were vomiting, and the rest weren't feeling too well—including me. We were happy to land at Pakse and get our feet on the ground. It was about ten-thirty in the morning.

Dr. "Bing Bing" Alegar, one of the Filipino doctors at Paksong, had driven down to meet us. Bing Bing was a slim, gangling young man, smiling and friendly. Before driving up on the Bolovens Plateau to Paksong, we had to stop at the USAID area co-ordinator's office. The area co-ordinators were the senior American officials in the six major Lao towns and the surrounding countryside. They were responsible for all American-supported projects and activities in their designated area. The AC as he was called, was also responsible for the security and safety of both resident and temporary-duty personnel. All Americans and third country nationals who worked for the US were required to inform him of their activities while in his area of authority.

In Pakse, the AC was John McQueen. We went to his office and I introduced myself as the new public health officer. Vitoy and Toots had known John for two or three years, and they were obviously good friends. After chatting a few minutes, they accepted his invitation to lunch later, and in the meantime left to take care of some business with Bing Bing in town. John then took the time to brief me on the various American projects in the Pakse area; give me a run-down on the local political situation; and introduce me to the members of his staff. By the time we finished talking, it was twelve o'clock.

John's office was in a large building which also served as the McQueen residence. Vitoy, Toots, and Bing Bing returned, and we went into the house for lunch. John and Polly McQueen were a delightful couple in their late forties. Polly was a tiny, vivacious sprite of a woman who bubbled when talking, whereas John was six-feet-two, big but trim, thoughtful and deliberate. He'd spent several years as professor of agriculture at Texas A &

M before going overseas to Haiti and then Laos. By remarkable coincidence, I too had attended undergraduate school at Texas A & M, and John and I had several mutual friends. There was the usual warm feeling between ex-"aggies," and so lunch turned out to be all but a festive occasion.

We thanked John and Polly for their hospitality and started for Paksong. To my surprise the road was asphalted and quite good. Paksong is 100 kilometers east of Pakse, and sits in the middle of the Bolovens Plateau—a roughly circular area about 200 kilometers in diameter, rising to an average height of 1,000 meters, and flat except for occasional low, undulating hills. The sides of the plateau are sheer, vertical cliffs, except on the northeast perimeter. Thick rainforest covers much of the surface, but many small areas are cleared to grow vegetables and fruit, particularly pineapple and strawberries. Under the forest canopy, a fine grade of arabica coffee is also grown, and this crop gives the area considerable economic importance.

During the rainy season, huge rivers cascade hundreds of meters off the cliffs that form the perimeter of the Bolovens, and if one is fortunate enough to take a small plane or helicopter around the edge of the plateau, these magnificent waterfalls are truly an unforgettable sight.

The inhabitants of the Bolovens are Mon-Khmer—from many different tribal groups, but of the same racial stock as the hilltribe *montagnards* in Vietnam. Most are hunter-gatherers making the transition to agriculture. They plant dry rice, and convert a large part of it to alcohol—which they drink to excess. Sometimes whole villages would start celebrating some occasion and stay drunk for several days. Although their languages are related, they are rarely mutually understandable. Often, different tribal groups living in bordering areas cannot communicate with each other. At the time, their social and economic structures were primitive, and their health was terrible. Infant mortality approached 50%—as high as any place in the world.

On our way to Paksong we stopped at three or four villages which had dispensaries established and supported by OB. The medics or health workers were native to the village in which they worked, and had been chosen by Toots and Bing Bing—in consultation with the village elders—and trained at Paksong. The training course emphasised the basic health principles of hygiene, sanitation, and nutrition, but OB had also taught the workers to use a few symptomatic drugs to alleviate common ailments, and above all to set a good example for the villagers.

This aspect of the program was immediately apparent when we walked into one of the villages. Although the medic's dispensary-residence was built of the same bamboo and thatch as all the other houses, its cleanliness and order was in strong contrast to the general squalor of the village. An attractive bamboo fence protected it from the domestic animals; flowers grew on the boundary and around the building; there was a kitchen vegetable garden; and young banana and papaya plants screened and shaded a well-constructed water-seal toilet. Many of the village families were beginning to follow the example of the health worker, and Toots was well pleased with her student's work.

We arrived at the little town of Paksong late in the afternoon to find one main street lined with two-story, unpainted, wooden buildings—most of which were shops of one sort or another. Off to one side was a long, wooden school, and a collection of dilapidated government office buildings. On a hill overlooking the town there was a small military installation surrounded by barbed wire—which provided protection for the town, and security in the adjacent area. The population probably numbered about 1,000, but few people were on the street, and there was an atmosphere of gloom and decay. This was the height of the monsoon, and the clouds were down to the ground. It was uncomfortably cold and damp, and I regretted not having dressed in heavier clothing. At an altitude of 1,200 meters, the temperature was several degrees cooler than at Pakse. To me, Paksong seemed an unattractive blemish on a beautiful landscape.

The OB hospital was located in the middle of the town. The central core seemed to be an old, wooden residence—used for office space, as well as living quarters for the Filipino staff. Two long wings had been added to the old building to accommodate the clinical and laboratory functions, and to furnish beds for about forty patients. The whole facility was cheaply and crudely built, but was nevertheless clean and attractive. The Filipino staff deserved commendation for running such a high-quality operation with a minimum of resources. All the beds were full, and to my surprise, many of the patients were from Pakse.

The Paksong leader was Dr. Ramon "Mon" Pablo, and the team was composed of the two doctors (himself and Bing Bing), Mrs. Pablo—the nursing supervisor, plus five nurses, a nutritionist, and a laboratory technician who also did the X-rays. There was also one support person assigned to maintenance, procurement, warehousing, and anything else that was needed to keep the team functioning. All the Lao personnel were trained on the job, except a few of the nurses who'd attended the nursing school at OB Vientiane.

That evening, the hospital staff gave a party and invited all the local dignitaries and their wives. The *chao muang*, military commander, school principal, and well-known merchants were all there with members of their staff. The Filipinos had roasted a pig, and also prepared *lechon, dinaguan,* and several other of their national dishes. After much drinking and eating, there was singing and dancing well into the night. There was no doubt the OB people were liked and respected in the community.

We rose at six the next morning to cold and foggy weather. There was no hot water, and I was shivering so badly that it was difficult to shave and shower. After breakfast, Bing Bing and I made rounds on the patients, while Vitoy and Toots discussed administrative matters with Mon and Mrs. Pablo. Bing Bing also showed me the laboratory where they were making vaccines for cattle, buffalo, pigs, and chickens. Vaccines for domestic animals were unavailable in Laos, but badly needed. Epizootics of potentially controllable diseases often caused the loss of large numbers of animals. With a minimal amount of equipment, a large measure of innovation, and at hardly any cost, they had isolated causative organisms, prepared cultures, and made effective vaccines. Such ingenuity was certainly remarkable.

We were to due take the milk run from Pakse to Attopeu before noon, so it was necessary to leave Paksong by nine. The flight around the edge of the Bolovens Plateau was spectacular, with the many rivers falling from the crest to the plain far below. Attopeu, our next stop, located just off the southern edge of the plateau, is on the west bank of the Sekong River. The Ho Chi Minh Trail is a few kilometers to the east, and its Cambodian extension—the Sihanouk Trail—is even closer on the south. The small town is an ethnic Lao enclave in a predominantly Kha (Mon-Khmer) tribal countryside.

The pilot didn't start to descend until we were directly over the dirt strip on the edge of the town. The plane spiralled down and made a tight, short approach. Security in the vicinity of Attopeu wasn't too good, and if the plane deviated from the immediate vicinity of the town, it might come under enemy fire.

Dr. Pedro "Pete" Joaquin, the OB Attopeu team leader, was waiting for us when we landed, and the hospital—a brief, five-minute drive by jeep from the airfield—was a few meters from the bank of the Sekong in a coconut grove. It looked similar to the Paksong hospital—in that it was an old masonry building expanded to make ward space and house the outpatient service—but it was much smaller and had only 12 beds. It wasn't busy, and the small capacity seemed adequate.

At the time of our visit, the OB team was restricted to the town of Attopeu, and couldn't venture into the countryside because of poor security.

Previously, they had developed a public health program in the surrounding villages, but under the present situation, it wasn't possible to continue it.

Pete Joaquin—short and very obese—was a friendly, cheerful man whom I liked immediately. He'd been in Attopeu for three years, and about two years previously had lost his wife and two children in a tragic accident when their boat capsized while crossing the Sekong near the hospital. Vitoy had wanted to transfer Pete to another hospital, but he'd insisted on staying at Attopeu.

That evening, OB Attopeu duplicated the Paksong party of the previous night. The local military commander was there, and we had an opportunity to talk to him about the security situation in the area. Vitoy was highly concerned about the team, fearing they might get trapped, since there was no way to leave Attopeu except by air. The commander admitted that security was bad—and that the Vietnamese might try to occupy the area. On the positive side, he thought their intelligence was good, and if there was a threat to Attopeu, there'd be plenty of time to call in aircraft to evacuate the team.

The next morning, Vitoy and I walked around the town and found an atmosphere of dejection and gloom. Everyone seemed to be waiting for something bad to happen. Vitoy tried to converse with some of the people along the street, but they appeared reluctant to talk—even though the Lao usually love to talk to strangers.

Later, we discussed the security situation once again with Pete. He was of the same opinion as the military commander. Without doubt, the Vietnamese were concerned at the proximity of the Lao troops around Attopeu to their vital supply lines into South Vietnam and Cambodia. It was highly likely there would be problems, but danger didn't appear imminent.

If the Vietnamese moved against Attopeu, Pete agreed there would still be time to evacuate by air. Fortunately, the hospital had a radio transceiver that netted with OB Vientiane, and Vitoy instructed Pete to come up on the radio—at six in the morning, noon, and ten in the evening—on a regular schedule. If security began to deteriorate, they'd maintain a 24-hour radio "watch."

When we heard the plane overhead at noon, Pete took us to the airport. We boarded an old DC3 and headed back for Vientiane. Vitoy and I felt considerable apprehension and concern about Pete and the rest of the Attopeu staff. They were in a potentially dangerous situation that could deteriorate rapidly. We would need to monitor it closely. Our flight was uneventful and we landed at Wattay airport about four in the afternoon. Vitoy and I agreed to work in our offices for two days, then make the trip to visit OB Sayaboury.

Two days later, Toots and Vitoy met me at the airport and we took the milk run north to Sayaboury town, the capital of Sayaboury province—which, together with Champassac in the South, is the only Lao province on the west bank of the Mekong River.

The sleepy, little town of Sayaboury had a population of about 2,500, but the surrounding area was quite densely settled, considering Laos's sparse population. It lies in a valley dotted with villages encircled by rice paddies. With the exception of three or four small valleys which are suitable for wet rice culture, the province is rough and mountainous. Meo and Lao Theung—who practice slash and burn farming on the mountain slopes, and also raise dry rice, corn, and opium—make up most of the population. Because of the opium trade, Sayaboury town had a long, well-maintained turf airstrip, suitable for DC3s.

When we got off the plane, Dr. Azul, the OB Sayaboury team leader, met us with a jeep and took us to the hospital. The airfield was inside the town, and was only several hundred meters from the hospital. All the commercial and residential buildings were solidly constructed of wood, but they were unpainted and appeared very old. The buildings were scattered at random, leaving wide open grassy areas where water buffalo were grazing. There was a drab, sleepy atmosphere about the place, but for some obscure reason it was rather attractive.

The hospital was similar to Paksong and Attopeu—an expedient use of whatever happened to be available—and the OB team was housed in an old, wooden residential building which had been renovated to provide both living and office space. Across the narrow, dirt street, a tobacco warehouse had been converted into a long ward and an outpatient clinic. We arrived mid-morning, and the clinic was overflowing with patients.

After we chatted and had coffee, Vitoy said we should go and see the *chao kweng*—who was the brother of the king—and pay our respects before we did anything else. Members of the *chao kweng's* family had been hospitalized several times at OB Vientiane, and he and Vitoy had become close friends.

We drove to the provincial offices in the middle of town, where several bare, weathered structures faced onto a wide field that appeared to be a parade ground. All the buildings were single-story affairs constructed on wooden columns about two meters above the ground—and the *chao kweng* used one for his office and residence.

We walked up the steps and entered a large reception room with a high ceiling. The floor was made of polished rosewood boards, and the walls and ceiling were teak. All the furniture was ornately carved ebony, some decorated with mother-of-pearl inlay. No screens were on the windows, and the wooden shutters were open. It was a cool, pleasant place.

There were three or four people sitting around, but before we could sit down, the *chao kweng* walked out of his office and welcomed us. He was pleased to see Vitoy, and greeted him warmly. We went into his office, and—over coffee—Vitoy explained to him my position in USAID and my relationship to OB. He was a tall, distinguished-looking man with a strong, vibrant personality. His French was excellent, and although my capability in the language was minimal, we were able to converse without too much difficulty. After chatting for a while, he invited us to dinner that evening. Realizing he was very busy, we excused ourselves and returned to the hospital.

The OB Sayaboury team was similar to those at Paksong and Attopeu, except that Sayaboury had an agronomist. The OB organization thought of their health program as primarily a vehicle for community development—and secondly as providing a needed service in health care. As part of their community development effort, all the teams originally had an agronomist—who tried to teach more productive agricultural techniques and breeding methods, and also introduce new, high-yield, disease-resistant seeds and breeding stock.

Each hospital had a farm which demonstrated improved methods, and also helped to feed the staff and patients. Policy-wise, USAID objected to these activities, and was pressuring OB to discontinue them. The pressure originated from the head of the agricultural division of USAID—who contended that OB was duplicating their efforts in the same area, causing confusion and unnecessary expense. I found such a viewpoint asinine. It derived from unfavorable comparison between the well-received OB program, and some inappropriate USAID agricultural activities.

Aside from the beautiful demonstration farm, the OB Sayaboury operation was much like that of Paksong. Toots and the team had developed a successful dispensary and public health program in several of the surrounding villages—chosen from a survey which showed that they had the worst health problems in the area.

That afternoon, we visited three of the village dispensaries. Although they provided simple clinical care, the main focus was on health education and environmental problems. Mosquito abatement, clean water supply, refuse disposal, improved nutrition, personal hygiene, and maternal and child care were all promoted in some simple, practical way. The statistics on infant mortality and malnutrition at the beginning of the program three years previously, and at the time, showed a huge improvement in each village.

That evening, Vitoy and I had a delightful dinner with the *chao kweng*. To my surprise, we were the only guests, and the atmosphere was relaxed and pleasant. Our host had been a student in France for several years, and he appreciated good food. The meal was outstanding.

After dinner, we talked for several hours—with Vitoy interpreting in Lao when my French broke down. I was able to learn much about Laos, and particularly the royal family. The *chao kweng* spoke with frankness and considerable humor about his many relatives, and I felt fortunate to have had the opportunity to listen to his stories. It was midnight when we thanked him for his gracious hospitality and returned to the hospital.

The next day, we took the milk run back to Vientiane. Our tour of the OB hospitals had been much too hurried, but there was work to be done at my office, and I also needed to get back up to Sam Thong. Nevertheless, I now had some knowledge of the OB operation as a basis for discussion and decision-making. Our trip gave me a most favorable impression of their work. They were doing an outstanding job economically—and often with considerable ingenuity and imagination. Their grasp of the problems, and how to solve them, seemed appropriate and effective—and both the Lao and the United States were getting a bargain for the small amount of money being spent.

Refugee Relief

During the Vietnam War era, the US mission in Laos was second in magnitude only to South Vietnam. It gradually increased in size up to the early seventies, and reached a peak of over 400 personnel. USAID's role mainly comprised economic stabilization and development, public works projects, rural development, manpower development, and refugee relief—through various loans and grants.

During my stay in Laos, some American assistance in health operated at the ministerial and provincial levels—as separate programs administered by the Lao through the normal RLG channels—but most efforts and resources in health were put into the rural development and refugee relief programs, as part of a more comprehensive approach.

The largest USAID program of the Lao mission by far—in terms of funding and personnel—was refugee relief. An annual cycle of fighting caused the displacement of large segments of the population—particularly in the Northern provinces of Xieng Khoung, Sam Neua, Luang Prabang, and Nam Tha.

In the ten-years from 1963 to 1973, the Vietnamese and Pathet Lao displaced approximately one million people from their homes at least once. In those four Northern provinces, 500,000 were displaced several times—and in some instances, six times or more. For one of the poorest countries in the world, with a population of 3.5 million, this was a catastrophic situation.

The refugee relief program undertook to feed the displaced people, provide basic necessities, and make available primary health care. In the longer term, it attempted to help the people to become self-sufficient in basic foodstuffs; re-establish the government infrastructure; construct and support primary schools; and provide primary and secondary health care. An abundance of traditional building materials—such as bamboo, thatch, and timber—made shelter readily available. Although the winter season can be uncomfortably cold and damp in the mountains, the climate is usually mild, and heavy clothing isn't necessary. Due to the low population density, land for building villages and for agriculture was seldom a problem.

However, there were many enclaves of refugees and dependants of the military that were in very insecure areas—and little farming was possible other than in small garden plots. In secure areas, most refugee groups grew their own rice and many other crops, and were self-sufficient after one annual crop cycle.

Because of the availability of farming land, refugees weren't confined to camps, but instead dispersed themselves over large areas in their usual village groups. This made rehabilitation and attainment of self-sufficiency easier— but created enormous logistical problems, particularly in the first year of resettlement.

A typical situation was for a village, or group of villages, to be overrun during the night by Pathet Lao or Vietnamese troops. People would flee, panic-stricken, through the jungle, often leaving all their possessions behind, with nothing but a few rags on their backs. They would run for two, three days, a week—however long it took to get to a secure place. If possible, they would try to get to another village, or any place that had a STOL strip or at least a chopper pad. If that was impossible, a strip and drop zone would be hacked out of the jungle. Working together with the local officials, the USAID refugee relief officers would contact them using a chopper or STOL aircraft.

These refugees would be exhausted, starving, and demoralized; many of them ill or wounded. Before anything else was done, a list was made of all the people, by family and village. No matter how many times they were displaced, they continued to identify with their home village. This refugee list was important for planning and administrative reasons, but also important as a symbolic gesture that the refugee leaders were starting to function again. After the list (*bansee*) was made, morale always started to improve.

The USAID officer had a transceiver for ground to air contact, and would have a message relayed to the air operation in Vientiane to drop rice at his location. The people would clear a drop zone and mark it with cloth panels, and within a few hours, a C46 or a C123 would be dropping rice. A USAID public health officer with basic medical supplies would normally also be with the refugees, and he would quickly evaluate their health status. Whatever additional supplies and personnel he needed, were flown in the same day. Rolls of black plastic for temporary shelter; rolls of black cloth for making clothes; as well as blankets, machetes, hoes, cooking pots, cooking oil, powdered milk, and canned meat, all came streaming into the site in the first few days.

Clearing an airstrip always had top priority at a refugee site without one—since it was the end of the lifeline through which all supplies flowed. But because of the rugged terrain, it was often difficult to find a suitable location. Regulations required that the strips used by our small STOL planes be at least 500 feet long. Often, this was impossible to achieve, so we built the strips on steep slopes, and the pilot landed uphill and took off downhill—allowing gravity help brake the plane, as well as accelerate it for take-off. In the worst cases, we flew out of strips as short as 250 feet. Freak winds in the rough terrain, fog, smoke, low cloud ceilings, thunderstorms, torrential rains, a complete lack of navigational aids, as well as enemy ground fire—all made flying a nerve-chilling, hair-raising experience.

On one occasion, a new pilot being checked out in a Helio had been flying in horrible weather for several days. The check pilot in the right seat was Al Rich, a veteran of thousands of hours in the Lao STOL program.

"Captain," the new pilot asked Al in a frustrated tone. "Isn't there ever any good weather in this damn country?"

Al got a thoughtful look on his face but didn't answer for some time. Finally, he turned to the new pilot. "Yeah, there was ... but I didn't fly that day."

Refugees would spread out in the vicinity of the strip and start to build their houses from bamboo and thatch, always retaining their village grouping. Top priority for construction was always the medical dispensary, and second would be an administrative center for the government officials or whatever leadership there happened to be. As soon as the situation stabilized, a primary school was added, too. If there was no teacher, any literate person might be picked to fill the role until one was available.

Seeds supplied by USAID would soon be sprouting out of the ground in garden plots by every house (wives often sewed small packets of vegetable and rice seeds inside their clothing as insurance if they were suddenly overrun), and—depending on the season—swidden-culture dry rice would also be planted. The displaced people were usually self-sufficient and off refugee status after one harvest cycle.

This type of operation required large inputs of air time, as well as commodities that were very expensive—and it was only possible through the generosity of the US humanitarian assistance program. However, the success of the relief operations was due to the dedication of the Lao and American personnel, who were willing to face great privation and danger in order to help these simple, peace-loving people survive the onslaught of a powerful and vicious aggressor.

Other than Pop, most of the refugee relief officers who worked out in the field were young Americans in their twenties. Most of them had come to Southeast Asia with the Peace Corps or IVS, and were fascinated with this part of the world. After finishing their tours with the voluntary organizations, they looked for ways to stay in Asia, and a few found employment with USAID. Charley Mann, the USAID director, usually required that Pop interview and evaluate the candidates—and if they were chosen, they worked under him until he was satisfied they could operate on their own

Tom Ward, Jack Williamson, Win McKeithin, Blaine Jensen, Joe Flipse, Ernie Kuhn, Paul White, Fritz Benson, Bob Dakan, Wayne Johnson, and George Cosgrove were the central core of field officers developed by Pop. One of his other proteges, Don Shustrom, sad to say, was killed by the Vietnamese on his first tour—when Na Khang in Sam Neua was overrun.

The usual tour of duty with USAID is two years. All of the above were in Laos from four to thirteen years. All were fluent in Lao, and in many cases spoke better Lao than the refugees with whom they worked.

No two of them were similar in personality or background, except that all were independent and worked best when they were in charge. Their most common attribute was a love for the Lao people, and a heartfelt empathy for the desperate plight of the refugees and their struggle against the Vietnamese. Nevertheless, there were certainly no bleeding hearts among this group. They were tough, pragmatic, and not awed by anything that walked on two legs. Jack, Win, Joe, Fritz, Ernie, Paul, and Wayne all married Lao or Thai women; Bob's wife is Indonesian; Tom and Blaine are still single; and George was the only one who was married before leaving the US, and the only one whose wife isn't Asian.

Most of the American mission in Vientiane worked a forty-hour week with weekends free. The refugee relief people lived out in the countryside with the refugees, and worked seven days a week, week in week out. Their day began at dawn and lasted until late at night—but there still seemed too little time to do all that needed to be done. The work was dirty, dangerous, and never-ending. No one asked or ordered them to work such a long and arduous schedule, and they received no extra compensation and little commendation from the American mission. As a matter of fact, most of the Vientiane administrators thought they were a pain in the ass. They were always bothering people on weekends, holidays, and in the middle of the night; everything they did was an emergency; and if they didn't get what they wanted immediately, they went screaming to the USAID director or the ambassador.

Although they received little commendation from the mission (with the notable exception of Charley Mann), the heartfelt gratitude of the refugees, and their own personal sense of accomplishment, was more than adequate compensation—and sufficient motivation to continue the struggle year after year.

There was also no doubt or equivocation on their part as to who was the enemy. They knew they worked for a just and important cause against evil forces, and they gave it their all. The grinding work schedule and the constant exposure to misery, catastrophe, and danger kept them weary, short tempered, and cynical. They were an ornery, recalcitrant bunch—and made no effort to hide it.

Pat was often their interface with the mission, particularly when they were having problems—whether operational or personal—and she was notorious for terrorising all the petty bureaucrats and making them shape up and produce on the refugee officers behalf. She gave them her complete support. She worked with them, laughed with them, cried with them, drank with them, fought with them, and took care of them at our house when they were sick.

One of the major problem areas in the program was education and schools. Refugee leaders, as well as Pop and myself, put high priority on establishing schools as part of the resettlement and rehabilitation process. However, the RLG required that all teachers be certified, and that schools be accredited by the Ministry of Education. But with the scarcity of teachers, there was no hope of schools or personnel being available for the refugees for many years—and the government had little interest in the refugees anyway, particularly if they were from the ethnic minorities.

To compound the problem, Dr. Smith, the chief of the education division in USAID, followed ministry policy and opposed the little bamboo schools we were building out in the refugee areas. He sarcastically referred to them as, "Buell's clandestine schools and bootleg teachers" and evidently thought that it was better to have no education and complete illiteracy, rather than support our crude but effective efforts.

However, this official opposition meant little in the remote areas where we worked. We recruited anyone who could read and write, and made them the teacher. Since we had no funding for teachers' salaries, I put these "bootleg teachers" on the USAID public health payroll as medics—and we scrounged money for school books and other supplies from friends in the international community. The Air America, Bird & Sons, and Continental pilots that flew us around the country were particularly generous. Early in the program, their contributions bought three quarters of all the supplies that went into the refugee schools.

Despite the crudity of the system, the children *did* learn how to read and write, and they also grasped the basics of mathematics. It was a giant step forward, and—later—they themselves became the teachers, medics, nurses, and officers in the military.

Gradually, over a period of years, we overcame the opposition in the Ministry of Education, and built a junior high school and school for teachers at Sam Thong. Some of the graduates were able to go to the new Lao-language High School and the Teacher's College in Vientiane. Eventually, the students returned to the refugee areas with official positions in the Ministry of Education—and Pop's "bootleg schools" achieved legitimacy.

It must always be kept in mind that the refugees being displaced were the population base from which the irregular or partisan military was drawn. Their welfare and survival were crucial to the war effort—because their sons and husbands were the only effective forces preventing the communists from taking over the country.

Cholera Outbreak

Hong Non, a tiny Meo village in Sam Neua province, sits high on a mountain ridge 11 kilometers from Sam Neua City, the communist headquarters for Laos during the war. Sheer cliffs and steep, rocky slopes make it difficult to approach on foot. The crest of the ridge—only 15-30 feet wide—was flattened to make a STOL strip 425 feet long. The strip was designated LS86.

This frightful postage stamp of an airfield had a 25% grade, and erratic winds gusted across it constantly. Only urgent business and a pilot deeply dedicated to the program could bring one to land at Hong Non on a windy day.

Dirt and rocks were dug out of the side of the mountain to form small, flat terraces where houses were built—and through community enterprise and much hard labor, two larger terraces had been made to provide space for the first hospital and the first school in the area.

In the first year the school opened, every student was in the first grade, regardless of age or ability. Barefoot Meo and Lao Theung children walked many kilometers each morning from their villages to attend, and the one teacher taught his sixty students—only nine of whom were girls—in the one large classroom. The mere existence of a school in this remote enclave, particularly with girls in attendance, was a small miracle that only Edgar "Pop" Buell could have accomplished.

Hong Non was the district headquarters for the civilian administration and the military. Its close proximity to communist headquarters at Sam Neua City made it crucial for intelligence gathering about enemy troop movements—and both civilian and military authority was vested in the one young Meo leader, Lieutenant Boua Chou, who was both the *chao muang* and commander of the local Auto Defense Corps (ADC) battalion. He had successfully defended the area against the Pathet Lao for three years, and had been careful not to take any major offensive action which might provoke the enemy—particularly the Vietnamese—into making a major effort to take Hong Non.

Because of the strategic importance of this advanced base, a PARU team was also stationed in the village to help Boua Chou in training and planning. There were four Thai soldiers on the team: the team leader, his assistant, a communications specialist, and a paramedic who went by the code name of Sam. He was a powerful bear of a man, but smiling and soft-spoken, and his kind and gentle manner had won him the confidence of the villagers—particularly the little children, who loved the games he played with them.

Sam had trained seven local young men as medics over a few months, and selected seven more for training. Villagers had just completed the bamboo hospital next to the school in the center of Hong Non, and Sam planned to build dispensaries in some of the larger villages in the area and assign medics to operate them.

All the activity in developing the school and medical programs—initiated and supported by Pop—was at VP's request. When the villagers completed the hospital, Pop felt that I, as the new USAID chief of public health, should be present for the inauguration. It would also be an opportunity for me to take a look at what Sam was doing in the way of training, and to evaluate his health program.

I arrived at Hong Non on the afternoon of August 10th, 1963, to take part in the opening ceremony for the new dispensary hospital. Pop and Major Thong Vongrasamy, the Lao military commander at Hua Muang (LS58), had preceded me by one day. Father Lucien Bouchard, a Catholic Oblate missionary priest, was also there, and had been working in the vicinity for a week. "Father B"—as most people called him—was a good friend of Pop's, and the two worked closely together.

When Jack Houston, the Air America pilot, brought our Helio Courier to a stop, the three of them were at the airstrip to meet me. They were accompanied by Lieutenant Boua Chou, along with Sam, the rest of the PARU team, and many of the villagers. The end of the airstrip was only about fifty meters from the center of the village. After exchanging greetings, we all walked over to the hospital, which—along with the *chao muang's* house, the PARU quarters, and the school—bordered a small, open court of bare, hard-packed clay.

Garlands of flowers and an arch of wild banana leaves framed the entrance to the hospital, and in the open court, mats were laid out to seat the guests—with a few crude benches made of rice-drop palettes provided

_____

_____

_____

_____

_____

_____

_____

_____

_____

_____

_____

_____

_____

_____

Just a note

for the luxuriant comfort of us VIPs. Children were out of school, laughing and running all over the place, and most of the village was crowded around—providing a festive atmosphere for the beautiful, bright, cool day.

As soon as we were seated, the ceremony began. Boua Chou made a short speech, followed by Thong. Pop was next, and then Father B translated my remarks into Meo and Lao Theung. No one was listening to the speeches, but everyone was having a fine time laughing and talking to each other. When the speeches were over, Sam and the medics guided the guests through the hospital.

Thin green parachute cloth from ammo drops lined the bamboo building, and the silky material gave the light that filtered through it, a pleasant, soothing glow that seemed especially appropriate for a hospital. There was a 14-bed ward, plus rooms for treatment, consultation, and storage. Walls, beds, shelves, tables, and cabinets were all made of expertly-crafted, woven bamboo. A large, shaded veranda with benches provided a waiting area, or—simply—just a pleasant place to rest and talk. Medics whose families were not at Hong Non used an adjoining building for living quarters. Ly Chai, the senior Meo medic at Sam Thong, had bought drugs, supplies, instruments, and equipment, and helped Sam get things set up.

This valuable new facility impressed and pleased everyone in the community. Not only would it serve the civilian populace, but it was badly needed for military casualties, who—if there were no aircraft to evacuate them to Sam Thong—had previously had no place to care for them locally. This had caused a grave problem in the past for Thong and the *chao muang*—and was devastating to the morale of their soldiers. At least in this modest, little hospital there was someone to dress their wounds; medicine to prevent or cure infections; warm, clean blankets; and hot food.

After the tour of the hospital was over, the rice wine and corn whisky began to flow. The sun had set and darkness was falling. A huge bonfire was made in the middle of the village, and we ate fried pork, roasted chicken, and glutinous rice in the flickering light. Thong started singing and beating a rhythm on a drum, and soon there were more drums and tin cans filled with pebbles following the beat. Everyone sang and clapped with the rhythm.

The Meo and Lao Theung don't normally dance, but Pop was quickly up and dancing a *lamvong* (a traditional Lao and Thai dance) in a circle, with a crowd of little girls laughing and jumping around him. The PARU soldiers joined in, and eventually even the Meo and Lao Theung men were shuffling around the big fire in their bare feet. It looked like a great party that would last most of the night.

Earlier in the evening, Father B had said he wanted to talk to me as soon as we had the time; a serious medical problem had arisen while he was visiting the surrounding villages during the previous few days. When there was a lull in the festivities, he got the *chao muang*, Thong, Pop, Sam, and I together in the *chao muang's* house.

Father B described a rapidly fatal diarrheal disease without vomiting or fever. The victims had a sudden onset of uncontrollable diarrhea, and within several hours were completely dehydrated, moribund, and liable to die quickly in a shock-like state. After some discussion, I agreed with Father B that the disease was probably cholera.

Cholera is endemic to much of Asia, and is of two different strains. The pandemic at that time had originated in a remote region of Indonesia in the fifties, and had spread all over the world. This new mutation, called El Tor, became endemic in Southeast Asia—along with a much older organism referred to as the Asiatic strain. Vaccines against the El Tor strain were not very successful. Immune response was low and shortlived. On the other hand, vaccines prepared for immunization against the old Asiatic strain were highly effective. In a remote, mountainous area of Northern Laos that had no contact with the outside world, the disease would undoubtedly be caused by the old Asiatic strain.

A small percentage of cholera survivors become chronic carriers of the bacterium—or vibrio as it is usually called. The carrier will have no symptoms, but will pass the vibrio in the stool for many years. An outbreak of cholera in the Hong Non area would most likely result from the fecal contamination of the water supply by a chronic carrier. If the epidemic should spread, it could not only cause much suffering and death, but also endanger military and intelligence operations from this important site.

We decided that I would leave as soon as we had a plane in the morning, and return to Vientiane. The nearest cholera vaccine was in Bangkok, and I would get a supply sent up to Hong Non as quickly as possible. In the meantime, Boua Chou and Thong would try to prevent anyone from entering or leaving the area where the outbreak had occurred, in an attempt to prevent spread of the disease.

I'd forgotten that the next day was a Sunday, and on arriving in Vientiane, found all the offices closed. Charley Mann was at home, and we talked over the phone. He understood both the importance of the Hong Non enclave to the security of Sam Neua province, and our concern about the cholera situation. We met at his office first thing next morning, and his staff made the necessary arrangements to have the vaccine delivered as quickly as possible. If things went well, I calculated that the vaccine should be in Hong Non in about 36 hours.

After leaving the office, I went to the embassy medical unit and was able to borrow a fifty-dose vial of cholera vaccine which Dr. Bush, the embassy physician, had just received. That afternoon, I flew up to Sam Thong and met Pop. We then went over to Long Chieng and immunized VP and the members of his staff who moved in and out of the Hong Non area, as well as Pop and myself.

We spent the night at Sam Thong, and the next morning my office in Vientiane informed us by radio that the vaccine from Bangkok would arrive there about noon. Pop called Air America and told them to hold Lee Mullins and the Helio Courier he was to fly to Sam Thong that morning until the vaccine arrived at the airport, so Lee could bring it to us. Everything went according to schedule, and by late afternoon, Pop, Lee, vaccine, and I were at Hong Non.

That night, with Boua Chou, Thong, and Sam, we worked out a plan of action and a schedule. The area of concern was approximately triangular in shape, with each side about 25 kilometers long. The apices of the triangle were the three major villages of Hong Non (LS86), Cha Tao (LS107), and Houi Khammoune (LS111). Fortunately, all three had STOL strips where a Helio Courier could land.

The population of the area was about 10,000—dispersed in many small villages throughout the triangle, and connected only by narrow footpaths barely wide enough for one person to pass. The terrain was rough and heavily-forested, with mountains in the area rising to crests of 2,000 meters.

The cholera outbreak occurred near the center of the triangle—at a Lao village called Muang Yut, and at a Meo village named Houi Hao. Muang Yut was located in a deep valley at the foot of Phu Pha Thi mountain (LS85), but Houi Hao—although nearby—was high up the slope of adjacent Phu Din Dan.

First, we would immunize as many people as we could near the three small airstrips, then—riding through the central area on horseback—we would try to immunize the rest. The procedure would be repeated in two to three weeks.

The first day, we worked at Hong Non and immunized about 1,500 people. Sam, and the medics he had trained, showed a skill and proficiency which exceeded my expectations. Thong and Boua Chou controlled the crowd, Pop kept the children amused with a good supply of balloons and candy, and the whole affair had a holiday atmosphere.

During the course of the day, Pop heard that there was extensive flood damage to the rice crop in a Lao village in the valley below Hong Non. Flood victims, in turn, heard that Pop was at Hong Non, and came to see if he would help them with rice. About mid-afternoon, he decided to go and check to see if the story was true. He hadn't worked with these villagers previously, and had some doubt about their story. He left on horseback with six soldiers for security, and promised to be back before dark.

In the late afternoon the weather suddenly deteriorated, and dark clouds moved in to cover the mountain tops. A cold mist was falling, and well after dark Pop had still not returned. We all began to worry, and around eight in the evening Thong decided that he and some of his soldiers should go and see what had happened.

Just as they were ready to leave, we heard Pop and his escort coming up the trail that descended into the valley. He was on foot and limping, and his horse was nowhere to be seen. When he got into the light, I could see that he was soaking wet and shivering.

When I asked him what had happened, he answered in a disgusted voice, "You won't believe it, Doc, but that sure-footed little pony went and slipped off the bridge crossin' the crick down in the valley. Fell right on top of me and bruised me up some. Still, I was real lucky."

"How's that Pop?"

"Well, thank God he's a small horse, Doc."

The horse itself had been too badly injured to be ridden, and Pop had to drag himself up the steep mountain slope.

Next morning, Ly Chai and I went to Cha Tao by Helio with vaccines and medicines—expecting Sam and Pop to follow us half an hour later. However, the Helio developed mechanical problems and had to return directly to Vientiane. Ly Chai couldn't speak any English at that time, so there was no one to interpret for me. Without Sam or Pop to help, I expected the day's activities to be a disaster. But, to my surprise, things didn't turn out that way. Ly Chai explained our purpose, and then, very quickly, he and the villagers constructed a shaded work area—from bamboo and old drop parachutes—as well as tables for our equipment and supplies.

Within a few hours we had immunized all 750 people in the village, and in addition I'd examined, and prescribed for, about sixty sick people—without exchanging a spoken word. The village chief had, in effect, acted as my interpreter by pointing out the significant parts of the patient's anatomy, then—through gestures and pantomime—we communicated the necessary information to diagnose and treat the patient. All went well, and by mid-afternoon we'd completed our work.

After an excellent meal of porcupine stew, cucumbers, and glutinous rice, we inspected the school, airstrip, and drop zone. Cha Tao was a Meo refugee village of people displaced from their homes about six months previously. They hadn't had time to plant crops as yet, and were almost totally dependent on USAID rice drops for survival.

Pop had been in the village during the previous month and was very upset by the poor condition of the strip and drop zone, as well as the dilapidated condition of the school. The village didn't have proper drainage, and the people scattered trash at random.

Before I left Hong Non that morning, he'd told me he intended "to raise seven kinds of hell if the place ain't cleaned up."

He was almost livid as he continued, "On the trip there a month back, when we flew over, the strip was all grown over to where you hardly knew where it was, and you couldn't see the drop zone. I told the pilot not to land, but after looking it over, he thought it was possible. We went in, but believe me, the plane was about every place it shouldn't have been. Ruts all over everywhere. When I got out, I was swarmed all over by people tellin' me they didn't have no rice. I told 'em it added up this way. I couldn't care less if they never have no rice since they nearly caused two Americans to get killed and lose an airplane. Until the strip was made better, drop zone cleaned up, village cleaned up, schoolhouse rebuilt, an increase from twenty to at least 75 pupils, and every face an' hands clean—no rice drop. Until that was all done, their rice is cut off. I gave 'em some drugs and school supplies for thirty kids and left."

It appeared that Pop's anger and threats had accomplished the desired results. Village, airstrip, drop zone, and a little jewel of a school sitting on that wild, green mountainside, were all in excellent condition.

The school building was made of the usual woven bamboo panels with a thatched roof—but at a distance it made a storybook picture. The land was cleared for about 100 meters around it, and the tallest and most magnificent shade trees were left standing. A low bamboo fence and a wide bed of marigolds enclosed the school yard; the grass was carefully trimmed; neat walkways were laid out, bordered with narrow beds of colorful flowers; and a huge Lao national flag flew from a towering bamboo pole.

Although Pop's goal of 75 pupils wasn't reached, at least the enrolment had doubled. Desks pegged together from hand-hewn boards of a shiny, dark rosewood were occupied by forty of the cleanest, brightest faces in Sam Neua—ten of them girls.

Unfortunately not all the students had a book, pencil, or writing pad. However, pieces of plywood from drop palettes had been cut to the size of slates and dyed black, and soft limestone rock carved into slate pencils gave everyone something with which to write. The teacher wrote with the same limestone crayon on a blackboard made of the same drop palettes.

Nai khu (literally, Mr. Teacher) was a youth from Muang Yut, the Lao village down in the valley. He had only finished five years of elementary school, and had no training as a teacher. His salary was paid by Pop, and he didn't relate to the RLG or the Ministry of Education, of course. Certainly this was one of Pop's better "clandestine schools with a bootleg teacher."

Late in the afternoon the replacement aircraft for our malfunctioning Helio Courier arrived, and took Ly Chai and I back to Hong Non. I was quite happy with how well things had gone during the day, since neither Pop nor Sam had been there to help me. Pop, however—when I related the day's events with considerable enthusiasm—seemed a bit disgruntled that I'd been able to survive without his being there to babysit me. I found out later that he routinely abandoned neophytes like myself in such situations to test them out. There was probably nothing wrong with the aircraft.

Soon though, the *lao hai* (rice wine) started to flow, and Pop was quickly in good humor again. In spite of his bruises from the previous day, he led the *lamvong* to the hottest drum north of Xieng Khoung, ably assisted by the small girls and the local militia with their ever-present pistols and rifles strapped to their waists and backs.

Sadly, Sam and I were not to join the party. Early in the evening, a young Meo couple from a nearby village brought their seriously ill, one-and-a-half-year-old daughter into the hospital. Previously robust and healthy, the little child had been feverish and unable to eat for two days. That day she'd been extremely irritable and crying with pain—and a few hours earlier she had suffered a generalised convulsion and lost consciousness. In desperation, the parents had decided to seek help at the new hospital in Hong Non.

By the intense light of the Coleman lantern, I could see the child lying on her side in the bed with her neck extended and back arched. Her muscles quivered and her eyes rolled back under the upper lids. She did respond to stimulation, however, and would whine when we moved her. It seemed highly likely that she had an acute bacterial meningitis.

We had no laboratory equipment, nor the usual simple instruments for doing a spinal tap. Nevertheless, I took a regular hypodermic needle, did a spinal puncture, and drained a few millimeters of fluid into a small medicine glass. In the lantern light the spinal fluid had a vaguely pearlescent appearance and sparkled slightly. Normal spinal fluid is clear and slightly yellow. The milky color and sparkle was due to white blood cells in the fluid. This left little doubt as to a diagnosis of meningitis. We would need to give the little patient massive doses of antibiotics intravenously if there was to be any chance of saving her.

Our tiny child was dehydrated and all her little veins were collapsed. I was unable to get an IV going, and so decided we'd have to do a cutdown. This is a simple procedure in which a small incision is made in the skin, and a vein dissected free. A small plastic tube is then inserted in the vein, through which large quantities of fluids and medications can be given quite rapidly. But there was one major problem. We had none of the small plastic tubing.

In desperation, I took a hypodermic needle, and—with a whetstone—ground off the sharp point and edges so it wouldn't damage the fragile vein. We did a successful cut-down that flowed well, and started large doses of crystalline penicillin and sulfadiazine. These were the only intravenous antibacterial agents that that we had, but they are suitable for this sort of problem, especially if the infection is due to a meningococcus—which was highly probable.

Everything went well, and Sam and I were optimistic for a few hours that our little patient would survive. I wish that I could write of a happy outcome, but it wasn't to be. As the night passed, the poor child's condition continued to deteriorate. In spite of our efforts, she died during the small hours of the morning.

The air was cold and damp, and I shivered as I crawled under the blankets on my bunk with tears in my eyes and the overwhelming feeling of depression and humility that only a doctor knows when faced with failure and death.

✦✦✦

We were up before dawn getting equipment and horses ready. Rather than Sam and I flying to Houi Khammoune to immunize the people at the third point of the triangle, we decided to send two of the medics instead. Pop, Thong, Boua Chou, Sam, and I would start the trek through the center of the triangle.

Boua Chou had 12 soldiers go with us for security: four as advance guard, four as rear guard, and four with the main group. Two horses carried our medical supplies and equipment, Pop and I got on two of the little mountain ponies, and everyone else walked. I would have preferred to walk, too, but Boua Chou insisted that we ride.

A narrow trail wound along the crest of a rough mountain ridge that was heavily forested. At times we'd be in bright sunshine, and then—seconds later—clouds would swirl in and envelop us in a damp, gray mist. Just as quickly, the clouds would blow away and the sun would be shining again. The view from the ridge was spectacular, when not obscured by the mist or the trees.

We slowly plodded along, hour after hour, without stopping. Although I weighed only 75 kilograms, my little pony—not accustomed to carrying such a load—quickly tired. By midday he could no longer support my weight, and I had to lead him along the trail. In the late afternoon, the weather worsened, and a cold, fine rain began to fall. Fortunately, soon afterwards, we arrived in the little Meo village of Houi Hao. We'd been on the trail for ten hours since leaving Hong Non.

Our party was warmly welcomed, and Pop and I were a great curiosity to the people. The only non-Asian they'd ever seen before was a French Catholic priest—Father Subara from the Oblate mission in Sam Neua City—who, three years previously, had fled into the jungle when the Pathet Lao and North Vietnamese had occupied the town. He spent one night in the village and barely escaped the next morning when a Pathet Lao patrol arrived in search of him.

Sam and Boua Chou quickly got the people organized, and we used the village chief's house to immunize everyone. When we were finished, I held sick call, and Pop sat with the men and discussed the problems and needs of the village. Apparently, the security situation prevented them from obtaining the iron bars that their blacksmiths used to make knives, axes, hoes, and other household utensils and tools. They also needed salt. This was a serious problem, and they asked Pop if he could help. Pop was rather non-committal but told them he'd do what he could.

At about nine in the evening we finally finished, and I was able to sit and relax after a long, tiring day. The village chief's house, where we were staying, was built of heavy timbers with a wooden, shingled roof. It was quite spacious, and was divided into three sections: a large, open area adjacent to the entrance was used for receiving visitors, dining, and as a bedroom for overnight guests; several curtained sleeping compartments for the family were along one side in the center of the house; and a corridor along the opposite side led to a large cooking area in the rear.

In one corner of the kitchen was a waist-high, clay platform with a fire cavity and various openings that formed a multiburner stove and oven. Spring water carried by a bamboo pipe filled a large, wooden receptacle that drained through the rear wall. Onions, garlic, peppers, strings of dried meat, and many other unrecognizable vegetables and herbs hung from the rafters. Pots, pans, storage jars, baskets, sacks, and all sorts of other containers filled the room. The hard-packed clay formed a black, marble-like floor that glistened in the fire light.

The women and girls preparing our evening meal were dressed in colorful embroidered black skirts, black strips of cloth wrapped around their legs from the ankle to the knee, and long-sleeved blouses with bright red and green sashes tied around their waists. They all wore the heavy, ornate silver necklaces and earrings common to the Meo.

By nightfall, the damp air had become uncomfortably cold, and a fire was built on an open hearth in the middle of the visitors room in the front of the house. After we finished working, all the men sat around the fire on low stools. Two girls brought Pop and I large basins of hot water, and after we washed our faces and hands, our little hostesses removed our boots and socks and had us soak our feet in the hot water.

Our host, the *nai ban* (village chief), brought in a metal tray with several small glasses of corn whisky, and passed it around to all the visitors. After two shots of the fiery liquor I had a warm, happy feeling, and all seemed right with the world.

When the girls had dried our feet and removed the basins of water, unobtrusive little ladies brought in two low wicker tables with bowls of steaming food. All the men commenced to eat. There was chicken, pork, venison, corn on the cob, fried corn bread, wild mushrooms cooked in chicken broth, and several different vegetables. I could scarcely believe the richness of the feast that was set before us.

During my short experience in Laos up to that time, I'd only seen the Meo refugee villages. Houi Hao was an old village whose inhabitants had never been displaced—and the standard of living contrasted sharply with that of the poor refugees.

After we finished the main meal, our hostesses served bananas and mandarin oranges. Later, we had a digestif of corn whisky flavored with wild mint and honey. I knew these products hadn't come from this high, windy mountain, but from Muang Yut, the Lao village in the valley. The people of Muang Yut and Houi Hao lived in a sort of symbiotic relationship; the skilled Meo blacksmiths trading their iron tools and other implements with the Lao for their homespun cotton cloth and farm products which would not grow on the mountain tops.

That night we slept with our feet to the open fire on a mat covered with a big, woollen blanket. I wrapped myself in a soft-tanned tiger skin, listening to the small sounds of the chickens, pigs, ducks, and horses sleeping in the stable a few feet away. It was all comforting and reassuring to a farm boy from Louisiana.

After breakfast the next morning, Sam and I immunized the people we'd missed the night before, and then treated several more who were ill. We also discovered the details of the cholera outbreak.

Three months previously, a third of the Houi Hao people had moved from the main village to a new site a short distance away. They needed to be closer to the new fields they were clearing and planting. In their haste to get the houses built and the fields prepared, they used water from a small creek below the village.

Traditionally in this area the Meo dig out a good spring above the village and transport the water to all the houses using bamboo pipes. Unfortunately, there must have been a cholera carrier in the group, and his or her faeces soon contaminated the creek. Within a week, 26 people died of a violent diarrhea only a few hours after its onset. Many more were ill but managed to survive.

The terrified people abandoned the village and fled. Most of them returned to old Houi Hao, but the *nai ban* made them build at a distance from the main village. This time they dug out the spring and piped the water to the new houses. Six more people died at this location, but then the disease disappeared.

Pop had a little ERK4 survival radio, and was able to contact the Helio Courier we had working out of Hong Non. Before leaving, he'd instructed the pilot to overhead us each morning in case we needed anything. He told the pilot to pick up iron bars and salt at Sam Thong, and make a drop at Houi Hao on his signal.

Before noon, the plane had returned and circled overhead. Pop told the pilot that a small area a short distance from the village would be the drop zone. A hundred iron bars and two sacks of salt soon fell from the sky, directly on the spot. When the people saw the objects hit the ground, they were afraid and wouldn't go to see what they were. Boua Chou had to go to the drop zone himself and get one of the bars and show the villagers that Pop had kept his promise. This miraculous incident caused a furore of speculation, and everyone agreed that Pop was the most powerful shaman they had ever seen.

With our work finished at Houi Hao we departed just before noon on a trail that steadily descended for six hours into the Nam Yut river valley. For most of the way, it wandered along, or in, a small creek which eventually flowed into the Nam Yut down below. A dense, triple canopy of rainforest completely shaded us from the sun. The floor of the forest was carpeted with a smooth, green, velvet layer of rotting debris, and was surprisingly open; the giant trees—rising fifty to seventy meters—that appeared so thick from the air, were actually widely spaced apart. Slim, graceful plants that grew in the soft, green-tinted light that filtered through the canopy, all had huge leaves to gather as much energy as possible.

Except for the noise of the little stream tumbling off a ledge, the forest was quiet and still. Only occasionally would the call of a bird or the high-pitched yell of a howler monkey be heard in the distance. A mystical air filled this natural cathedral, and for some inexplicable reason we moved along as quietly as possible without speaking. No one wanted to disturb the tranquillity.

We descended into the valley and entered the little village of Muang Yut late in the afternoon. Fifty or sixty bamboo-and-thatch houses high on stilts stood on one bank of the clear, sparkling river, and on the opposite side was a large paddy area. Coconut palms, papaya and banana trees were scattered through the village and along the riverbanks. Since leaving Houi Hao six hours earlier, we'd descended from the cool, misty mountains into the warm, humid tropics

After exchanging greetings and slaking our thirsts with cool coconut milk, we bathed in the Nam Yut. In the middle of the river there was a hot spring that gushed up and mixed with the cool water off the mountain slopes. Below the spring, a series of rock pools had been formed, each one decreasing in temperature as less of the hot water reached the lower levels. The practice was to start at the coolest pool and gradually work up toward the hottest that one could tolerate. After soaking in the hot pool for a while, the bather reversed the process to cool off before getting out of the water. It was a delightful way to shed the dirt and fatigue of the long trail down the side of the mountain.

While we bathed, Thong sat on a high rock where he had a good view of the surrounding area with his rifle across his lap. After everyone else had bathed, two of the soldiers took his place on the rock, and he got in the water.

By the time we finished bathing, darkness was falling, but Boua Chou and the *chao muang* had assembled all the people for immunization. By candlelight, Sam and I vaccinated everyone, and then treated the many that were ill. We found out that six people had died, and several were ill, of what was most likely cholera, soon after the outbreak at Houi Hao. Two of the patients we saw were probably recovering from the disease, but no new cases had occurred in several days.

After Sam and I finished our work, we joined Pop and Boua Chou at the *chao muang's* house where we would spend the night. Two large jars of *lao hai* were already in the center of the floor, and two of the young village girls invited us to drink with them.

Lao hai is a rice wine that is drunk extensively at parties and ceremonies throughout Laos and Thailand. Unhusked rice is placed in a large masonry jar, yeast is mixed in, and just enough water is added to dampen the rice thoroughly. After the initial fermentation, the mouth of the jar is sealed with a heavy clay plug to preserve the brew until it's ready to drink. When the plug is removed, the husks are damp, but there is very little fluid in the jar; the potent alcoholic brew having absorbed into the rice. Water is then poured over the husks until the jar is about to run over, and slim, flexible bamboo straws are used to suck up the wine.

The men always have a young village girl as a drinking partner, and two or three couples drink at the same time. Each pair drinks a measured amount controlled by a winemaster who adds water out of a buffalo horn— replenishing exactly the quantity that is drunk. Much laughing, singing, and hand clapping accompanies the drinking. Men accuse the girls of shirking their duty by not drinking their share, and the girls make the same accusations of the men. When the alcoholic content becomes too diluted, a new jar is opened. Often the ritual will go on for hours. The *lao hai* has enough alcohol to make everyone feel good, but is dilute enough that no one gets very drunk.

That evening the drinking didn't last long because our meal was ready—and we were all famished after a long, hard day on the trail. By this time, Pop—in his own inimitable way—had made friends with everyone in the village. After a good Lao dinner, he talked to the men well into the night—one good farmer to another—with understanding and sympathy. He was just as much in his own environment as if he'd been back on his farm in the Midwest United States.

Sam and I were up early in the morning to check two seriously-ill patients we'd seen the previous evening. Fortunately they had improved, so we immunized the remainder of the people we'd missed, and saw a few more villagers who were also ill. About mid-morning we said goodbye to the kind people of Muang Yut, promising to return, and began the long climb up the slopes of Phu Pha Thi to Cha Tao, the Meo village where Ly Chai and I had worked three days before. The trail was very steep and difficult, and my poor little Meo pony gave out completely after the three hard days of riding. I almost had to carry him myself, to keep from abandoning him.

We arrived at Cha Tao around three in the afternoon, but before Pop would sit down and talk to the people, he took a close look at the village, airstrip, drop zone, and—particularly—the school. Everything was as I'd reported, so he promised the local leader he'd start the rice drops again that week. A Helio Courier arrived about four o'clock, as we'd scheduled, and shuttled us all back to Hong Nong—a ten-minute trip that had taken three days on the ground.

When we landed, Father B was waiting at the strip. He'd told us, before we left for Houi Hao and Muang Yut, that he'd be going to Phia Kham on foot. He wanted to remain there for about a week, and—if it was possible—would like for us to send a plane to pick him up. It surprised us that he had returned so quickly and not waited for the plane.

Phia Kham is located ten kilometers north of Sam Neua City, and about fifteen kilometers northeast of Hong Non on the same high mountain ridge. On a clear day, one can look to the northwest and see the country around Dien Bien Phu. Phia Kham is actually three small villages of Meo farmers, all within several hundred meters of each other. These courageous and determined mountain people had resisted the aggression of the communists for many years—and on three occasions the Pathet Lao, with Viet Min cadre, had overrun their villages. Three times they had taken their wives, children, and old people to the security of the mountain peaks; regrouped; and thrown the enemy out.

Catholic missionaries had worked in the area for several decades, and most of the people of Phia Kham were converts. This was very unusual, as few missionaries of any faith had made converts among the mountain people. In happier times the Oblate fathers had a mission house in Sam Neua City—but they'd barely escaped with their lives when the communists occupied the town three years previously.

In the past year, Father B—with Pop's help—had been able to fly into Hong Non and make contact with the Phia Kham people. He had them hack out a chopper pad and a Helio strip, but they were seldom used because the area was insecure and the air traffic called undue attention to the place.

When I jumped out of the plane, Father B grabbed me, and above the roar of the engine, shouted in my ear, "Doc, there're several wounded men at Phia Kham. They've been shot. We must go get them."

He and I climbed back into the Helio, and in ten minutes we landed at Phia Kham.

It was indeed a bizarre sight. Seven men—all elderly, and none soldiers—had high velocity wounds through their thighs. As badly injured as they were, we would need to send them to Sam Thong. The little hospital at Hong Non wouldn't be adequate. I asked our pilot to see if he could contact another Helio by radio, as one plane couldn't carry all seven casualties, and there wasn't enough daylight left to make two trips to Sam Thong.

With Father B's help, I dressed their wounds and splinted the ones that had fractured femurs. The pilot reported that another plane would be landing in a half hour. We loaded the three worst cases and sent the pilot on to Sam Thong, hoping he'd have enough daylight to return and take us back to Hong Non—as Father B considered it unsafe to spend the night at Phia Kham. Before long, the second Helio landed, and we evacuated the other four wounded men. While we waited for the first plane to return, we heard the strange and sickening story of how the seven old men had been shot.

Late the previous evening, a Pathet Lao patrol had infiltrated the village through the outposts, and found all the armed men gone. A few young, unarmed men had been in the village at the time, but when the PL appeared, they quietly slipped away. Had they remained, there was a strong possibility they would have been conscripted for labor.

The people were apprehensive, but not unduly alarmed, because this had happened before. Pathet Lao soldiers would harangue and threaten them, and take rice and other foodstuffs—but never had they injured unarmed civilians. A similar scenario seemed to be unfolding on this occasion. The villagers listened to their propaganda, treated them politely, fed them well, and put them to bed comfortably. Next morning, they fed the enemy soldiers again, and also gave them food to take with them. When they were ready to leave, however, the soldiers lined up all the adult males in the middle of the village—the seven old men—and slowly and deliberately shot each one through the leg. They said not a word and left.

Fortunately, the previous day, Father B had been held up in a village on the way to Phia Kham. He arrived two hours after the enemy patrol had left. When he saw the condition of the old men, he immediately started back to Hong Non to get help—and arrived there just at the time we landed.

Our plane returned just before dark. Father B and I took off from Phia Kham and went back to Hong Nong. There was barely enough light to land, and the plane had to RON. That night, Boua Chou, Thong, Pop, Father B, and I sat around the fire—and I searched their knowledge and experience to find an answer to the disturbing event at Phia Kham. It was difficult for me to comprehend the horrible and seemingly irrational atrocity that had occurred.

Thong explained it to me this way. When the communists were trying to win the sympathy of a group of people who had military security and support from the RLG, they would work side by side with them. They would help to plant the rice, build a new house, clear land, haul water, and never ask anything in return. They would show how much more they cared for the people than the Royal Lao Government, and would develop a spirit of cooperation and camaraderie.

However, in circumstances such as Phia Kham—where the villages were isolated from the RLG and had a minimum of military security—the communists used terrorist tactics to control the people. Since they weren't influenced by any humane considerations, a simple expedient solution such as the shooting of the seven old men was usually effective. It saved much time and effort, and the message was clear: your government *cannot* and *will not* protect you. Cooperate or you will be destroyed. More often than not, the realistic and pragmatic peasant farmer bowed to the plain facts—and cooperated.

Next morning, Pop and I returned to Sam Thong. Chan had evacuated three of the wounded men with shattered leg bones to the OB hospital in Vientiane. The other four were stable and would probably be able to return home in two or three weeks. At noon, Pop and I flew over to Long Chieng and had lunch with VP, Tony, and Vint. We briefed VP on the activities in Sam Neua, and—after a long bull session—Pop returned to Sam Thong, and I headed for Vientiane.

This episode, early in my sojourn in Laos, was without doubt an important factor in my decision to stay for such an extended period of time. It marked the beginning of my love affair with Laos and the Lao people. The grandeur of the wild countryside, and the exotic tribal people and their graciousness and hospitality, were overwhelming. Most of all, being able to provide a medical service where there was such a desperate need, was a dream come true for any doctor devoted to his profession, and to the alleviation of suffering.

I felt that I'd found something I'd been seeking all of my life.

To Stay or Not to Stay

There was much excitement and satisfaction in developing and working in the medical program, and we had a strong desire to remain in Laos. Nevertheless, only a few months after our arrival, Pat and I were seriously considering leaving, and trying to find similar work in some other developing country. Things weren't working out well for Pat. We couldn't get anyone to focus on the commitment in Washington by USAID to hire her. Actually, she was working full time, all over the country, in what we now called the village health program—but wasn't employed by the USAID mission, and wasn't being paid.

There was no funding for medical programming at that time, and there appeared to be little likelihood of any in the near future. The stocks of medical supplies left by the White Star teams that we were using at Sam Thong were almost gone, and even though Charley Mann had lost his initial hostility and our relationship had become quite amiable, he still seemed hesitant to support a greater commitment in health, other than the OB contract.

In retrospect, the main problem was our lack of insight into the bureaucratic process of program planning, review, approval, and funding. Although the USAID mission director has some flexibility, in the usual course of events, the time lapse from the initial planning of a program to the beginning of implementation is at least 18 months, and often two years. Also, creating a new position and getting it approved is time consuming. Bureaucracies just don't move fast.

On the other hand, after working with Pop out of Sam Thong, and traveling all over the country with Vitoy to visit the OB hospitals, Laos fascinated us—and so did the challenge it offered. Becky, Ray, and Walter had fallen in love with Vientiane and the Lao. They were already communicating with their new friends in their own language, and thought the big, smelly morning market in the center of town was much better than the department stores in the US. Above all, we were deeply impressed by the desperate struggle that the people in the rural areas were making against the invader of their beautiful country. We desperately wanted to help them in their fight to save their homes and their simple, happy, peaceful way of life.

To me, the political and moral issue was as clear cut as when I'd been fighting the Japanese in World War II. I was the good guy and the Japanese were the bad guys. In this case, the Lao peasant fighting for his home was the good guy and the Vietnamese, seeking their centuries-old goal of domination of Southeast Asia, were the bad guys.

I flew up to Sam Thong to talk to Pop about our tentative thoughts on leaving—and the reasons that were influencing our decision. In the short time we'd known each other, I thought we'd become good friends—but when I mentioned the possibility of quitting, he went red in the face, paced the floor cursing to himself, and finally started raging at me.

"You're just like all the rest of them damn ed'cated fools comin' up here. I thought maybe you was different but you're all the same. Come up here and tell me how much you wanna help and soon as I think I can depend on you a little, you tell me you gotta go. This ain't no goddamn Vientiane cocktail party. Takes real guts to stick it out and help these poor people. I guess you ain't got none. Go on. Go anywhere you damn well please. I sure in hell don't care. . . ."

This went on for nearly an hour. He stormed around the office throwing things on the floor and cursing. I was crushed. He was so right. I couldn't say a word in response.

Eventually he calmed down a little, but when I tried to talk to him, he completely ignored me.

Finally, he stopped and looked at me. Shaking his finger in my face he said, "Don't do nothin' for a week."

I wanted to ask him what would be the point of delaying for a week, but it was obvious he wouldn't tolerate any further discussion.

I worked around the hospital for the rest of the day, and late in the afternoon went up to the strip to catch a plane back to Vientiane. I didn't see Pop, and asked where he was. To my surprise he'd left earlier for Vientiane, without saying anything to me, knowing I had to return to Vientiane also.

The next morning, shortly after arriving at the office, my secretary said Mr. Whitehurst was on the phone. "Whitey" Whitehurst was the CIA station chief. I didn't know him well, but we had met at social affairs in Vientiane, and at Long Chieng a couple of times when he was visiting VP. I had a very favorable impression of him. He asked if I could come over to the embassy and see him that morning.

Whitey dated back to the World War II OSS days. Personable and highly capable, he was well liked and respected by all in the international community in Laos. We made an appointment for later in the morning.

When I walked into his office at the embassy, George Koularis, Whitey's deputy, was with him.

Whitey opened the conversation. "Doc, all of us here, from the ambassador down, are impressed and pleased with the work you and Pat are doing—particularly up in Xieng Khoung and Sam Neua. We know it's really tough up there."

"Thanks," I replied half-heartedly. "Glad to know someone appreciates what we're trying to do." Then I got straight to the point, since the opportunity had arisen. "But I'm surprised anyone *here* has noticed. USAID certainly doesn't show any interest in the medical program."

"Well, I'm not sure that's true, Doc," Whitey replied defensively. "Sometimes it takes a while to get things done. The red tape in Washington is pretty tough to break through. Still, the reason I wanted to get together with you, was to see if my office could help out a little. We heard you and Pat were thinking about leaving because you're not getting the support you need. Is that true?"

"Yes, it is. Pat and I don't want to go, but with no program, no funding to start one, and no interest from USAID, it seems foolish to stick around. Also, maybe you're not aware of it, but Pat's working on a voluntary basis. She hasn't been paid a cent. Washington told us the Lao mission would hire her under contract when we arrived, but nothing's been done. As a professional, this is embarrassing to her—and makes both of us pretty damn mad."

"I don't blame you, Doc. It would make me mad too. Anyway, how about giving us your most urgent requirements to keep things going for the next ninety days. We'll try to get what you need as quickly as we can. I have a hunch that Charley Mann will get USAID geared up and give you all the support you need before too long."

Not having worked in this context before, I was surprised and puzzled. However, there seemed to be everything to gain and nothing to lose.

There were two pressing problems. First and most important were drugs and other medical supplies. Second, I needed local currency to pay medics, trainees, and other local personnel, plus Thai baht to make miscellaneous purchases in Thailand of items not available in Laos.

After some discussion to clarify exactly what I had in mind, Whitey asked me to give George a list of the drugs and supplies as soon as I could get it together, and he'd have his sources obtain the items as quickly as possible. If I would give George a figure for local currency—kip and Thai baht—right there and then, they'd take care of that immediately.

I thought for a second or two, and gave George my rough estimate. He left the room for a few minutes, and returned with a large, brown paper bag. I was handed the bag with the following admonition.

"For Christ's sakes, Doc, don't keep any receipts. And when you need more, just let me know."

When I left the embassy, I wanted to jump up and click my heels, but I was afraid I'd drop the big bag of money George had just given me. It took only a few hours to get the lists of drugs and supplies together—as I'd already made a lot of notes, and I only had to alter the amounts to fit the ninety-day requirement period. My estimate of the cost was about 200,000 dollars. George had the lists early the next morning.

On the same day, Charley Mann called me to his office and we reviewed the details of a position for Pat. While I was still there, he called Mr. Moore, the personnel officer, and instructed him to send a cable to USAID Washington telling them that it was urgent that the mission receive immediate approval of the position requested for Dr. McCreedy. This was the first I knew that Charley had already sent my request for the position for Pat to Washington. This boosted my morale considerably.

That evening, I went over the day's events with Pat, and for the first time in weeks, dinner was a really lively affair. We opened a second bottle of Tavel and drank several toasts to Whitey, George, and the CIA. The kids thought we'd cracked up.

Things had really taken a turn for the better. I suspected what had happened, but wanted to be sure.

Some time previously I had befriended Ambassador Leonard Unger's secretary by helping her with a minor medical problem when the embassy doctor was away. The next morning I called her.

"Mildred, this is Doc Weldon. How are you?

"Oh, I'm fine thank you Doc. Can I help you?

"Have you seen Pop Buell lately?

"No I haven't seen him, but a couple of days ago he called and wanted me to set up an appointment for him with the ambassador. The ambassador was busy, but he hadn't seen Pop in a while and he wanted to talk to him. He told me to invite Pop to have dinner with him that evening."

"Thanks a lot Mildred."

"You aren't going to tell me what this is about?"

"Not now, but maybe the next time I see you."

There was no doubt that Pop had brought up Dr. Weldon and Dr. McCreedy in their dinner conversation. Ambassador Unger sincerely admired the old man, and would do anything within reason for him.

Three days after I gave George Koularis the list of drugs and supplies, a US Air Force C130 delivered everything I requested, from the Department of Defense medical depot in Okinawa, to Udorn in Thailand. The same afternoon they arrived, we shuttled the stuff up to Vientiane.

About a week later, USAID hired Pat—and we didn't think about leaving again for the next 11 years.

Still, it took weeks to get back in Pop's good grace. "Damn ed'cated fools can drive a man crazy."

The Problem

At the time of our arrival in 1963, health care by Western standards was non-existent in Laos. During the colonial era, the French had established crude hospitals in the larger towns, but they were badly staffed and poorly supplied. No effort of any sort was made to develop health services in the rural areas.

At the village level, illness was treated with herbs or by shamanism—depending on the sick person's perception of the cause being natural or supernatural. Some diseases of a physical nature weren't even thought to be abnormal, and certainly not preventable. It was simply part of the human condition, and one did not seek or expect treatment. With patience and luck—it was believed—the condition would most likely disappear.

When Laos gained its independence in 1954, responsibility for health shifted to the new Royal Lao Government, and the Ministry of Health took over the dilapidated French institutions. With no budget for maintenance and supplies, health care deteriorated even further. Although the French gave the Lao little financial support, they continued to furnish a small team of doctors, nurses, and medical technicians, as part of the French military mission. There were usually about ten doctors and an equal number of nurses and technicians. Half worked at Mahosot, the main hospital in Vientiane, and the other half were scattered around the country at Luang Prabang, Savannakhet, Seno, and Pakse. The French army doctors were all specialists—particularly general surgeons—and acted as consultants to the Lao staff.

When we came to Laos, there were a total of seven Lao MDs in the entire country—all of whom had studied in France. Four were government officials who filled administrative positions in the ministry and at Mahosot Hospital—none of whom performed any clinical services; two of the seven were in the military—and headed the staff at the military hospital in Vientiane; and there was one in private practice—Maniso Abhay, a specialist in obstetrics and gynecology. She was also the wife of Khamphay Abhay, who was to become the minister of health (in 1964, and remained in the position until the communist takeover in 1975).

In other words, on the civilian side, the doctor-population ratio for Laos was about 1:500,000—to my knowledge, the lowest in the world.

In addition to the doctors, approximately forty Lao had been trained as *medcin assistants* in Hanoi, Saigon, and Phnom Penh. A *medcin assistant* had nine years of primary education, and was then exposed to a four-year medical curriculum without any prior basic sciences or other pre-medical education. On graduating, they went directly into practice—with no internship, no residency, or any further post-graduate training.

Schools for *medcin assistants* had been established early in the colonial period in Vietnam and Cambodia, but the French didn't establish any in Laos before independence. Over the years, six or eight Lao were selected annually to go to those schools, and a small percentage of the newly-graduated *medcin assistants* were picked to go to France to study for medical degrees. Those graduates were chosen from influential families on a political basis rather than scholastic merit. This para-professional—the *medcin assistant*—staffed the hospitals throughout Indochina, and held important administrative positions in the Ministry of Health or at the provincial level.

In 1963, there wasn't a single Lao nurse that had finished a diploma course and qualified as an RN. Historically, the hospitals had recruited young boys and girls locally, and gave them on-the-job training as practical nurses. The administrators always preferred boys to girls for such training because a majority of the girls married in their mid- to late-teens, and seldom continued to work after their marriage. In some instances, older, more experienced practical nurses were put in charge of small government dispensaries in rural market towns. These facilities received little support or supervision, and the nurses in charge operated them for their own financial benefit.

After independence in 1954, a *medcin assistant* school and a practical nursing school were established in Vientiane with the assistance of the World Health Organization. They were the initial phase of a plan to establish accredited schools of medicine and nursing that would train MDs and RNs.

By 1963, they were turning out well-trained and better health workers than the country ever had previously. In the late sixties, these institutions made the transition to fully-accredited schools of medicine and diploma nursing. Both institutions were assisted by WHO advisors. France assumed the financial support of the medical school, while USAID built and supported the nursing school, and provided an American nurse educator to work with the WHO nursing advisors.

In the sixties, the paramount problem in health development (as in other areas of development), was basic education. Of the many different ethnic groups in the country, the Lao had the highest literacy rate, but that probably didn't exceed 20%. Taking into consideration the total population of the country, only about 10–12% could read and write the Lao language.

The Lycee in Vientiane was the only high school in the country, and there was no educational institution at a higher level. There wasn't a single high school that taught in the native tongue. The Lycee was staffed, in large part, by French and Vietnamese expatriates; classes were taught in French; and the school turned out an average of ninety graduates each year. With the huge demand by all the different agencies of the government for educated young people, not very many of the ninety high school graduates could be expected to go into nursing and medicine.

Teacher training schools were located in the four largest towns of Vientiane, Luang Prabang, Savannakhet, and Pakse. The teachers were formed from students who had completed six years of elementary school. The teacher training lasted three years, and then the new teachers were sent to work in the six-year elementary schools. The subjects they taught were almost exclusively the "three Rs"—by the method of endless repetition. There were few books or school supplies, and all the students wore uniforms. The schools were usually one long building with a veranda down one side, and divided into rooms by thin partitions with open windows and doors. The most common construction was wood, with corrugated tin roofing, and woven bamboo walls.

When school was in session, the chorus of rote teaching pouring from every room produced a cacophony of discordant sound that could be heard all over the countryside. But in spite of the system, the children did learn to read and write, and also learned some basic arithmetic. That was a giant step forward, but unfortunately, such educational benefits were only available to children in the ethnic Lao areas. The other half of the population—the ethnic minorities—had no schools of any kind.

Against this poverty of human and institutional assets, was opposed a disheartening array of health problems. Malaria was holo-endemic; 90% of the population had positive tests for three or more intestinal parasites; liver and lung flukes were common; TB ravaged the small, urban population;

hundreds of lepers were segregated in special, isolated villages; and the childhood diseases that are so easily controlled in modern countries by immunization were rampant. Children died of measles, polio, whooping cough, diphtheria, as well as malaria, diarrhea, malnutrition, and ignorance. The infant mortality rate varied—in different areas and circumstances—from 180–500 per 1,000 live births. Add to this a war that displaced hundreds of thousands of the country's peasant farmers, and produced 25,000–50,000 casualties each year, and the problem was truly overwhelming.

After getting some grasp of the problem, I decided that US health assistance to Laos should have two distinct aspects that paralleled the realities of the political situation. The focus of the RLG was on the towns and villages along the Mekong and its tributary river valleys that were ethnically Lao. There was little official interest in the other half of the population which lived in the hills and who didn't speak Lao. However, this non-Lao half of the population occupied three quarters of the land area of the country, and were the prime target of the Pathet Lao and their Vietnamese masters. These were the people who were fighting desperately for their lands and their traditional way of life. And the enemy knew that if they conquered and controlled the countryside, the towns would fall without effort.

The United States was interested in helping the RLG develop a stable and effective central government, but was also deeply concerned—for both political and humanitarian reasons—about the desperate plight of the hilltribes and other minority groups. The program of health assistance had to be a balanced one that helped meet the needs of the RLG in building health institutions and infrastructure, and also met the urgent, emergent needs of the people struggling in the mountains and jungles. In the latter case, it was obvious that we—the Americans—would have to take the lead, because of the almost complete lack of interest by the RLG. Such would be the situation not only in health, but also in military assistance, refugee relief, education, and many other programs.

As a consequence, over my many years in Laos, I found myself in an ambiguous and almost schizophrenic role. One day I would sit around the table in the Ministry of Health with the minister and his staff planning a new, US-financed hospital, or discussing a contract to bring in technical expertise to upgrade the lab at the medical school. The next day I'd be in a war in the middle of the jungle, running a medical program that had a budget three times that of the Ministry of Health, and which the minister and I never discussed. At least we never discussed it officially at the ministry.

Khamphay Abhay was minister of health for ten years of my stay in Laos, and we became quite close friends. He was a member of the influential Abhay family from Khong Island, the southernmost province of Laos that borders on Cambodia.

On Sunday afternoons or evenings particularly—when I happened to be in Vientiane—we'd get together at his house or mine, have a few drinks, and talk for hours. Although I was never able to get him personally involved in any aspect of my activities in the field, he gave me invaluable guidance in how to solve many difficult problems. All the bilateral aid-funding documents of the separate activities in which I was involved had to be cleared through the ministry, and Khamphay always implemented the clearance process rather than impede or prevent it—as often happened in other ministries.

Within this dual context, and under the titles of "national health development" and the "village health program," US health assistance was developed and administered. Those parts of the program which we planned and implemented with the Ministry of Health under national health development were of two types. First, new hospitals were built, or old hospitals were renovated, in all the major towns—to replace the horrible, crumbling buildings from the French colonial period. This process was phased and relatively slow, as personnel had to be trained and organized to staff the new facilities as they were completed.

The second element was to provide health care in the more isolated ethnic Lao areas that had significant concentrations of population, but where small hospitals and dispensaries had been abandoned or had never existed. In this instance, medical and public health services were provided through a contract, financed and administered by USAID through OB.

OB usually had about 120 doctors, dentists, nurses, technicians, and administrative people who ran the four small hospitals at Vientiane, Sayaboury, Paksong, and Attopeu. In later years, the number of hospitals varied from six to nine at any particular time, as the sites were often overrun by the enemy. When the hospitals were lost, we'd set them up again in another location. The nurses, technicians, and other medical auxiliaries were all young Lao that the Filipino professionals trained on the job, or—in the case of nurses—at a school in the main hospital in Vientiane. The chief of staff, in later years, was a Lao *medcin assistant* assigned by the Ministry of Health who worked with a Filipino counterpart.

The little OB hospitals out in the provinces were health centers in a true sense. The Filipinos developed community programs—in maternal and child health, nutrition, environmental sanitation, and potable water supply—and often became the focus of many other social and educational activities.

OB was a flexible, dedicated organisation that—in emergency circumstances—could set up operations within a few days, with whatever facilities that might be available. Over the years, they worked in many different places in Laos, as priorities and security changed. The United States furnished the funding, but the contract was with the RLG—and policy dictated that they be located in predominantly ethnic Lao communities.

Although the OB hospitals were in Lao areas, and their primary purpose was to serve the Lao, we located them so they could also be used as reception centers for the emergency evacuation of casualties when fighting flared up. In addition they served as backup for the less sophisticated facilities we operated in support of the refugees and minority groups under the village health program.

OB had operated for a few years in the late fifties in South Vietnam, and had received funding from the CIA through a front organization. This relationship had become public knowledge, and although the OB operation in Laos had no connection with the CIA, and certainly was never involved in espionage, this past history occasionally caused unfounded accusations and embarrassment. The OB field teams were completely apolitical, and always had good relationships with whatever Pathet Lao elements happened to be in their area.

On at least five occasions, the towns in which OB had operations were overrun by Pathet Lao and Vietnamese troops—but in all instances the PL gave the Filipinos advance warning and made certain they were out of danger before the attack. On the other hand, they always destroyed and burned the physical facilities, as they considered them American.

The USAID public health office had the responsibility for administering the OB contract, and Pat became the contract representative, along with her many other responsibilities. Over the years, there was much friction in OB contract negotiations between USAID and Oscar Orellano at the Manila level, but Vitoy and Pat never allowed this to harm their harmonious personal and working relationship.

Although they both looked out for their own organizations' interests, Pat protected Vitoy from USAID, and Vitoy protected her from Uncle Oscar and Manila. Later, we created a special position—for a USAID-OB contract administrator—to relieve Pat of some of her huge workload. Nevertheless, she and Vitoy still maintained their close relationship.

In later years, under USAID auspices, we developed a national family planning program, and established a national detoxification center for drug addicts. Dr. Maniso Abhay, was in charge of the family planning program, and—in spite of the unfavorable circumstances of war, political instability, logistical difficulties, illiteracy, superstition, and dozens of other problems— it was well accepted and successful. Meechai Veeravaythaya, the dynamic Thai who has played such a large part in the success of the Thai family planning program, gave Maniso invaluable assistance in developing the Lao program.

The National Detoxification Center in Vientiane was undertaken as part of a US policy to induce the Lao into making an effort to suppress the production and trafficking of opium in the early seventies. Dr. Joseph Westermeyer, professor of psychiatry at the University of Minnesota Medical School, and an adviser to the US President on drug problems, was our adviser on this project.

Several years before, Joe had been my deputy in Laos for a two-year period, and was well qualified to help us develop this program. With Dr. Westermeyer's assistance, Larry Berger from my office, and Dr. Sudaly from the Ministry of Health, put together a very innovative and well-received drug rehab program. Larry was a young sociology major who had come to Laos as a community development officer. Today he's the vice president of the largest psychiatric hospital in the US.

There was a wide spectrum of activity by USAID at the national level in helping the Ministry of Health develop infrastructure and provide health services, but this was not our major effort or emphasis. Most of our time, money, and energy was spent out in the countryside, in the mountains and jungle where the war was being fought. We called this effort the village health program, and it was developed and run with only token participation by the ministry. It attempted to serve the health needs of the refugees and those people in the remote areas of the country that had been neglected by the government in the past.

Geographically, the program had three divisions that reflected political and ethnic considerations. By far the largest was in Northern Laos that included Xieng Khoung, Sam Neua, Luang Prabang, Borikhane, and parts of Vientiane, Sayaboury, and Khammouane provinces. Headquarters for the operation was at the Sam Thong-Long Chieng complex in Xieng Khoung, and the dominant group involved were the Meo under the leadership of VP. However, there were also large numbers of Lao Theung, Tai, and small, isolated groups of ethnic Lao. All together about one million people were involved in the Northern program.

In the Northwestern province of Nam Tha—as well as Western Luang Prabang, and Western Sayaboury—the headquarters for the operation was in Nam Thoui—a refugee village north of the old Mekong port and French fort (Carnot) at Ban Houi Sai. This area, which borders on China, Burma, and Thailand, has many different ethnic groups, and the leadership was very fragmented. However, Nam Thoui was a Yao village, and the leadership was vested in Chao Mai, the hereditary Yao clan chief, and his younger brother, Chao La. There were slightly less than 15,000 Yao, but they were the dominant group in the area. The Lao Theung were by far the largest group, but their leadership was weak, and they were poorly unified. Small, isolated pockets of Meo, Lao, Tai, Lu, and Akha were also scattered throughout the area.

The contiguous parts of Laos, Burma, and Thailand in the Northwest are often referred to as the Golden Triangle. This has been an important trade center for many centuries—originally because of salt produced from brine wells, and not the opium of the modern era. It was the only salt available in a vast area of Southern China, Eastern Burma, and Northern Thailand and Laos. The population that benefited from American assistance in the Northwest was about 200,000.

The Southern program was based in Pakse—a Mekong river port and agricultural market town, trading in rice from the Sedone Valley, and coffee from the Bolovens Plateau. There were many small American assistance projects in this area, particularly in agriculture and community development—and health programming was often adjuvant to, and part of, these efforts. However, priority in health was given to working with the Kha (an unfortunate term meaning slave, used to identify the aboriginal Mon-Khmer people in Southern Laos; the same people called Lao Theung in other regions) tribal groups on the Bolovens Plateau and around its eastern and southern perimeter. There were several Kha tribes, some with as few as 500 or 600 people, and the largest with only a few thousand, each with a distinctive language.

Historically, the tribes had vied for land and hunting rights, and often fought bloody inter-tribal wars. However, in the late colonial period, they had been organized by a dynamic leader, Sithone Khommadam, and became a formidable insurgent force against the French. During the sixties and seventies, the leadership had been assumed by Colonel Vuk, a Laven tribal chief from the Saravane area. Vuk, fortunately, was strongly opposed to the Pathet Lao, and was a very important paramilitary asset. In the South, the program probably affected about 250,000 people.

Most of the fighting in the struggle against the aggressors was done by irregular military units formed from the ethnic minorities—those most menaced by the Vietnamese and Pathet Lao. The hundreds of thousands of refugees who were being displaced from their homes by the fighting, were the families or neighbors of these soldiers. Completely neglected by their government, and ignored by the international community, they struggled, bled, and died in the jungles and mountains that were their homes. They died of the most trivial wounds because they had no dressings or medicines, and they had no one who knew how to use such things, had they been available. Even under the best of circumstances, they lived in perilous balance with malaria and parasites, but the disruption of their farming and the destruction of their animals resulted in malnutrition and weakness—which tilted that balance with disastrous effect.

During the first few months after my arrival, the health problem seemed overwhelming. Not only were there no trained medical personnel for us to organize and support in some sort of program, there were no people with enough basic education to train and staff programs of the conventional type. With no roads, nor any kind of land transportation, the logistics of supply and evacuation could only be carried out by air at very high cost.

By far the most discouraging aspect of the problem however, was the apathy of the RLG and lack of interest on the part of USAID concerning health. Fortunately, at least from my standpoint, it turned out that this lack of interest was not shared by the American Embassy and the CIA. After a time, USAID gave complete support to the medical program, too.

As I traveled the country and became better acquainted with the wide spectrum of health, political, and security factors involved, the basic principles for the development of the village health program began to form in my mind. First, from an epidemiologic standpoint, the pathology in order of priority was: war casualties, malnutrition, malaria, and the acute infections of infancy, especially diarrheal diseases. There would be a minimal number of professional and paraprofessional people available, and the necessary human resources would, in most part, come from the youngsters recruited locally in their early- and mid-teens.

Because of the diversity of languages among the various groups concerned, and also for political considerations, the language of instruction would have to be Lao. Since a majority of the trainees wouldn't be able to speak Lao—and almost none would be able to read and write it—they would have to be taught to speak, read, and write their national language. Hopefully, much of this problem would be obviated in four or five years by the elementary schools that were being established.

Since war casualties were a priority problem, physical facilities would be needed, but construction would be as simple as possible, and of local materials, to keep costs and maintenance as low as possible. Time was often a critical factor. A good bamboo-and-thatch hospital or dispensary could be put up in a few days, or even a few hours if necessary. If the facility was overrun, there was no significant loss. The major emphasis of the program, aside from war casualties, would be at the village level—and focus on the problems of malnutrition, malaria, and infantile disease, in a prophylactic and preventive context.

Obviously, there would be many diseases and much trauma which our personnel and resources wouldn't be able to handle. I had to develop a basic philosophy that it was better to focus on the 80 or 90% of the problems that we could handle, and not waste time and resources on the others—no matter how much I empathised with their suffering. The health program would be an integral part of the co-ordinated effort in refugee relief, primary education, agriculture, and other community development projects such as water supply and protein sources from fish ponds, pigs, and ducks. Because of the war and the regular, sudden displacement of huge numbers of people, the capability to react immediately to large emergency situations would need to be mandatory.

Apart from national health development and the village health program, there was a third aspect to health assistance that was unofficial and trivial in some ways. Nevertheless, it was highly important to a good working relationship between Minister Khamphay and myself. This had to do with everyday logistical and operational problems that plagued Khamphay constantly.

A truck was needed to transport supplies to Savannakhet. The visiting World Health Organization survey team needed a plane to go to Khong. Mahosot Hospital was out of X-ray film. An operating room air conditioner was broken and needed a part from Bangkok. The ministry had hardly any logistical or maintenance capability, and such things were always brought to the attention of Khamphay. He was expected to solve the problem, and would lose face if no solution was forthcoming. As a consequence, he would have someone call his friend, Doc Weldon, and ask his help. I was always made to understand that the request had come from Khamphay, but there was never any mention of the matter between the two of us. That would also cause loss of face. Taking care of these little headaches probably bought USAID more goodwill from the ministry than all of our more substantive efforts.

As the program developed, I was more and more pressed for time. Seven days a week was just not sufficient. I would spend one or two days in the office, and then go into the field for a few days. Often, the few days would extend to two weeks or more. As a result, there were constant complaints by various offices in the mission that I neglected my responsibilities. But if there was some epidemic situation, I always felt it necessary to be on the spot to organize its containment. If people were being displaced by the enemy, I had to be there. The bureaucrats thought I was an administrator who should sit in Vientiane attending meetings or answering emergency cables from Washington. I, however, knew that my professional skills were better used in administering the program in the field, and delegating the office work to my staff. Fortunately, Charley Mann—who was in Laos for eight of the 11 years I was—agreed with me.

Over the first few years, I was able to build up a staff of about twenty Americans who filled our two basic requirements. One group took care of administrative and logistical needs in Vientiane, and the other group supervised the field program—in particular, village health.

In the field, there were usually five or six people. All were ex-Green Beret or Air Commando medics who were assigned on a geographic basis, and there was one RN who supervised the Sam Thong hospital. Don Dougan, former Green Beret B Team leader, honchoed this group, and worked countrywide. Fred Michaels, and—later—Earl Reynolds, a retired US Army colonel, did a great job of developing and running the medical supply facilities that supported our widespread field operations.

One of the major causes of pain and suffering was in dental health, and up until 1966—with the arrival of Dr. Frank Becker—we had almost completely ignored this area, having no resources to provide care or training. A dentist with a post-graduate degree in public health, Frank had a wide range of expertise and experience—which we would now be able to utilize to develop a training program for dental medics.

Frank and I had first met in American Samoa, when I hired him to run the dental program for the territorial health services—and I'd been particularly impressed with the training program he'd developed for dental hygienists. Samoan youngsters with elementary education were taught to do several useful dental procedures with a high level of skill within only a few months of training. After four years in American Samoa, Dr. Becker was ready to move on, and I had persuaded him to come to Laos.

A tall, trim, crew-cut man, always neat and meticulous in his dress, Frank was quiet, polite, and a real gentleman. But he was tough as nails. As a paratrooper in World War II, he had jumped into France on D-day. When he was in private practice in the US, he raced sports cars on a Ferrari-sponsored team in his spare time. In Samoa—by default, since we were the only two divers on the island—he and I were the unofficial diving and salvage officers. We had become close friends, and I was happy to see him again.

A problem peculiar to the military situation in which we worked had forced me to focus on the tooth problem. Many teams were going out on road-watch missions on the Ho Chi Min Trail, and doing other intelligence work behind the enemy lines. Often they'd be out for several weeks at a time. It was extremely dangerous for them to break radio silence and request an emergency pick up. The little Lao or Meo soldier could bear the pain of a gunshot wound or the debilitating agony of a malaria attack—but not a toothache. If he had a throbbing, aching molar, within a short time, he would break radio silence requesting a chopper to pick him up—no matter how dangerous it might be. Hopefully, we'd now have better screening and prevention of dental problems so this situation wouldn't arise.

Of course the main reason for developing some dental capability was to provide services to the hundreds of thousands of civilians we were supporting. Poor dental hygiene with plaque build-up caused a chronic inflammation of the gums, with loss of teeth that were otherwise healthy. The dental medics could attack such problems effectively, with simple education in dental hygiene and the removal of plaque. The service most in demand, however, was extraction of an aching tooth that was too damaged to salvage.

Frank and I landed at Sam Thong, and over his first few weeks, he would travel with me and become familiar with the program. First however, he had to pass the rigorous and nerve-wracking inspection by Mr. Edgar Buell.

I was always a little anxious about introducing a new employee to Pop. Sometimes he'd take an immediate dislike to a person for reasons which weren't always clear to me. Fortunately, on this occasion, my concern was unfounded. Before we'd finished the first bottle of corn whisky that night, it was obvious that Pop had given his stamp of approval to Frank, and had admitted him to the fraternity.

As the years passed the American personnel came and went, most after two or four years. Only Pat, Don Dougan, Frank Becker, and I remained to give the program continuity.

Partisan Warfare
in Sam Neua Province

Sam Neua province (see map) in Northern Laos borders on North Vietnam. Sam Neua City, located about 35 kilometers from the Vietnamese border, is the provincial capital. It had been the Pathet Lao headquarters since 1953. Colonial Route 6 starts at Hanoi, travels southwest into Laos at Sam Neua City, then turns south to join Route 7 at Ban Ban on the eastern side of the Plain of Jars. Route 7 forms a junction with Route 13 south of Luang Prabang, the royal capital of Laos on the Mekong River, travels east through the Plain of Jars, enters Vietnam just east of Ban Ban, and ends at Vinh on the South China Sea. Route 6 is an important line of communication and supply route into Laos from Vietnam—and during the Vietnam war also fed into the Ho Chi Minh Trail.

For these geographical, political, and logistical reasons, the Vietnamese and Pathet Lao placed high priority on controlling Sam Neua province. However, the population of the province was strongly rightist, or—possibly better stated—strongly anti-Vietnamese and anti-Pathet Lao. They vigorously opposed the communists' efforts to take over their homelands.

Like most of Northern Laos, the terrain of the province is mostly heavily forested, rugged limestone mountains. Travel and communication are restricted to narrow trails, by foot or on the backs of small mountain ponies. The few tiny valleys with land suitable for paddy farming are occupied by some ethnic Lao, but a large part of the population is Tai Dam (Black Tai) and Tai Daeng (Red Tai).

The Tai and Lao are closely related, and their dialects are usually mutually understandable. Some Tai are paddy farmers, but most live in the hills and are slash and burn farmers who raise dry rice. Several million Tai are found in Southern China, Northeastern Burma, and Northwestern Vietnam. In both China and Vietnam they live in so-called autonomous zones, and retain some small measure of self determination. In Burma, where they are called the Shan, they have been in rebellion against the central government since the end of British colonialism after World War II. Generally speaking, they are fiercely independent, and none of the countries have successfully integrated them into the communist system. At the higher levels in the mountains of Sam Neua, are many scattered groups of Meo and a few Lao Theung.

In the sixties, when the struggle for control of Sam Neua was at its height, the center of resistance to the Vietnamese invaders was at Hua Muang. Before its destruction, this large Lao village was located about eighty kilometers southwest of Sam Neua City, in one of the deep valleys that had a small area of flat, alluvial land that the villagers used for paddy rice farming.

The village was located on the west bank of a beautiful river, and rice paddies surrounded it on three sides. A sheer cliff rose 200-300 meters immediately from the east bank of the river, to a small plateau on which a dirt airstrip about 400 meters long had been built by the people of Hua Muang so the Corsican opium buyers from Vientiane could pick up the opium produced in the area. The strip was minimal in length for the old Beechcraft C45s that the Corsicans used for this purpose, and the tangled wreckage of one of these planes at the base of the cliff below the strip was testament to that fact. On the other hand, it was more than adequate for our STOL aircraft—including planes as large as the Caribou.

The resistance in Sam Neua was a partisan operation, and the hard military core that did most of the fighting consisted of about 1,000 men divided into two units. They were designated BV26 and BV27. The name BV, or *battalion volontiere*, was a holdover from the French colonial period. The 23 officers in the two units were mostly Lao from Vientiane and other Mekong lowland towns, but many of them had family ties in Sam Neua. The non-commissioned officers and other enlisted men were Lao and Tai volunteers from Sam Neua.

In many of the larger Lao and Tai villages there were men armed and trained by BV cadre. These village militia could prevent harassment and coercion by small units of the enemy troops, but when faced with any serious threat, they had to fade into the jungle until help arrived from one of the BVs.

To the north of Hua Muang, near Sam Neua City, were the three Meo enclaves—Hong Non, Houi Khammoune, and Pha Thi—with a total of 350 armed men. Located on mountain crests that were difficult to approach from the ground, all three were strong defensive positions.

Although these troops were poorly trained, they were courageous in the defence of their homes, and it would take a large, well-organized enemy attack to displace them. Each enclave had a small, dirt STOL strip about 150 meters long. They were rough and narrow, and the winds on these mountain tops blew strong and erratic. It took a cool, experienced STOL pilot who enjoyed a challenge to sit a Helio Courier down on one of these strips. The passengers usually closed their eyes and prayed.

BV26 was under the command of Colonel Khamsao Keovilay, while Colonel Thong Vongrasamy commanded BV27—and they had worked out an arrangement between themselves which exploited their personalities and capabilities to the maximum. Both were from Vientiane, and both had gone through officer's training school at Dong Hene at the same time. General Khamkhong Boudavong had been commandant of the school at the time, and he had later organized the resistance in Sam Neua when he became the commanding general for Military Region 2. Khamkhong hand picked his old students for the difficult job of leading the fight against the Vietnamese invaders and their Pathet Lao allies. Khamsao was a good organizer and planner, and Thong was a leader and fighter. Khamsao ran the headquarters, did the logistics, and organized the civilian population support base, while Thong was the field commander who saw to the training and discipline of the troops, and led them in battle.

Before 1966 they had no tactical air support—and logistical air support was minimal. A C47 flying out of Region 2 headquarters at Paksane on the Mekong below Vientiane made an occasional ammo drop, and Air America planes flying out of Vientiane dropped rice to the troops and refugees each month. The one or two Helio Couriers and a chopper that Pop and I used when we worked in the area were the only other air support available to them. Our USAID Air America contract aircraft were their only contact with the outside world.

The operation was 300 kilometers deep in enemy territory. Between 1962 and 1966, Pop and I, along with the pilots who flew us, were the only Americans allowed in the area by our embassy—and no other foreigners had the means or desire to visit it.

Civilian leadership rested with the *chao muang* of Hua Muang. A tall, quiet man in his early forties, the *chao muang* had been born and raised in the town, and his father had been *chao muang* before him. He exerted his authority with dignity and firmness, and the people in Sam Neua respected him for his honesty and ability.

Khamsao was a small, smiling man with a happy, outgoing personality who liked to party and socialise. Thong was quite the opposite. A tall, handsome man with a pale ascetic face, he seldom spoke, but when he did, one was immediately attracted to him. His language capability was considerable. In addition to Lao, he spoke English, French, Vietnamese, and Meo. His men believed that he had magic powers, and there was an aura of the mystic about him. One could only describe him as charismatic and a natural leader of men. Both Thong and Khamsao were in their mid-thirties.

The three men—the *chao muang,* Khamsao, and Thong—liked and respected each other, and worked in perfect harmony. They had organized the entire population to carry out the struggle against the enemy. The young, able-bodied men were the soldiers in the BVs and the home guards; the women raised the rice and did the farming, with the men helping them as the security situation permitted; the elderly men and women took care of the small children and the home; and the children from five to about 14 years of age were in school if there was no threat from the enemy.

If attack was imminent, school was out. The girls helped their mothers in the fields and with the livestock, or helped prepare the food, which they took to the fighting men. The boys carried ammunition and supplies to their fathers and older brothers, and slept in the outposts to help listen and watch for the enemy. They went on patrol, and also acted as messengers to maintain contact with headquarters. Small, barefoot, and inconspicuous, they slipped through the jungle quickly and silently.

Good intelligence was the critical factor in success and survival. Khamsao and Thong had to know at all times exactly where the enemy was and what he was doing. Everyone had responsibility for reporting enemy movements and activities. The partisan group maintained a highly efficient and sophisticated network of observation and reporting. Particularly effective agents were the girls aged nine or ten years old. They were well trained and could go anywhere without being suspect.

The backbone of the partisan base was the women. The men were on one side of the mountain fighting a bloody, little war, and the women were on the other side trying to scratch out a living and hold the family together. It was a total effort by every man, woman, and child.

The *chao muang's* wife was a sweet little lady who made a significant contribution, but the leader of the women was Mrs. Khamsao. An attractive, quiet lady, good mother and housewife, she was completely fearless, with a will of steel. She could handle a light machine gun or lay a mortar as well as any man, but mainly she set an example of hard work, courage, and optimism that was an inspiration to all.

Thong's tactical headquarters was twenty kilometers to the east of Hua Muang, on a mountain ridge called Phu Kuk. His positions in this area controlled the mountain passes that led to Hua Muang and the heart of Sam Neua province. Across the valley, about five kilometers northeast from Phu Kuk, is Muang Peun. At that time, Muang Peun was an important Pathet Lao military base on Route 6 that guarded the southern approach to Sam Neua City.

By late 1963, I'd been to Hua Muang and the Hong Non area several times, but had never had occasion to go to Phu Kuk. On one particular trip in mid-1965, Pop and I decided to spend the night with Thong at his headquarters. On previous trips to Sam Neua, he had always met us at Hua Muang, but this time he wanted me to check out the new dispensary the people had just built at Phu Kuk. Pop had brought school supplies for the little bamboo school, and USIS had given us an operator with a portable generator and projector to show movies. Thong met us at Hua Muang, and we flew to Phu Kuk late in the afternoon.

There was the usual short, rough STOL strip, and a few bamboo-and-thatch buildings inside a perimeter of sandbagged bunkers. However, when we landed, there was a large crowd gathered at the strip to meet us. Most of the people were Tai Daeng (Red Tai) from the surrounding villages. A long line of women and children stretched from the airstrip to the military compound, and each person had a bouquet of flowers. As Pop and I passed down the line, each one knelt and presented their flowers to us.

The building where Thong and his staff lived, and where we would sleep, was beautifully decorated with greenery and flowers, and already the big jars of *lao hai* had been set out. Soon, in accord with the local custom, Pop and I—the honored guests—were sucking the rice wine through long, slim bamboo tubes with two pretty little Tai girls to help us. All the crowd sang and clapped their hands in encouragement.

After a good meal, we all did the *lamvong* to the accompaniment of Thong's drum and the clapping and chanting of the spectators. Thong didn't drink or dance, but he loved the drums and was a very good percussionist.

About ten o'clock, the dancing stopped and the film started. This was a rare treat, and in fact many of the people had never before seen a movie. First, there was a government propaganda piece, and then a series of Disney cartoons. Everyone—man, woman, and child—was enchanted with Donald and Mickey.

Suddenly, a few minutes before eleven o'clock, Thong stopped the movie and ordered all the lights extinguished. He had Pop and I climb on top of a bunker where we had a good view across the valley toward Muang Peun. Thong commanded everyone be quiet and watch. It was all very mysterious, and no one knew what to expect. Thong wouldn't answer our questions, and told us we'd see for ourselves what was to happen in a few minutes.

At exactly eleven o'clock we saw the flash of several explosions in the area of the Pathet Lao military positions, and—several seconds later—we heard the sounds of the explosions mixed with that of small arms fire. Fires began to burn brightly on the horizon.

In three or four minutes, all the noise subsided, and only the flames could be seen. Thong had the projectionist start the movie again. Everyone was curious, but in spite of our pleas, Thong wouldn't say what had happened across the valley. He said to be patient and we'd find out the next morning.

The next morning, Captain Duangtha arrived with twenty of his soldiers and three Pathet Lao prisoners. They had raided Muang Peun. Duangtha was Thong's second-in-command, and although a rough, fearsome-looking man, a huge smile and a ready laugh revealed a kind and pleasant personality. In time we were to become the closest of friends.

They also had 15 AK47s besides their own weapons, as well as various other trophies of their raid on the PL camp. Fortunately, there had been no casualties, and all the men looked remarkably fit after a hard night's work. With much animation and laughter, they related the details of the raid and the capture of the prisoners.

They were especially proud and happy to have the AK47s. The Vietnamese had just started to arm the PL with this excellent automatic weapon, and these were the first they had captured. We were all greatly impressed. As an ex-Marine infantry officer, I appreciated the difficulty of carrying out such an operation on the exact time schedule, as planned, particularly at night.

Thong had ordered the operation, not just to harass the enemy, but specifically to take at least two prisoners. He hoped to confirm information he had about new Vietnamese units moving into the area for an attack on Hua Muang. No such units had yet been committed, and were apparently held in reserve for the present—if they existed at all. If this information was true, the Pathet Lao soldiers at Muang Peun should know about it.

I was curious to see how they would go about getting information from the prisoners. Visions of physical cruelty and torture came to mind, but it didn't work exactly that way. The method was much more refined. First, Thong talked to all three of them at the same time. He talked to them in his usual quiet, polite manner, but when they looked into his eyes, none doubted that he would do exactly as he said. Any one of them who didn't answer his questions would be killed. He would talk to each of them separately, and if each man's answers to his questions weren't essentially the same, he would kill all three of them. If the answers they gave seemed reasonable, he wouldn't harm them, but would hold them prisoner until future events proved that they'd told the truth. When this happened, he would release them and see that they returned safely to their people. If he found that they had lied to him, he would shoot all three.

I found out later that the psychology had been effective. Although they couldn't give Thong all the information he wanted, he was satisfied that they'd told him all they knew, as accurately as they were able. Future events proved that they hadn't lied, and—true to his word—all three were later released.

After the excitement of Duangtha's return had subsided, Thong and I inspected the new dispensary and talked to the two medics who would operate it. Neither had much training, and we decided to take them one at a time to Sam Thong and put them through the basic training course. In addition, Thong would select two more boys to be medics. One would also go to Sam Thong for training, and one would help in the dispensary. When the first two finished their training, Thong would then send a second pair. I made a list of drugs and supplies the dispensary needed, and would have them sent from Sam Thong in the next few days. Ly Chai, our medic supervisor, would bring the drugs and supplies, and when he returned, he'd take the two boys back to Sam Thong with him for training.

At mid-morning Pop, Thong, and I flew back to Hua Muang. Thong was worried about the enemy build-up, and believed an attack could come within the next three or four weeks. He wanted to hold a meeting with Khamsao and all the other leaders, and decide on a plan of action. Thong's intelligence indicated there were at least seven battalions with a minimum of 3,500 Vietnamese troops moving into position.

Pop remained at Hua Muang, but I had to get back to the office in Vientiane. Over the following four weeks, I made three or four quick trips to Hua Muang and Phu Kuk. Pop was spending most of his time there, and the enemy was expected to attack at any time. Khamsao and Thong believed that they had to hit Phu Kuk first, as it guarded the best approaches to Hua Muang. When this happened, Thong would fall back to Hua Muang and try to slow the enemy as much as possible.

Suddenly, the Vietnamese started to move. Phu Kuk was attacked, and Thong began his withdrawal. He had few casualties, but his troops took a heavy toll of the Vietnamese and slowed them down in plenty of time for Hua Muang to prepare. Khamsao had his troops in a semi-circular defensive screen to the east of Hua Muang facing the enemy. Over the next few days, Thong gradually pulled back into this defensive perimeter.

At the same time, refugees started to stream into Hua Muang as their villages were overrun. Our troops were beginning to take casualties as the fighting intensified. Pop and I remained at Hua Muang to be sure that the refugees were cared for, and that the casualties who were too serious to be handled at the little dispensary hospital were evacuated to Sam Thong. We only had two Helio Couriers and one H34 chopper, and we kept them shuttling back and forth constantly.

In the mornings, however, the fog was very bad around the airstrip (3,500 feet above sea level) on the plateau above the Hua Muang Valley, and it often didn't burn off until ten or eleven o'clock. The cloud hung about 15 feet above the surface of the strip—with a very sharp, distinct ceiling—and extended upward to around 6,500 feet. Horizontal visibility in the 15 feet of clear air below the fog was about two kilometers. This blanket of fog extended out over the valley in a flat plane, so the valley remained clear.

We had a portable, low-power homer (radio direction finder) the size of a Kleenex box with a range of forty to fifty kilometers, which we sat on the end of the runway where the cliff dropped off into the valley. The strip ran due east and west, perpendicular to the north south valley—which was about two kilometers wide, with high mountains on the west rising to 6,000 feet.

Lee Mullins, the Air America chief STOL pilot, would take off in a Helio from Sam Thong at first light in the morning and head for Hua Muang. Flying a compass course just above the overcast at 6,500 feet, he would pick up our little homer and call us on his radio. If we had an emergency—particularly if there were badly wounded we couldn't care for at our crude bamboo hospital—I would describe the weather and visibility around the strip and over the valley. Lee would then head toward the radio homer, its signal getting louder and louder in his earphones.

When he was directly overhead, he would hit the small cone of silence over the homer, and the signal would suddenly fade. He knew he was then over the end of the runway. Immediately, he would take an easterly heading for about five minutes, maintaining his 6,500 foot altitude, then make a tight 180-degree turn and fly back to the west until he overheaded the homer again.

The instant he hit the cone of silence, he pulled back the throttle, turned on the carburettor heat, cranked on full flaps, and sat the Helio on its nose. His descent had to be almost vertical or he would hit the mountains to the west of the valley. The plane dropped down 3,000 feet through the fog, and broke into the clear at 500 feet above the valley floor. Lee had about three to four seconds to make a recovery before he would crash.

After he was in level flight again and had his bearings, he slipped the Helio into the 15 feet of clear air between the ground and the fog, and taxied up to where we were standing at the far end of the strip. Everyone would be waiting anxiously, and when the Helio appeared in the little patch of daylight at the end of the airfield, wild shouting and cheering would break out.

The handsome, trim, grey-haired pilot, with his cigar stuck in the corner of his mouth, would kill the engine, nonchalantly climb out of the plane, and ask, "What the hell's all the noise about?"

The pressure continued to build up, and within a few more days the enemy was fully committed to the attack. As Khamsao and Thong had anticipated, their 1,000 men were facing about 3,500 Vietnamese troops driving toward Hua Muang. They were not only outnumbered, but the enemy troops were much better armed and supplied. Our troops had ancient World War II, M1 rifles and carbines, whereas the enemy was armed with new, automatic AK47s, and modern rocket and grenade launchers. The situation was truly grim. Khamsao and Tong couldn't possibly engage in a set-piece battle to defend Hua Muang against such a numerically superior and better armed enemy. They had to take the initiative away from their opponent.

The two commanders, the *chao muang* and their staffs held a meeting, with Pop and I as interested spectators. The meeting went on for several hours, with various plans presented and discarded. I was surprised how little Thong involved himself in the discussions, although he paid close attention to everything that was said. He only responded when someone asked him a direct question. Finally, he stood up, raised his two hands for silence, and began to speak in his quiet but authoritative voice.

"This is what we'll do. I'll take 250 men and march to Hong Non. The rest will remain here and defend Hua Muang. We'll take 48 hours to get there without rest. When we reach Hong Non, we must rest and prepare for one day. The next day, we'll move into Sam Neua City and occupy the town. This will cut the enemy's supply line and endanger his rear areas. He'll be forced to pull his troops back to drive us out of Sam Neua City. You must hold back the enemy here for four days. By then I'll be in control of the town, and the enemy will begin to withdraw.

"*Tan* Pop will let us use the planes for the next two days to carry ammunition and supplies to Hong Non for the troops to take into Sam Neua City. I'd like for *Tan Maw* Weldon to stay at Hong Non with the helicopter until we pull out of Sam Neua City, to help us evacuate casualties. If you agree with this plan, I'll get my troops ready and leave for Hong Non in four hours."

Thong had spoken, and no one questioned his plan. If he said he could march his men the sixty kilometers to Hong Non through the rugged mountains and jungle in two days, and then occupy Sam Neua City, it would be done.

Hong Non sits high up in the mountains 11 kilometers to the west of Sam Neua City, and was the perfect jumping-off place to attack the town. Four hours later, in the fading light of the day, Thong and his 250 men quietly departed Hua Muang.

In the mid-afternoon of the second day, Pop and I flew to Hong Non. About five o'clock, Thong arrived—and within the next hour, all 250 of his troops were with him. The men were tired but in surprisingly good condition after the gruelling march. They had stopped only twice for about three hours each time during the two days since leaving Hua Muang.

Lieutenant Boua Chou, the Meo commander and *chao muang* at Hong Non, had cleared out the school and some houses so Thong's soldiers would have a place to sleep—and the villagers cooked rice and two pigs that Pop had brought from Hua Muang. They ate their meal quickly, and by dark everyone was asleep, including Thong. It was well into the morning before anyone stirred the next day.

Thong and his officers spent the day going over his plan of attack, and the troops worked on their weapons and equipment. As usual, Pop and I had brought a good supply of balloons and candy. We amused ourselves with the little children by blowing up the balloons and organizing contests for candy prizes. When Thong had a free moment, I got him off to the side and asked him if I could hold sick call in Sam Neua City after the invasion.

"If you think it's possible, send word and I'll take the chopper with a lot of medicines, I'll see as many civilians as possible," I told him.

I could tell from his expression that he didn't like the idea, and I was sorry I'd spoken. But after a moment of consideration he replied, "All right *Tan Maw*, if I think it's safe enough I'll let you know."

That evening at dusk, Thong and his men started down the mountain for Sam Neua City. Just before dawn the next morning they attacked. Although there were probably 300-400 enemy soldiers in the town, they were disorganized, and were caught completely by surprise. Thong's troops quickly routed them and occupied the communist's headquarters.

After three days, most of the enemy troops in the attack on Hua Muang pulled out and moved north on their way to relieve Sam Neua City. As soon as the North Vietnamese and Pathet Lao started to put pressure on his troops, Thong began to withdraw. Four days from the time of departure, they were back at Hong Non, and had suffered only a few casualties—three killed and seven wounded.

Thong and his 250 men had made almost 4,000 experienced Vietnamese troops look like a bunch of fresh recruits. It was a great tactical victory in the military sense, but was an even greater moral victory for the Sam Neua partisans defending their homes against the hated Vietnamese.

Unfortunately, Thong never sent word about the sick call, and my grandchildren would never hear the tale about when Grandpa saw his patients in the routed communist's headquarters.

The enemy called off the Hua Muang campaign, and that was the end of their offensive for that year.

The Ambush

All the airstrips at the upcountry sites had a panel code which the villagers displayed before an aircraft could land. The panels were made of white cloth about one foot wide by four feet long, and were placed near the landing area to form a designated letter of the alphabet. This letter identified the site to planes dropping rice and other commodities, and also indicated to the pilot that it was safe to land. The rules forbade putting the signals in place until the aircraft was overhead, and also forbade leaving the signals in place after the aircraft landed.

This simple practice prevented our pilots from landing at a site captured by the enemy during the night, or since the last time the site was visited. Supposedly, no one was ever to land on an unmarked strip. Regrettably, both the villagers and the pilots would sometimes become negligent—particularly at sites not often visited, where the procedure might not be followed.

Ban Lao is a small ethnic Lao village on the Nam Beng River in Luang Prabang province, located just a few kilometers north of Pak Beng—a local trading center and port on the Mekong River at the mouth of the Nam Beng. In this area, the Chinese were building a road from Southern Yunnan province through Northwest Laos that would tie into the Mekong River at Pak Beng. The last part of the road would follow the Nam Beng Valley. This project begun as assistance to the Lao coalition government formed under the Geneva Accords—but ceased soon after it started, as China's relations with the RLG deteriorated.

By 1965, the Chinese resumed construction on the road without consulting the RLG—likely as a result of their commitment to support the Pathet Lao and the communist insurgency in Northern Thailand. They corveed Shan in Southern Yunnan to work on the road, and the conditions were terrible. As a consequence, we had over 9,000 Shan flee into Nam Tha province to escape from the Chinese—and USAID Laos was supporting them as refugees through our Ban Houi Sai headquarters. From the bank of the Mekong opposite Pak Beng, it is only a few hours walk across a narrow strip of the Lao province of Sayaboury to reach the Thai border in Nan province.

Ban Lao was a friendly village opposed to the Pathet Lao, but its location in the path of the advancing Chinese road construction put it in a very precarious situation. Undoubtedly, the PL would make an effort to eliminate this obstacle in the near future. The village had a defense unit of local men trained by the FAR with the help of PARU and CIA instructors, but they couldn't hold out against the large PL units in the area.

We had built a dispensary and a school in Ban Lao, and Joe Flipse, the USAID community development officer stationed in Ban Houi Sai, had been helping the people with medical and school supplies, and also with some agricultural support in the form of seeds and farm tools.

Joe—a young American from Tennessee—had come to Laos with the IVS. When he had finished his two-year tour, he'd been hired by USAID. He was married to a lovely Lao girl, Suzie; spoke fluent Lao; and was a competent and highly-motivated worker who was liked and respected by all the local officials, both civilian and military. The hilltribe leaders considered him a devoted friend, and he had their complete trust and cooperation

Joe, Terry Burke—a young CIA field operations officer, and one of the Thai PARU soldiers had been working in the area for a few days. Terry and the PARU soldier had decided to stay the night in the village, while Joe flew back to Ban Houi Sai that evening, saying he would return the following day to finish some work he had started.

Early the next morning, Joe left Ban Houi Sai in a Pilatus Porter for Ban Lao, and about a half hour later was over the village. The pilot circled, but no one put out the signal panel, even though people could be seen on the ground. After circling the field three or four times, still no one put out the signal. Nevertheless, the pilot decided to land, since he knew Terry had spent the night there, and he assumed that the security situation was normal.

But Joe sensed something was wrong, even though he couldn't say exactly what. In any event, it was strange that Terry hadn't come up on his little VHF radio transceiver when they continued to circle the strip. Perhaps he wasn't in the village at the time.

The pilot had already turned on final approach when Joe made him pull up and head back for Ban Houi Sai. He would check with the military, and if there was trouble at Ban Lao, they would probably know through their radio net.

On the way to Ban Houi Sai, Joe had his pilot put out a call to all aircraft in the area instructing them that the Ban Lao strip was closed to all traffic until he gave the word that it was open again. Ernie Brace, flying a Continental Airlines Pilatus Porter, was on his way to Ban Lao at this time to deliver five passengers and to pick up Terry. Apparently, he didn't hear the instruction from Joe that closed the Ban Lao strip.

We don't know why Ernie landed at Ban Lao that morning, since it is highly unlikely that the villagers displayed the signal. Possibly he made the same error in judgement that Joe's pilot made when he'd started to land. In any event, Ernie landed and then realized something was wrong—because he quickly turned the aircraft around and started to take off. Pathet Lao soldiers lying in cover on the side of the strip riddled the Porter with automatic weapons fire. The turbine was hit and ceased to function before he could get airborne.

Miraculously, Ernie wasn't hit, even though all five passengers were seriously wounded and the plane was badly damaged. The Pathet Lao soldiers rushed up to the Porter, pulled the American out of the cockpit, and quickly lead him out of the village into the foothills toward the northwest. The five wounded passengers on the plane were thrown out on to the ground and were shot again to ensure they were dead. One of the victims was a soldier in green fatigues, and for some reason—possibly there was yet some sign of life—one of the communist soldiers ripped open his abdomen with a long knife. After a short while, all the Pathet Lao departed.

While this was happening, Jack Williamson and I were in Xieng Lom, an isolated but rich Lao paddy area in Sayaboury province, visiting some dispensaries that we supported. The local military commander was a personal friend of Jack's, and we intended to spend the day with him. Jack had taught the commander and some of his men how to play basketball, which resulted in close friendships.

Xieng Lom is only a few kilometers south from Pak Beng and Ban Lao, but on the opposite side of the Mekong. It had a long, grass airstrip that had been built many years before for C47 traffic that was still in good condition but seldom used. We were in a village near the strip and heard a chopper, a Porter, and a Caribou land in close succession. So much traffic on this remote airstrip was unusual.

I was wondering what was causing the activity, when someone drove up in a Jeep and said I was wanted at the strip. Although there were no roads, the FAR had a Jeep to shuttle people and supplies from the planes to their small headquarters nearby. I got on the Jeep and the driver took me to the strip.

Several people were standing in a group talking when we drove up, and I recognized Bill Lair and Major Decha. Bill was in charge of all CIA field operations for Laos, and Major Decha, a military advisor in the Thai PARU, worked closely with him. The three of us had known each other since my arrival in Laos, and were good friends.

Although Bill was assigned to Laos, his office was in Thailand, at the Udorn air base. He had received word through the military radio net that there was trouble at Ban Lao—and Terry and the PARU officer were missing. Immediately, he and Decha had flown to Xieng Lom to organize the search and rescue effort for their men. I hadn't been aware of the problem, and the two of them briefed me on the situation. They wanted me to be on hand because of the high probability that they'd be bringing in wounded from the search.

Decha took off in the chopper, and within an hour was back with Terry and Wichan—the PARU officer, as well as several wounded Lao soldiers and civilians. Terry was in good shape, but Wichan had a high velocity round through his right thigh. As I worked on the wounded, Terry told us what had happened.

About midnight, they were hit by a large force of Pathet Lao troops. With great numerical superiority, the enemy had quickly overrun Ban Lao. Wichan was wounded early in the fighting, but with Terry carrying him, the two had been able to escape into the brush. They had slowly worked their way out of the vicinity of the village without being seen by the enemy. Terry had his small radio transceiver, and when Decha's chopper got into the area, he guided it in for the pickup.

Decha continued to search the area around Ban Lao for casualties and bring them into Xieng Lom. One of the wounded men that Decha picked up had seen Ernie Brace captured on the airstrip and led away by the Pathet Lao. As soon as Decha heard this, he took off again to search for the American and see if there was any possibility of rescuing him. Decha correctly guessed that the Pathet Lao would be moving north on the main trail in the area, and he soon spotted Ernie with a large escort of troops.

The PL troops made no attempt to hide from our unarmed aircraft, hoping to tempt it into firing range. There were also troops strung out along the trail, both in front and behind the group with the prisoner. The chances of Ernie breaking away from his captors and being picked up were zero. A Porter was in the air, so Decha instructed the pilot to try to keep Ernie in sight. He would return to Xieng Lom and see if Bill had any ideas about what might be done to rescue the pilot.

The situation appeared almost hopeless. Decha and Bill decided that a thin possibility might be an air strike on the trail immediately in front of the PL guarding the American. If it could be done suddenly and unexpectedly, there might be enough confusion for Ernie to make an escape. Decha would be hovering as close as possible in the chopper and would try to rush in and make the pick up if there was any chance of success.

Two problems occurred to us that further complicated the picture. First, to be effective the strike had to be close enough to Ernie to cause plenty of confusion, but far enough away not to injure or kill him. The second problem was political. Bill had the authority and radio capability of contacting US jet bombers on station over Laos to come in and make the strike, but all our aircraft were forbidden to approach the area in which the Chinese were building the road. The vicinity of Ban Lao was well within this no-fly zone.

However, Bill was in constant contact with Ambassador Sullivan, who was urging him to do everything possible to rescue Ernie—including using the jets. Certainly the jets were not the ideal weapon for the pinpoint accuracy that was required, but there was little choice.

Bill contacted the aircraft on station over Northeast Laos, explained the situation to the strikeforce leader, and gave him the co-ordinates of the target. They estimated that they'd be overhead in twenty minutes. Decha would try to bring them in at exactly the right spot from his chopper.

In the early afternoon, we got another chopper and used it to pick up additional wounded. Most of the Pathet Lao had left the vicinity of Ban Lao, and it was possible to search the area without too much difficulty.

By late afternoon we had 28 wounded soldiers and civilians lying on the dirt floor of a bamboo shack by the strip at Xieng Lom. Earlier in the day, when we realized that we'd be getting casualties, I ordered supplies brought in from our medical warehouse in Ban Houi Sai. There was no lack of dressings, splints, IV fluids, stretchers, and other necessities, but all I could do under the circumstances was to cleanse the wounds, stop the bleeding with pressure dressings, and get the IV fluids started. Nevertheless, these simple procedures could be life saving. Fortunately, I had the medic from the nearby dispensary to help me. Several of the wounded were shot to pieces and barely breathing.

One of the wounded was the soldier on the plane with Ernie Brace that morning—whom the Pathet Lao had shot and then knifed open. This poor man was hit by six bullets. One grazed the left side of his head; two went through the left arm; one hit his left flank; and two went through his left thigh, shattering the bone. Two loops of small intestine were protruding from a long, gaping wound in his abdomen. To my utter amazement, he was still conscious, responsive to questioning.

We irrigated the loops of bowel with saline solution and cleansed them as well as we could. After stuffing the protruding bowel back into the abdominal cavity, we strapped the wound closed with tape, and applied a dressing. With his other wounds bandaged, a traction splint on the shattered leg, and IV fluids containing massive doses of antibiotics going into his veins, he asked for a cigarette! Between puffs he told the following story.

None of the passengers had suspected anything was wrong when the plane landed at Ban Lao that morning, until the pilot suddenly swung the plane around and seemed to be taking off. At that moment, our patient was hit in the leg and side by small arms fire, and the plane came to a stop. A few seconds later, the enemy pulled the door open, dragged him out of the plane, and threw him on the ground. Again, there was firing, and he felt the bullets hitting his head and arm. Lying on his back, he remembered seeing the Pathet Lao soldier take the knife out of his belt, and he knew he would be stabbed with it. At that moment he lost consciousness.

When he regained his senses, everything was quiet and no one could be seen other than three or four bodies lying around the plane. He cried out to them for help, but soon realized they were all dead. The river was about 100 meters away, and he slowly and painfully dragged himself toward it. He had a terrible fear that the Pathet Lao would return. If he could reach the river and crawl into the water, possibly he could keep afloat, and the current would carry him away from this horrible nightmare.

He dragged himself a short distance, then fainted from the pain and exertion. Gradually his mind would clear, and he would struggle on toward the river. This was repeated many times over until he finally slid his shattered body very gradually into the river. The cool water felt good, and his head was clearer for it.

It was shallow along the bank—and using his good arm and leg, he was able to propel himself with the current for a while. Then the water began to get deeper and it was difficult for him to stay afloat. He clung to the bank, too weak to drag himself out of the water, afraid he would drown if he let go and tried to float with the current again.

A path followed the side of the river, but he had seen no one since he regained consciousness at the airstrip. Suddenly, a little boy and girl came hurrying down the track. He cried out to the children, but when they saw the body in the water, with the face torn by the bullet, they were terrified and began to run away.

Desperately, the dying man continued to plead and cry for help. The children stopped, and slowly returned to where they could get a better look at him. Suddenly, they realized he was from their village, and with great excitement tried to pull him out of the water.

He resisted their frantic efforts, explaining that he was badly wounded and couldn't get out of the water. Nearby was a field with an old bamboo shelter. Under his direction, the children tore the shelter apart and made a raft from the bamboo. They helped him get the upper part of his body on to the raft, and then pushed it out into the current. As he floated away, he told the boy and girl that they had made much merit, and he would pray to the Buddha to reward them.

The man hoped that he'd be able to float downriver to the Mekong and get help at Pak Beng. This little river trading post was more-or-less politically neutral. Since it was useful to both the communists and rightist factions, neither side bothered the merchants and residents who lived there.

However, the wounded soldier's luck took a turn for the better, and there was no need for him to go that far downstream. Our chopper that was out looking for wounded, saw the raft floating on the river and went down to investigate. The ordeal was over. About 15 minutes later, he arrived at Xieng Lom.

It was getting late in the afternoon when Bill and I heard jets off to the north. Shortly after, the muffled thunder of exploding bombs could be heard. We waited for Decha's return, and prayed that we'd see Ernie get off the chopper with him. It wasn't to be. The strike wasn't close enough to have the desired effect, and it was likely that the plan was flawed from the beginning. I felt sorry for Bill, for we heard later that the jets had hit a village, and there were serious casualties—which was certainly upsetting.

Both of our choppers continued the search for casualties until dark, and the Air America Caribou was standing by for me to take the wounded to the OB hospital in Vientiane. As soon as the choppers broke off the search, we loaded the wounded on to the plane and took off. It goes without saying that we didn't like to fly out of this unlighted strip in the dark, but there was no choice that day. Still, Ed Dearborn, the pilot, had flown everything with wings—in war and peace, in half the countries of the world—and it was reassuring to know he was at the controls.

The flight from Xieng Lom to Vientiane would take about an hour and 15 minutes. There were 32 people on board: 28 wounded, the pilot and co-pilot, the kicker, and me. Some of the wounded could sit up, but stretchers covered most of the floor of the aircraft.

The take off from the dark field was uneventful, and we were at cruise altitude about 25 minutes into the flight. All my patients were quiet, and seemed to be resting. Their IVs were running okay, and there was no unusual bleeding. Suddenly, I noticed a flickering light outside the windows on the left side of the aircraft. At first it didn't register that something might be wrong. However, when the light increased in intensity, I threaded my way through the stretchers and looked out the window. A cold chill of fear flashed through me.

The left engine was on fire.

I was nursing a planeload of wounded people with nothing below us but a sea of darkness—and the goddamn airplane was on fire!

Climbing a small ladder that allows access to the cockpit from the cargo compartment of the Caribou, I stood behind Ed and the co-pilot and gave them the good news. Ed activated the fire extinguisher system but it wasn't effective. He killed the burning engine, but had difficulty feathering the propeller. Fortunately, after a minute or two, the fire gradually extinguished itself, and Ed got the prop feathered. We all said a silent prayer of thanks.

After Ed trimmed the aircraft for single-engine flight, it couldn't hold altitude. We were descending at about 200 feet a minute. When power was increased on the one engine to maintain height, it would overheat, and Ed had to back off.

We were still 45 minutes from Vientiane, at an altitude of 6,500 feet. I did some quick mental arithmetic, and calculated that we would hit the ground about twenty miles short of the runway. However, Ed said that our rate of descent should slow a bit as we lost altitude. If we got too low, he would increase power to hold altitude, and hope the engine would last long enough to get us home safe.

It was a long 45 minutes—with the last five minutes of the flight at tree-top level. Fortunately, the approach was straight in, and Ed greased the sick Caribou to a perfect landing, with its one red-hot engine glowing in the dark.

We'd been in radio contact with Tom Crohn, the air operations manager for Air America from the time the fire started, and when we landed, fire trucks, ambulances, and what looked like half the people in Vientiane were waiting for us. Tom had already thoughtfully phoned Pat and told her that her husband was in a burning Caribou over Sayaboury province. Pat was at the house with Pop, who I'd made come down from Sam Thong to rest for a few days because his heart was acting up and his chest pain had been worse.

When Ed brought the Caribou to a stop, Pat ran out and Pop was following her, rubbing his chest and popping nitroglycerine under his tongue. If Tom hadn't been such a good friend, I would have strangled him.

✪✪✪

Several months later, I was walking down the street in Vientiane, and a Lao man, who limped slightly and had a jagged, red scar across his face, came up and greeted me like a dear old friend. He seemed elated to see me, but quickly realized I didn't recognize him. To refresh my memory, he raised his shirt, and there was a long scar on his abdomen from below the umbilicus up to the rib cage. I finally recognized my disemboweled patient from Ban Lao. We embraced, and laughed. That evening, we had dinner together, and reminisced over that horrible day at Ban Lao.

The next day, I put him on a plane for Ban Houi Sai with a note to Joe Flipse, asking Joe to help him find his family. Joe was working with the Ban Lao refugees and would know where to send him. It would certainly be a miraculous and joyful reunion for him and his family—who undoubtedly believed he was dead.

✪✪✪

Ernie Brace paid a harsh penalty for breaking the security rules. With much abuse, beatings, prison cages, and aborted escapes, a trail of horror took him through Laos to the Hanoi Hilton. He survived, and was released in 1973 after being a prisoner for seven years, ten months, and seven days.

Epidemic

I had just returned to Vientiane from a trip to Southern Laos in mid-1966 which had lasted much longer than anticipated, and I was at the office, buried in a mountain of paperwork, when the radio room called.

The operator said Pop was trying to get me, and asked could I talk to him. I told him to patch me in. When he came through, his voice was urgent.

"Doc, this is Pop. You gotta get up here right away. I just sent a plane down for you and it should be landing in about forty minutes. Get out to the airport quick as you can."

"Pop, I can't come now. I've been out of the office all week and it's going to take me two days to get caught up. What's the problem? Can't it wait a day or two?"

"Hell, no! VP says there's a smallpox epidemic at Phou Nong, and kids are dyin' all over the place. You gotta get up here now."

About three hours later, I landed at Sam Thong. Pop, VP, and Father B met me at the airstrip. VP had been to Phou Nong the previous day, and had found the place in uproar. At least 65 children had died in the previous week in this community of 4,500 people, and everyone was terrified.

I asked VP why he thought the children had died of smallpox. He replied that all of them were covered with red spots that looked like pox at the time of death. It seemed highly unlikely that the disease was smallpox, and I knew from previous experience that *any* illness with a skin rash was usually called smallpox by the Meo. Nevertheless, it was obvious that some very serious disease had broken out.

Phou Nong was a small enclave high in the mountains on the east side of the Plain of Jars. Completely surrounded by Pathet Lao troops led by Vietnamese cadre, it was a community of about 3,000 Meo and 1,500 Lao Theung, defended by approximately 150 of VP's Meo soldiers under a tough little lieutenant called Shu Ya.

Phou Nong was strategically important because of its location—just southwest of the junction of Route 6 and Route 7 near the town of Ban Ban. Route 6 ran north in Eastern Laos through Sam Neua City into North Vietnam, and eventually reached Hanoi. Route 7 started south of Luang Prabang, ran east passing through the Plain of Jars, and terminated at Vinh in Central North Vietnam on the South China Sea. Ban Ban was the area headquarters for the Pathet Lao and North Vietnamese, and control of the area was crucial to the supply and communications of all the Vietnamese operations in Northern Laos.

Shu Ya and his troops, in addition to providing security for the Phou Nong enclave, also carried out the important intelligence function of observing and reporting movement of troops, vehicles, and supplies.

After some discussion, I decided to make a quick trip to Phou Nong to find out what was happening, and then return to Sam Thong for whatever supplies, equipment, and people we might need. We had little in the way of medical capability at Phou Nong—only a one-room bamboo dispensary and two military medics with Shu Ya—but Father B had some Catholic parishioners in the area, and knew it well. He generously offered to go along and help me, and I gratefully accepted his offer. Pop had a chopper standing by, so we took off immediately.

Phou Nong was only about sixty kilometers from Sam Thong in a northeasterly direction, but a direct route would cross the Plain of Jars, which was heavily defended by anti-aircraft weapons. To be safe, we followed a circuitous flight-path to the south of the Plain of Jars, over the mountains, and approached Phou Nong from the east. The old chopper—a Sikorsky H34—flopped along at about seventy knots, so it took us about an hour-and-a-half to reach our destination.

On a high, jagged karst ridge we saw several hundred bamboo-and-thatch houses jammed together at random. The pilot slowly maneuvered the chopper to a landing in a small, open area—blowing up a cloud of thatch roofing, drying clothes, chickens, and trash—and sending people, pigs, and dogs, screaming, grunting, and barking.

When the commotion of landing settled down, people began to gather in large numbers, and Shu Ya soon came to meet us. He was overjoyed that we'd come, and wanted to take us straight to his house. We politely declined his invitation because it was immediately apparent what deadly disease was killing the children.

In the crowd of people around us were hundreds of coughing, red-eyed, rash-covered infants in arms, and tots clinging to skirts. They had measles—rubeola. The hacking cough and blood stained sputum drooling down some of their chins was a foreboding of death if help wasn't quick in coming.

It was getting close to mid-afternoon, and I had to leave immediately if we were to get back to Sam Thong, load up the necessary medicines and supplies, round up medics to help, and return to Phou Nong before dark. I told Shu Ya what I intended doing, and although he understood the necessity, he was visibly upset that I was to leave. When he realized that Father B was staying, however, he brightened up a little.

Fortunately, we made the trip in record time, and we were back before nightfall with the medicines, supplies, and four medics—three Meo and one Lao Theung—to help us. We moved everything to the one-room bamboo dispensary as quickly as possible, I gave the medics some general instructions in how to handle the children, and we were soon seeing patients by the light of our lone kerosene lantern.

Hundreds of parents with their coughing, miserable little children patiently waited outside in the cool night. The medics saw the patients first, triaged them, and sent the more seriously ill for me to examine. Father B and Shu Ya kept traffic under control, and helped in instructing the parents how to give the medicines we prescribed.

Children seldom die from the measles virus itself, but from the secondary bacterial infections—particularly pneumonia—which they are so prone to develop during the course of the disease. Several of the children were deathly sick with pneumonia already, coughing and gasping for breath. Since we had no place where I could observe them overnight, all I could do was give the parents their medicines and some simple instructions, and ask them to bring the poor little things back in the morning—hoping against hope they'd still be alive. It was heartbreaking, but there was little else we could do under the circumstances.

By about one in the morning we had seen most of the seriously ill children, but Shu Ya told me there were many still at home that badly needed attention. We left the medics to care for the last patients at the dispensary, and Shu Ya, Father B, and I went from house to house seeing those that remained. Shu Ya, good leader and commander that he was, had already checked which houses held seriously ill children—but still, we continued our round of house calls until almost five in the morning before he was satisfied we had seen those cases that were truly emergent.

It had been a long day and night since Pop had called me in Vientiane the morning before. I was so tired, I could no longer think clearly. It was getting close to dawn however, and I wanted to return to the dispensary because I knew as soon as there was light, the people would start bringing the children. In spite of my protests, Shu Ya insisted we go to his house and rest for a while.

The house was one of the few made of wood in Phou Nong. The sides were hand-hewn boards, the roof split shingles, and the floor was hard-packed earth polished to a black, marble-like sheen. It was quite cold up in the mountains, and there was an open fire in the middle of the floor for warmth.

The house was—as usual—a large room with curtained-off sleeping compartments down one side. In the rear of the room was the cooking area, where the women were preparing food on a stove made of clay; a flat platform with a cavity for a fire chamber, and openings above the fire where the pots sat. The women preparing breakfast were Shu Ya's two wives, being helped and hindered by his several children.

I remember drinking some hot tea and starting to eat a bowl of rice with egg and chicken soup. The next thing I knew, Father B was rousing me from a deep sleep. Apparently, I'd drifted off while eating, and Shu Ya had laid me on a pallet and covered me up. They allowed me to sleep for about two hours, but after a glass of tea and some cold water on my face, I felt fairly good, and was anxious to get to work.

We hurried down to the dispensary, where a large crowd had already gathered. The medics had started much earlier, and several of the more serious cases they wanted me to see were waiting. We followed the routine of the previous day, with the medics seeing the patients first, and screening out those they felt I could better handle. Shu Ya and Father B were invaluable in maintaining order, translating, instructing parents, helping to dispense medicines, and dozens of other things.

As the day wore on and there seemed no end in sight, I was becoming increasingly concerned about not having the more seriously ill children where I could watch them. About noon, I decided something had to be done.

I called Shu Ya and Father B, took them outside where things were less chaotic, and we discussed the problem. It was one o'clock in the afternoon. I went back to work, and within a few minutes, things began to happen outside the dispensary.

Shu Ya mobilized about 300 people. Some were sent to cut bamboo; some were sent to cut grass for thatch; some were splitting the bamboo as it was brought to the site; and others wove it into wall panels. Another group made thatch roofing by tying grass to wooden stringers that would be laid like shingles on the roof frame. Father B was the architect, and Shu Ya was the construction foreman. Dozens of holes were dug in the ground and filled with heavy bamboo posts—tall ones as supports for the roof and walls, and shorter ones as the bases for beds, tables, benches, and shelves.

This amazing activity continued on all sides of the little dispensary—without disturbing the activities on the inside. Walls went up; the roof was thatched; and all the beds, tables, benches, and shelves were made. There was one large ward with forty beds; a treatment room; a pharmacy and medical storage area; an outpatient dispensary; a living and sleeping area for the medics; and a waiting area.

The entire building was lined with the usual nylon camouflage parachutes—previously used for ammo drops—that let in a soft green, soothing light, and the whole thing was built over our heads and all around us while we worked. It was finished at six o'clock—only five hours after the villagers started.

The new hospital completely enclosed the little dispensary—which was torn down while I continued to work, and disappeared through the door in pieces. I wound up sitting in the middle of the hospital, and had never moved from the dispensary. Shu Ya and Father B had performed an incredible feat, and were justifiably proud of themselves.

Soon, I had most of the forty beds filled with coughing, feverish, dehydrated children. Now I could monitor their condition, control their medications, and rehydrate them with intravenous fluids. Many of them were nauseated and vomiting, and the IV lines could be used to administer life-saving doses of antibiotics. One or more of each patient's family stayed at the bedside at all times to help with the child's care.

We had shuttled the chopper to Sam Thong three times during the day for supplies, and on one trip, Pop had sent 300 blankets. Although it was quite warm during the day, we were at an altitude of 1,300 meters, and the nights were damp and cold. The blankets made the bamboo beds warm and comfortable.

By nine that night, the situation was under control. We had seen all the outpatients who came to the hospital, and the inpatients were stable and doing as well as possible under the circumstances. During the day, Shu Ya had made a list of houses with sick children not seen at the dispensary (now hospital), and we started to make the rounds as we had the night before. By midnight, we had visited all the homes, and felt satisfied that all our little patients would survive the night. A quick round of the hospital, and then we went up the hill to Shu Ya's house.

Although it was close to one in the morning, both Mrs. Shu Yas were busy putting a hot meal on the table. Before we ate, Shu Ya broke out a bottle of fiery Meo corn whiskey. It was a clear bottle that had the usual big, brown centipede in it to give body and flavor. Our host, Father B, and I had a couple of shots of this outstanding aperitif, then devoured a delicious meal of rice, fried pork chops, and vegetable soup. It was two o'clock in the morning. Shu Ya showed us our beds, and in seconds I was asleep.

✛✛✛

Over the next three or four days we continued the same routine, but the epidemic was slowly diminishing in intensity. There were fewer out-patients, and fewer children needed hospitalization. We were also discharging some patients so we weren't running out of bed space as I had feared at one point.

Shu Ya said he had checked carefully with all the civilian leaders, and found that a total of 75 children had died in the eight-day period before we opened the new hospital. However, in the four days since then, not a single child had died. Certainly, we were all grateful for this small miracle. Although the patient load was still very heavy, and the outpatient "department" didn't clear until late at night, the worse seemed to be over.

The next morning Father B woke me up at seven o'clock. "Dammit Father," I said to him. "Why'd you let me sleep so late?"

"Well, you looked so tired, Doc. And you were sleeping so sound, I hated to wake you."

As I rushed around the place dressing and grabbing a bite to eat, he seemed to want to ask me something. Finally, he said, "Doc, do you know what day it is?"

I had no idea. "No Father, What day is it?"

"Sunday, Doc."

"Oh?"

"Yes, and I'd really like to say Mass today."

"Well?"

"If you could spare me for about an hour, I'd really appreciate it."

He sounded like a small child asking a parent for something he felt sure was forbidden. I laughed, almost with tears of affection, for this generous and devoted man. His compassion for the sick outweighed his responsibility to his priestly duties in this time of need.

How could I say no. "Okay Father, but please make it as quick as possible."

I rushed off to my patients, and he hurried off to say his Mass. Before an hour had passed, he was back with me, helping with our sick children.

Within a few more days it was evident that the epidemic was disappearing rapidly, and I felt that the medics could handle things by themselves. I had Shu Ya send a coded message through his military net to Long Chieng for Pop to have a chopper pick us up. When it arrived, Father B and I thanked Shu Ya and his gracious wives for their kindness and hospitality, and took off for Sam Thong. We picked up Pop, and went over to Long Chieng to have lunch with VP to let him know the problem at Phou Nong was under control. VP thanked us profusely for helping his people.

That afternoon I returned to the office in Vientiane—and reluctantly made the transition from doctor to bureaucrat once again.

The Magnificent Seven

The most interesting aspect of the Lao experience, and certainly the most difficult to develop from a programmatic standpoint, was the training of the various medical auxiliaries we used in the village health program. Very early in the planning phase, it became apparent that we needed two basic types of health workers. One would be male, working at the village level in an outpatient dispensary. He would focus on first-aid, hygiene, environmental sanitation, plus symptomatic and curative treatment of simple ailments. The second would be female, and she would work in the hospital environment doing nursing tasks.

As the program developed, selected boys and girls from these two groups received further training to carry out other tasks. In the case of the boys, some would become military medics. However, these students were usually selected—before their basic training—with the specific intention of going into the military. The male students were also given additional training to become laboratory, X-ray, and dental technicians.

When there were sufficient girls trained to staff the hospitals, we began to develop the public health nurses, who also carried out midwifery tasks, maternal and child health care, and family planning. They worked with the male medic, and formed the health team in the village.

At the beginning of the program we faced several difficult problems. The most significant by far was the lack of literate candidates for training. Very few of the young people in the remote areas could read and write. We had made the decision that all training would be in the Lao language, but in many instances the Meo, Yao, Kha, and Lao Theung couldn't speak Lao— or they spoke it very poorly.

The combination of illiteracy and lack of a common language for communication was a formidable problem. As a consequence, we had to devise a method of teaching in which we could start the training, and at the same time teach the students how to read, write, and—often—to speak Lao.

The teaching method was mostly demonstrational. The students would watch the teacher perform a simple task several times; a student would then assist the teacher with the task; and then the student would perform the task without assistance but under the supervision of the teacher. When the teacher was satisfied the student was capable, he or she would be allowed to carry out the task alone. The method was effective, but required a great amount of time and patience.

Early in the game, we found that the expatriates made very poor teachers, even if they were fluent in Lao. The only good teachers came from our brightest and best graduates, and very few of these turned out to be entirely satisfactory. The teacher was really a role model who inspired the student to want to emulate the teacher. It took five years to develop a teaching staff of about 25, but this was a sufficient number to supervise the training of the 3,500 medical workers who eventually participated in the village health program.

It was amazing to see how rapidly these illiterate young people progressed. They had good minds and were highly motivated and determined to succeed. At the beginning of the program, most of the trainees were very young. The boys were 14 or 15, and the girls were only 12 or 13. Nevertheless, they were far more mature than Western youngsters of the same age. Most of the older boys in the tribal groups were already soldiers, and weren't available to be trained as civilian medics. The girls usually married at 15 or 16, and when they did, they most often quit working—or at least they did so early in the program. As a consequence, there was a high attrition rate for both boys and girls, and it was necessary to start them in training at this very early age.

With the limited educational backgrounds of the students, we found that their basic training started to reach a plateau in a very short period of time. After much experimentation, the initial or basic training was shortened to four months. In the case of the male medics, upon completion of the basic course, they'd be sent out to work in the villages for several months under the supervision of more experienced medics—after which they returned to the school for further training. Ideally, we brought them back into training each year, but in some instances we could only do so after a longer interval.

However, everyone was recycled at least every two years, and no one was ever considered to have reached a level where training was no longer necessary. In the case of the hospital personnel, both nurses and technicians remained in a structured, continuous training activity as part of the daily work routine. Over a period of several years, and several training cycles, most of them reached a high level of proficiency.

Since the communist takeover of Laos in 1975, a large number of these medical auxiliaries have fled the country and emigrated to the United States. Many of them are now successfully working in modern medical institutions as technicians of various kinds. This is a truly amazing accomplishment when one considers that the only formal education they had was in the little jungle training schools of the village health program.

As mentioned previously, we lost many of the boys to the military. I say lost, but it was tacitly understood that the military always had priority on personnel. However, after they became soldiers, many of them did not continue as medics. Most had been selected for training because they were bright and intelligent. Their training gave them literacy and some Lao language capability, as well as a certain level of sophistication. They became the officers—particularly company and battalion commanders.

Probably the most frustrating problem in the early years of the village health program was in persuading the leaders to accept the idea of a girl becoming a nurse—or, indeed, any sort of health worker. Unfortunately, traditional medicine in all the tribal groups was male dominated. Men were the healers, the shamans. Women had no place in the scheme of things outside of the home and laboring in the field. It was strictly a man's world.

Chao Mai, the Yao leader, was a little more liberal than most of the other tribal elders. He reluctantly gave his consent, and we were able to get Yao and Lao Theung girls into training at Nam Thoui without too much difficulty.

At Sam Thong, however, the feeling about females was much different. VP and the other clan chieftains were strongly opposed to the training of girls. Many reasons were claimed as to why such training was impossible: married women couldn't work in a hospital; the unmarried girls were too young; the male patients wouldn't accept nursing care from a woman— particularly not from a young, unmarried woman; women didn't have enough sense to be trained; women were too lazy to do such work; if the unmarried girls lived at the hospital, the boys would seduce them.

We made little progress until Diana (Dee) Dick arrived at Sam Thong. Dee was an American RN who'd come to Laos with IVS. She was assigned to a project in school health in Vientiane, but Pop and I were able to talk Walt Cowart, the head of IVS, into reassigning her to Sam Thong.

For a pretty, young, single girl from the US, the jungle of Northern Laos wasn't the most desirable and pleasant place to live—and to be thrust into that savage atmosphere in the middle of a war to supervise a primitive hospital filled with battle casualties was a soul shaking experience. There had never been a Western female worker at Sam Thong—or any other site north of Vientiane—and of course, the staff at the hospital was all male at that time.

We hurriedly built Dee a little house, and she moved in and took charge. If she was ever scared or nervous, she never showed it. In spite of the mud, filth, and blood, she always looked immaculate in her fresh, starched white uniform and nurse's cap. It would have been much more practical to wear slacks, but that wasn't Dee's style. She took much pride in her profession, and her appearance and dress were a reflection of that. She worked seven days a week from dawn until late at night, and although usually sweet and kind, she could fly into a rage if things weren't going right, and terrify everyone in the hospital until they shaped up.

Soon after Dee's arrival, we hired a Meo girl to work with her. Chua was married to a Lao boy who worked for USIS in Vientiane, and they had two children. Although she was a Meo from Xieng Khoung, Chua had lived in Vientiane with relatives, and had gone through nurses training at OB. She was an intelligent, mature young woman, and—being fluent in English, as well as Lao and Meo—was the ideal counterpart to Dee, and an invaluable asset to the program.

About the same time that Dee and Chua arrived at Sam Thong, VP was able to have two Lao military doctors from the FAR assigned to Military Region 2. VP sent them both to the Sam Thong hospital. Both Lieutenant-Colonel Khammoung and Major Bounthan turned out to be outstanding men from a professional and a personal standpoint. Dr. Khammoung was a fully qualified MD, trained in France; and Bounthan was a *medcin assistant* of considerable capability and skill.

With Dee and Chua working in the hospital, Dr. Khammoung was able to get two female operating-room military nurses assigned to Sam Thong by the FAR. At a somewhat later date, I was able to hire an American doctor through USAID to work at Sam Thong.

In addition, when the American Forward Air Controller (FAC) team— the Ravens—was assigned to Long Chieng, it included an Air Force doctor. Since his total responsibility at Long Chieng was (initially) five healthy Americans, General Harry "Hienie" Aderholt, who started the FAC program, very kindly assigned the doctor to the Sam Thong hospital. If one of the Ravens needed attention, it was only a short flight to Long Chieng. Through a combination of design and luck, we had come up with a much better nucleus of a hospital staff than I'd ever thought possible in the middle of this Lao jungle.

Things were looking up, but we still couldn't get VP and the other Meo leaders to let us start a regular training program for girls. But in spite of their resistance, we went ahead and recruited seven girls who functioned as apprentices to Dee and Chua. Two were Meo, two Lao, two Lao Theung, and one Tai Dam. To our surprise, no one screamed too loud when they saw the girls working in the hospital. We were getting our foot in the door. Maybe in a few months or a year, we could start something substantial.

✪ ✪ ✪

That year, 1965, the Vietnamese and Pathet Lao decided to take the whole area in the mountains east of the Plain of Jars. Sites began to fall, and tens of thousands of desperate, terrified people fled through the jungle seeking refuge. We set up a reception center at Muang Cha, a large, grassy park-like valley about forty kilometers southeast of the Sam Thong-Long Chieng complex.

Some of the refugees were able to come directly to Muang Cha on foot. Others were cut off from safety to the south, and had to go far to the east to escape. When they reached an airstrip that was long enough to take one of our larger aircraft such as the De Havilland Caribou, we'd pick them up and fly them to Muang Cha.

Within a two-week period we were caring for 30,000 people—and every day, more and more straggled out of the jungle. Most had lost their few possessions, and some were almost naked. All were starving and demoralized.

We set up a large, tent-like shelter of canvas to receive them on arrival. Here they could rest while we gave them clothing, blankets, sleeping mats, and food. Most importantly, the village leaders could make the *bansee* and get them organized, once again, into family and village groups. After they rested for three or four days, they were assigned an area in the Muang Cha Valley, and they began to build temporary villages out of bamboo and thatch.

We also set up a large dispensary in the reception area with six of the medics from Sam Thong, and they took care of hundreds of patients each day. As the refugees dispersed through the valley and moved into their temporary villages, we built two additional, smaller dispensaries in other areas to prevent patients from walking long distances.

The main medical problem was malnutrition, with the whole gamut of protein, calorie, and vitamin deficiencies. Fortunately, we had the food and vitamins to correct this problem quickly. At least we had sufficient protein for short-term care, in the form of canned meat (a gift from the Mennonites)—but in a few months, protein deficiency would again be a serious problem. There was plenty of milk (Public Law 480 farm surplus— see *Metrical*) for the children, but not enough protein food to supplement the rice diet of the adults for very long.

Pop and I were sleeping in the big reception tent with the refugees, and each day we would talk to the new arrivals and find out from where they came. None of the Phou Nong people had arrived, and we were terribly worried about them and Shu Ya.

Phou Nong was right in the middle of the enemy offensive, and had been surrounded very early in the action. Within three or four days of its isolation, the ground fire became too heavy to get planes or choppers into the area, and two days later, Long Chieng lost radio contact with Shu Ya. The last time VP talked to him, he said he was getting low on ammo and wouldn't be able to hold out very long. He told VP that he would try to slip out of the perimeter with all the people that night, rather than take the risk of being overrun. They would head for Muang Moc, which was at least 12 days walk to the east, over extremely rough, mountainous country.

Each day, VP would fly to Muang Cha and talk with Pop and I, and check the refugees. The days passed, and two weeks after VP's last contact with Shu Ya, none of the Phou Nong people had arrived at Muang Moc. We knew that the combined Vietnamese and Pathet Lao forces in the attack on Phou Nong outnumbered Shu Ya's soldiers at least five to one—and although we tried to be optimistic, everyone believed that they hadn't been able to break out, and had been captured or killed.

Luckily, we were wrong. One morning, VP landed at Muang Cha— very happy—and told us that he'd just received a radio message that some of the Phou Nong people had arrived at Muang Moc. Pop and I jumped on the plane with him, and took off to see them.

When we landed, there were already several hundred sitting and lying around the airstrip. More were coming in all the time. They were in terrible condition. As they staggered up to the strip, they would collapse and lie on the ground as if in a coma. Although they were accustomed to walking over the mountains barefoot, their feet were torn and bleeding from their panic-stricken flight. Many had bullet and shrapnel wounds. Some of them couldn't talk coherently, and they wandered about aimlessly, even though they could hardly stand. What little clothing they had was ragged and filthy, and most of them were half naked. I had never seen such a pitiful, heart-rending sight before.

We had our pilot get on the radio and tell Vientiane to send us some Caribous to start shuttling them to Muang Cha. No one had seen Shu Ya for several days, but they were certain he was alive and would probably arrive in Muang Moc in a day or two with his troops.

We returned to Muang Cha, and later in the day the Caribous started bringing the Phou Nong people from Muang Moc. Many of them, especially the old, couldn't walk the 300 meters from the airstrip to the reception center, and had to be carried. Everyone seemed to have expended the last of their energy to reach Muang Moc. Some of the mothers in particular were so exhausted that they couldn't care for their babies. They had carried and dragged their poor little infants and children as far as they could. It was terrible to see a mother drop to the ground in the reception tent and fall into a deep exhausted sleep with three or four whimpering, frightened children clinging to her tattered dress.

I got the old man off to the side and said, "Pop, we need some help and we need it bad."

"Yeah, I know exactly what you have on your mind. I've been thinkin' about it too."

"Oh, yeah? And what's that?"

"You're thinkin' about our girls at Sam Thong. You want to bring them over here."

"Well, yeah. You're right. I think this is the ideal time. If they can cut it in this mess, nobody can possibly object to our starting a training program. Should we talk to VP first, or just go ahead and do it?"

Pop thought for only a second or two. "Damn it Doc, let's just go ahead and bring 'em in. If VP wants to raise hell, we can handle that, too."

Pop took a plane to Sam Thong late that afternoon, and early the next morning he brought Chua and our seven nurses to Muang Cha. Later in the day, VP showed up—and was surprised to see them there. Nevertheless, he didn't say anything to Pop or me, and we didn't say anything to him. He exchanged a few pleasant words with Chua and the nurses, and everyone acted as if nothing out of the ordinary had occurred.

Pat.

Becky.

Ray.

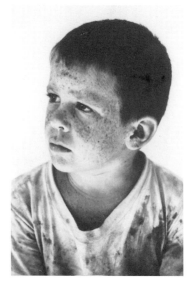

Walt.

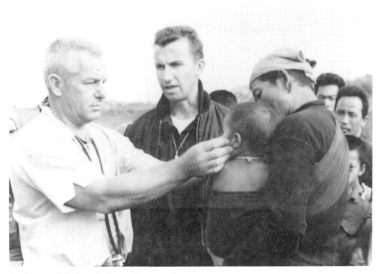

Author and Father B discussing a patient.

Pop in the office at Sam Thong.

Pat.

Dee.

Thong Sar.

Nai kong, Bleu Vu.

Typical refugee dispensary.

Medic graduation class at Nam Thoui with author at left.

Helio loading at Sam Thong.

"Clandestine school with bootleg teacher."

Tom Ward, Mrs. Khamkhong, Gen. Khamkhong, Pat, and Thong Sar.

Jack Williams, Gen. Khamkhong, and Ly Tou Yia.

Jack Williams and medics.

Mrs. Khamkhong, Thong Sar, Pat, and Pop.

Old hospital at Sam Thong.

Medics ready for inspection at Sam Thong.

Nam Yut river valley.

Vaccinations at Hong Non during the cholera epidemic. Author and Pop observe proceedings.

Pop and villagers open up the *lao hai* as Capt. Duangtha (right) looks on.

Father B joins the party.

Pop leads the *lamvong*.

Father B at a leper village.

Capt. Duangtha (left) and Col. Thong.

Pop, Duangtha, and troops at Phu Kuk the morning after the raid on Muang Peun.

VP and Pop.

Meo soldiers and civilians at Lao Tha.

Soldier at Phu Kuk.

Pop and "the Seven."

Flood in Vientiane, 1969.

Typical Meo village scene.

Two days later, Shu Ya landed at Muang Cha. Pop and I were happy to see the tough little commander, and he was likewise delighted to see us. Other than a considerable loss of weight, he seemed okay. He had walked into Muang Moc the day before with his family, and they'd been flown to Long Chieng. He was anxious to see the Phou Nong people, and after a night's sleep at Long Chieng, he'd asked VP to send him to Muang Cha.

That night, we sat around the open fire under a beautiful, clear, starry sky with Shu Ya and some of his people. They related the horrifying events of their tragic, two-week flight through the jungle.

The breakout from the Phou Nong enclave hadn't been difficult. Shu Ya had gathered the civilian leaders in the afternoon and told them to get their people ready to leave the same night. He explained the military situation to them, and that they wouldn't be able to take the short, direct route south to safety. Instead, they would have to make the long, difficult march to Muang Moc. Since the trek would take at least 12 days, they should try to travel as light as possible. They must leave all their possessions behind, and conserve their strength to carry food and to help the old people and children. There were about 8,500 people in the group.

About midnight that night, Shu Ya sent a platoon of 15 men out along a little-used trail to the southeast. He had information from patrols that had checked the area the last two days that this route wasn't closely guarded by the enemy. The platoon ran into light resistance, but were able to clear the way without too much trouble.

At one in the morning, the civilians started to move out of Phou Nong as rapidly as possible along the trail. Shu Ya had divided his soldiers into two units. Half were scattered out along the trail with the long column of civilians to guide and protect them, as well as maintain discipline and keep them moving. Shu Ya and the other half of his men left their positions in the perimeter after all the civilians were on the trail.

The Meo commander thought the main danger would come from the enemy troops besieging Phou Nong. When they realized that the place had been evacuated, they would try to catch the people and stop them. Shu Ya and his troops would form a rear guard to halt the pursuit or slow it down as much as they were able.

The evacuation went smoothly, with little confusion, but by the end of the second day, Shu Ya was getting hit by sporadic fire from pursuing enemy units. By the fourth day, the enemy pressure was increasing, and the fleeing people hadn't been able to stop and rest since leaving Phou Nong. They were dead tired, and Shu Ya knew they could go no farther without a night of sleep.

At midday he halted his troops and set up a defensive position. However, he sent word up the trail that the people were to continue moving until nightfall—then they would make camp and rest until the next morning. At daybreak they would start walking again. Shu Ya hoped to hold his position until the middle of the next day. That way, he would be able to delay the enemy long enough for the people to get some rest, and also put some distance between them.

The night passed quietly, but then—just after dawn—Shu Ya and his troops suddenly heard heavy automatic-weapon fire and mortar explosions in the distance where they knew their people had spent the night. Immediately, they realized what had happened. The enemy had bypassed their position in the night, and ambushed the main body of civilians.

The horror of that terrible dawn is difficult to describe. I still choke up with tears as I write this thirty years later and think of the holocaust that descended on those poor, innocent people. They had stopped to spend the night in a small, bowl-shaped depression on the side of a mountain. While they slept, they were surrounded by the Pathet Lao and the Vietnamese. At dawn's first light, the enemy fired a few shots into the air and shouted to them that they were surrounded and would be killed if they resisted. They were to prepare immediately to return to Phou Nong. Everyone panicked and began a mad flight down the trail to the east they'd been following.

The enemy began firing at random into the mass of terrified people with automatic weapons and mortars. The Pathet Lao soldiers physically blocked the trail to prevent the people escaping. They clubbed some with rifle butts; some were stabbed with bayonets; women and children were thrown off the cliffs and their bodies broken on the rocks below; infants were grabbed by the legs and their brains bashed out as they were slammed against the tree trunks. The slaughter went on for an hour.

The survivors of the blood-soaked killing field were fortunate. For some reason the enemy didn't follow, and nor did Shu Ya make contact with them when he came upon the hundreds of mangled bodies. After the massacre, the Pathet Lao and Vietnamese troops apparently gave up the pursuit and withdrew.

But although the worst was over, there were still ten days of hell ahead for the refugees as they struggled to reach Muang Moc. Most of their rice and other foodstuffs had been lost. The burden of carrying the children and helping the old people had been difficult from the beginning, but now they had many wounded in addition. Each day, people were dying along the way. Some of the old people who could no longer keep up begged to be shot and buried, but their relatives and friends somehow managed to support and half drag them along the trail.

When they reached Muang Cha and the village chiefs were able to make up the *bansee*, it was found that 1,260 people had died since leaving Phou Nong. Over 1,100 people had been brutally massacred that terrible morning by the Pathet Lao and Vietnamese.

✪

The male medics were doing a good job in caring for this mass of exhausted, bleeding, demoralized humanity, but when Chua and the seven nurses arrived and went to work, there was no doubt as to who were the more suitable and capable workers in handling such a situation. The girls knew instinctively how to manage the dispirited mothers, the frightened children, and the debilitated and often disoriented old people. Pop and I were proud of them, and vowed to get regular training courses started for girls—whether VP and the tribal hierarchy liked it or not.

It was obvious when VP came to visit again that he was very interested in what Chua's girls were doing. He always spent time talking to them, and assured them that if they had any problems or needed anything, they were to let him know and he would take care of it. They were flattered by his interest, and even looked forward to his visits.

About ten days after the nurses started working at Muang Cha, VP called Pop and I aside. He was very serious and said, "*Tan Maw*, I've been wanting to talk to you for several days about the nurses."

"Well, what's the problem General?" I replied, smiling—sensing what was coming next. "Pop and I think they're doing a great job."

"Yes, I agree. Their work is very good, but we need many more. Why haven't you trained more of them?"

As I guessed, he was simply trying to tell me that he'd been wrong without losing face. Still, I couldn't resist getting even with him for obstructing the training of the girls in the first place.

"Well, I thought medicine was men's work, General."

"Certainly not. Women can take care of sick people just as well or better than men."

"Well, many Meo men have told me that women aren't smart enough to be nurses. Isn't that true?"

"That's foolish," he answered impatiently and a bit angrily. "Who told you such a stupid thing?"

VP knew what I was doing, but as a politician he wanted to save face—and also not miss the opportunity to say that he was responsible for starting a good program.

Soon after the Muang Cha episode, Dee inaugurated regular training courses for girls, and the program was even more successful than we'd anticipated. In the first few years, most of the girls would get married when they were 15 or 16, and drop out of the program—but soon they were resisting parental pressure and beginning to postpone marriage so they could continue their training. And, over time, more and more of them found that they could continue to work, even after marriage. We gave them maternity leave, and—if their husbands were soldiers, teachers, or officials transferred from place to place—we would re-assign them to be with their husbands. Later, when some of them became instructors or supervisors themselves, and had to be re-assigned to new programs, we could, in most instances, have their husbands transferred with them.

The fact that they were nurses who had trained at Sam Thong gave these girls new status—and greatly increased their marriage eligibility and their bride price. This, no doubt—especially the latter—influenced other parents to allow their daughters into training.

The original seven nurses that had gone to Muang Cha with Chua to help the Phou Nong refugees came to be known as "the seven"—and they held a special place in everyone's esteem. It was an honor to be one of the seven, and they were always pointed out at parties and ceremonies, and received special attention and courtesies.

Having broken some of the rigid bonds that tribal custom and tradition placed on women, they were indeed courageous pioneers. Dee had not just taught them technical nursing skills, but had also instilled in them the basic ethic of the nursing profession—service to suffering mankind.

Coup Survival

In late 1964, Pop and I had been working up in Sam Neua for about two weeks. The North Vietnamese had started their expected offensive, and refugees were pouring into Pha Thi from the villages just west of Sam Neua City. About ten thousand Meo and Lao camped on this barren, butte-like mountain, waiting to see what the Vietnamese would do next. We had been so busy that we'd forgotten that Vientiane and the outside world existed.

Around mid-morning one day, VP landed in a chopper. He jumped out, obviously excited and upset. When the dust and noise settled down, he told us that he'd just received news that fighting had broken out in Vientiane that morning between troops supporting General Phoumi Nosovan, and troops supporting General Kouprasith Abhay.

VP was beside himself with disgust and anger that such a thing could happen at that crucial time. How could these two feuding generals put their personal ambitions above their obligation to their country? Such behavior outraged the Meo commander. He needed every bit of assistance and cooperation possible from Vientiane to stop the Vietnamese before they took all of Sam Neua.

After some discussion, Pop and I decided to try to make it into Vientiane. It was important that the flow of military and refugee supplies not be held up for any significant length of time. All the "hard rice" (munitions) came out of Udorn in Thailand by direct flight, so that wouldn't be a problem. However, food and medical supplies for both the soldiers and civilians came out of Vientiane through our USAID support facilities, on USAID aircraft.

With the sudden displacement of people and casualties resulting from the fighting, we were already getting short on supplies. Once in Vientiane we would try to get as much stuff up country as possible. I was also concerned about Pat and the children, and wanted to be certain they were safe.

The winds were so strong and turbulent on Pha Thi that it was impossible for a fixed-wing aircraft to use the tiny STOL strip on the side of the mountain. Pop called in a chopper and we took off for Hua Muang where we had a Helio Courier waiting to take us to Sam Thong.

When we landed at Sam Thong, Tom Ward was on the radio trying to contact Vientiane, but had been unsuccessful. Apparently, the radio room at USAID wasn't manned. This produced a long tirade of cursing from Pop—how it proved what he always said about the incompetence and lack of feeling on the part of the people who were supposed to be supporting him.

Tom had been talking to Long Chieng on the radio, but they had no more information than VP had already given us. There was fighting in Vientiane between two groups of FAR soldiers; one backing Phoumi Nosovan, and the other Kouprasith Abhay. Automatic weapons and artillery could be heard all over the place. The military and political situation was chaotic and confused. Pop and I got back on the Helio and had the pilot head for Vientiane.

When we were airborne, the pilot was able to contact the air operations office at the airport. The operations manager told him the airport was closed, and under no circumstance was he to land at Vientiane. He was either to RON at Sam Thong or Long Chieng, or continue to Udorn. All the contract aircraft in Vientiane were being flown to Udorn as fast as they could round up off-duty pilots and get them out to the airport—but the American Embassy had passed the word for everyone to remain at home and stay off the streets.

These conflicting instructions had produced a certain amount of confusion, and most of the planes were still on the ground. Pop tried to coerce the pilot into landing, in spite of his orders to the contrary, but he pleaded he'd surely be fired if he did. Pop relented and we flew on down to Udorn. It was getting close to dark, and there wasn't enough daylight left to get back upcountry.

After landing at Udorn, we walked over to the bar in the recreation area near the strip to look for Ed Reed. Ed, an Air America chopper pilot, was a close friend who lived near the air base. He and Chay, his Thai wife, had an extra bedroom. We would ask them to put us up for the night.

The bar was filled with pilots talking about the coup, but no one knew what was going on. We learned that Ed was upcountry, but we phoned Chay and found her at home. She was glad to have us, and told us to come on over to the house.

As soon as we got to the Reed's place, I asked Chay to try to get Pat on the phone at our home in Vientiane. Somewhat to my surprise, she got through almost immediately.

Pat was almost screaming. "Where the hell are you?"

"I'm in Udorn. Pop and I are spending the night with Chay."

"What in hell are you doing down there? Don't you know there's a goddamn coup going on here. We're getting shot at."

"We tried to land at Vientiane but they wouldn't let us. What's happening?"

"I'll tell you what's happening. I'm on my belly in the living room answering this goddamn phone. A mortar round just blew the windows open and every now and then we get small arms fire. I'm going to hang up and crawl back under the stairwell with the kids and servants."

"Is everyone all right?"

"No one's been hit yet. Now hang up."

"Okay, but I'll call back in a little while."

"I'm not going to answer. There isn't a damn thing you can do from Udorn."

"But. . . ."

But nothing. She'd already hung up the phone.

During the short time we'd been talking, I could hear shells exploding and small arms fire rattling in the background. No doubt about it, a pretty good little war was going on in Vientiane.

Three hours later I called again. Fortunately, things had quieted down, and Pat did answer the phone. Everyone was all right. Tong Sar, Pop's adopted son, happened to be in Vientiane, and had come to the house as quickly as possible to see if Pat and the kids needed help. A rain storm had dampened the soldiers enthusiasm for the coup, and most of them had melted away into the night seeking shelter.

The next day, we got in to Vientiane and found things quiet and peaceful. The Kouprasith forces prevailed, and Phoumi slipped across the Mekong and headed for Bangkok. After a few days of political tension, the situation returned to normal. Pop and I went back up to Sam Neua and our refugees waiting on bleak, windswept Pha Thi.

Becky's first-hand account of the coup in her diary notes, entitled *Coup Stories,* gives a much better account of the events that occurred at that time than I can. With her permission, I repeat *Coup Stories* in its entirety. She was 14 years old at the time of the Phoumi-Kouprasith showdown.

I was baking a cake when Ray and Walter pelted into our kitchen behind the house yelling about the gunfire up the street.

"Where?"

"At the corner."

"I don't hear it."

"Come out front and you will."

So with the dogs in attendance we all three ran to listen. The boys would have been out the gate had I not yelled at them to stop for by that time machine gun fire was clearly heard fairly close. I decided to call Mom—Dad was up country, so I got the boys inside. Our servants, Tin and his wife Hua, had been washing and cleaning that morning and I yelled out the back door for them to come into the house. The gun fire was getting loud by the time I got hold of Mom—she panicked—didn't know anything. She told me to get the mattresses off the beds upstairs, shut all the shutters, lock all the doors, put the mattresses in the stairwell to sleep and turn the dining room table on its side to provide a barrier at the stairwell. Get food and water inside from the kitchen and get flashlights. Wait for her—she would be home shortly. Well we were all excited and scampered in all directions getting this and getting that. The cake just got turned off and moldered over night in the oven. I got a few books to read to Ray and Walter and Ray got out the chess set as usual. Walter stood guard at the glass windows in the living room waiting for Mom.

She soon arrived, brakes screeching, horn blaring, a security guard in tow and we all ran out to greet her for to tell the truth we were getting very scared by then. Everyone was jittery and it sounded like a war outside. Soon as we were all out front—kids and servants—Mom yelled at us to get back inside and the door clicked shut before us. A horrified look dawned on Hua's face as she realised she had locked the door behind her. There we were outside, soldiers running down the street, bullets flying and our nice safe home locked up as well as any vault with us on the outside. Well, the driver, the security guard and Tin, the cook managed to knock the door down and as we poured in, scrambled to nail it shut again.

We settled in quickly. Mom went upstairs to change and get a radio and an automatic carbine. After surveying our food supplies—peanut butter, jelly and bread, she sent Tin, the cook, out to the kitchen for something more substantial. The kitchen was outside the house in a separate building. Mom then went to call the embassy with a status report. As she crossed the room to the telephone which was in a cool corner surrounded by windows, a mortar landed next to the property and the shutters popped wide open, gunfire resounding through the room and she hit the floor to return to the stairwell. The phone rang. We burst out laughing and Mom started cursing as she crawled toward the phone—it was Dad.

"Yes, goddammit, there's a coup going on."

"Where in the hell are you?"

"Hum, have a great time. I've got to get back under cover if you don't mind."

Bang went the phone as she slammed it down. We pretended to be reading when she returned to our enclave.

"Where's Dad?"

"Playing poker in Udorn."

Which we thought was just great but seemed to irritate Mom to no end.

So it went on, the coup, the bullets flew, the phone rang, until there was a commotion in the front yard and then a pounding on the door. We all sat still overcome by awe with the sight that appeared before us. Tongsar in a cowboy outfit—hat, boots and sixshooters. No kidding. He had come to protect us and went right through the lines in the paraphernalia he had picked up in the U.S. when he went home with Pop. Well, Tongsar being one of our favorite people, we were all cheered up considerably—Mom no less than anyone.

It appeared that the opposing sides were shooting over our compound at each other. Tongsar just went out and told them to move some other place which they did and the shooting faded and I took up reading Peter Pan to Ray and Walter until the rain fell and the coup was over.

Becky's stories continued in later years as the coups became a regular occurrence. . . .

I remember the 1966 coup too. That was the first of General Ma's wild escapades. It was my first day at the Lycee, a sunny clear October morning. School had started late because of the big flood and I nervously entered my home classroom with Chou Chou, Patricia Theodas, and sat down at the front and center desk thoughtfully vacated for me. If the teacher asks me something I'll die I thought. But he didn't. Monsieur stood up and announced that as tenth grade students we were to embark upon a voyage through 19th century literature starting with the giant, Victor Hugo, and that there was no better place to begin than with the poignant poem he wrote upon the death of his young daughter, "Demain des l'aube". Rocking on his heels, book in hand, spectacles on his nose, his short fat body tense with concentration, he began.

"Demain, des l'aube, a l'heure ou blanchit la compagne, je partirai!"

He paused to breathe and a bomb resounded toward Chinaimo Army Camp.

"Vois - tu, je sais que tu m'attends."

More bombs closer.

"*Jirai par le foret. Jirai par la montagne.*"

Planes began to dive toward the school and he paused and peered out the window.

We were transfixed in our seats, like dogs rooted stock-still by a thunder storm, our eyes riveted on the professor, our ears full of war. The planes began strafing over the school as they dived for the radio station and we all scrambled under our desks. Glass shattered above us as bullets went through the louvered windows at the upper reaches of the classroom walls. The planes made a long pass and veered off into the distance—bombs could still be heard in the background as we cautiously stood up—teachers and students staring at each other. Footsteps pelted outside and a messenger told the teacher to tell us all to go home. The classroom emptied. Chou Chou took me in tow. Outside was pandemonium. The streets were full of panic stricken people yelling, motorcycles revving, Bicycles spinning down the grade into the street. Chou Chou's boy friend, Jean Claude, was waiting for her by his motorcycle along with his friend Camille. Camille was to take me to Dad's office at USAID as our house was six kilometers out of town toward the army camp that had been bombed first. By the time we got around the Parliament, the road was deserted. Camille left me at the entrance to the USAID compound nearest the office. I stood there looking around. It appeared empty. No signs of life; I'd never seen it that way and it felt very strange as I walked through the gates which were wide open. No sooner was I through the gates when the door to the attaches' office on the right flew open, scaring me to death. A young Marine crawled out on his stomach and yelled, "You goddamn idiot what in hell are you doing? Get inside." I started crying and ran to Dad and Mom's office. I was never so glad to see them in my life. We waited all day but the planes never came back. Many people died or were wounded that day at the military camps, but we were all fine. General Ma fled to Thailand and the coup attempt was over.

In 1973 General Ma almost killed me again. Planes came in strafing across the river toward the Chinaimo Army Camp a little after 5 a.m.—with the first light. General Khamkhong's son, Boun Oum, was waiting outside for us to awaken. I opened the front door to let the dogs out and there he sat on the low wooden barrier along the parking area as calm as could be. How did he know this would happen? Not five minutes before as I packed my evacuation bag, Inta, the maid, had sobbed to me that it must be the Communists and for me to take her with us. And now, looking at me very coolly, sat my Lao teacher, a person that I knew for a fact to be a PL cadre. But it was not yet to be, it was only General Ma. He crashed and they cut his throat that day no more surprise

morning raids. But now years later, it's the pathetic look in Inta's eyes and the
arrogance revealed to me in Boun Oum's face that I remember best.

The Phoumi-Kouprasith coup had a profound effect on the course of
the war in Laos that is not usually understood or appreciated by students of
Lao history. Phoumi Nosovan was commander-in-chief of the Lao Armed
Forces. General Khamkhong Boudavong was Military Region 2 commander.
The troops in Xieng Khoung and Sam Neua under General Vang Pao were
part of Region 2, and VP answered to General Khamkhong.

Khamkhong's Region 2 headquarters was in Paksane, a small town on
the Mekong River in Borikhane province. Before being made commander
of Military Region 2, Khamkhong was commandant of the Officers Training
School at Dong Hene in Central Laos. A quiet, scholarly man, he did an
outstanding job at the school in turning out young officers who were real
leaders.

Khamkhong had taught his students that the war would be won by the
side that gained the confidence and respect of the people in the countryside.
When they graduated, they had a solid background in community affairs
and development, as well as military skills. Khamkhong was a patriot and
nationalist; a man of complete integrity and honesty who tried to pass his
ideals to his students. Having known and worked with many of the officers
who were his students, I was impressed with his success.

Realizing that Sam Neua was crucial to the defense of Laos, he had
organized the partisan resistance around the guerilla FAR units BV26 and
BV27 in the late fifties and early sixties. He staffed these units with his
hand-picked students from Dong Hene. Khamkhong and VP worked well
together, and considerable success was achieved in defeating the Pathet Lao.

As the war escalated and VP's role became more significant, it was decided
by Phoumi—probably with some pressure from US interests—to reorganize
the chain of command. A new Northern Command would be created that
would include Military Regions 1, 2, and 5. Khamkhong would head this
command, and VP would be Region 2 commander.

Some cynics viewed these changes as simply a way to kick Khamkhong
upstairs and appoint VP as Region 2 commander without rocking the boat
too badly. However, most of us who knew both Khamkhong and VP well—
particularly Pop and I—thought it would be an ideal arrangement. Having
Khamkhong co-ordinating the activities and providing support to all of
Northern Laos seemed a great step forward. Certainly the promotion would

boost VP's morale and prestige. These changes were put into effect a few days before the Phoumi-Kouprasith coup.

When the Kouprasith forces started to take over Vientiane, Phoumi ordered Khamkhong to move all his available men to Vientiane to support him. Most of the Region 2 units were tied up in active combat situations in Sam Neua and at Tha Thom, north of Paksane—and Khamkhong would never consider jeopardising the security of the country by pulling out these troops to assist in a political brawl in Vientiane.

However, since Phoumi was his superior, he had to make some kind of token move. He collected most of the headquarters troops at Paksane and began to march them on foot to Vientiane, hoping the situation would resolve itself before the ragtag bunch reached their destination.

In any event, Kouprasith prevailed, and Phoumi fled. Khamkhong's troops returned to Paksane, but Kouprasith—now commander of the FAR—still considered Khamkhong a political threat, and connived to have him arrested as a traitor. However, no one was willing or courageous enough to go to Paksane, relieve Khamkhong of his command, and arrest him.

This situation of continued tension was intolerable, as it was damaging the war effort in Region 2—where most of the action was taking place. The new American ambassador, William Sullivan and the country team were deeply, and rightfully, concerned.

Sullivan sent an American military attaché to Paksane who talked Khamkhong into going on an overseas trip, supposedly in an attempt to let the situation cool down. The attaché picked up Khamkhong in a US aircraft and promised to return him to Paksane when they returned to Laos. They went to Taipei for a few days, but on their return, the attaché had the plane land at Vientiane where Kouprasith's men were waiting to arrest Khamkhong. He was imprisoned at Ritaville north of Vientiane for a few months, and then placed under house arrest for three years in Luang Prabang. Several of his best staff officers were murdered, and several were imprisoned. Kouprasith and Sullivan had dealt a more devastating blow to the war effort than the Pathet Lao and the Vietnamese combined.

As an American, I was shamed and appalled. It was the most despicable act I ever saw in my career with the government. General Khamkhong and I were close friends, and remained so after the events. Pat and I helped him and his family in small ways while he was under house arrest, and when he was released, I was instrumental in finding him a good job with Continental, of which he was most appreciative.

We often got together socially, but he never mentioned the treacherous act that was committed against him by the Americans. And whenever we did get together, I always had a vague feeling of shame and uneasiness in his presence.

Floods

In August and September the Mekong is at flood stage, with a swift current filled with driftwood and debris. Huge trees, thirty or forty meters long and over a meter in diameter float downstream, along with a mass of smaller animal, mineral, and vegetable matter. People in boats gather the wood and stack it on the bank to use as firewood. The larger logs and trees that are too heavy to drag up the bank are tethered with ropes so they'll be stranded when the flood waters recede.

At this time of year Ray, Walter, and I loved to take a boat several kilometers upriver and then float back down to the house on the driftwood. After our stay in Samoa, the boys were completely at ease in the water; the turbulence in the Mekong was minimal compared to the surf of the island.

It was great fun to throw each other off the logs and joke with the Lao boatmen gathering firewood. However, Pat couldn't swim well, and was somewhat afraid of the river. She would get extremely angry with me when the boys and I indulged in this innocent lark. Because of her fear and anger, we finally restricted this activity to the times when she wasn't at home.

Unfortunately, on one occasion she returned home earlier than expected and was out on the terrace watching the river when the three of us came bobbing along on a piece of driftwood. She was livid, and I was in the doghouse for several days. In her opinion—which she wasted no time sharing with me—if I was stupid enough to drown myself, at least I should have enough sense not to drown our sons, too. I had work stacked up at the office, but when Pop called on the radio, I was happy to have an excuse to leave town.

The headwaters of the Mekong River lie in the snows and glaciers of the Himalayas. During the southeast monsoon, this mighty stream is also fed by dozens of rain-swollen tributaries throughout its winding 4,500-kilometer journey to the South China Sea. Every year, the combination of snow melt and rain results in a flood that inundates large areas of Laos, Thailand, Cambodia, and the delta region of South Vietnam. The flood waters usually crest around the end of August or the first half of September. Alluvium deposited from the muddy water renews and enriches the rice paddies that feed millions of people.

In some years, when snow and rain are both exceptionally heavy, the water overflows the dikes and levees, flooding the towns. Most often, little damage is done. The riverside residents anticipate such natural occurrences, and houses are built on stilts above the highest watermark. Occasionally, the rice crop suffers, but rarely is it lost completely. But this is also expected and accepted philosophically as the price paid for the renewal of the land. Enough rice is always stored to last through a bad year.

Our children loved the annual flood. It was a time of excitement, and if they were lucky, it disrupted the opening of school. Everyone traveled around town in boats, and stayed wet and muddy. It was more like a vacation at the beach than a natural disaster. There was also a lot of work to do, particularly for the boys. Sandbags had to be filled and put in place to protect the lower floor of the house. Ray had to get up several times during the night to check the fuel in the standby electrical generator. The city electrical supply always ceased to function during the flood. If the generator stopped, the sump pump stopped, and the house flooded in spite of the sand bags. There were snakes all over the place, and Walter was in charge of serpent control— a job which he performed with great enthusiasm and expertise.

Later, when they were going to school in Europe, their departure usually coincided with the height of the flood. They hated to go, not because they were leaving Pat and I, but because they'd miss the fun and excitement of the deluge.

Their departure was quite an adventure in itself. They piled all their gear on a longtail river boat that would take them from our house to That Luang—the site of an old Buddhist temple in the middle of town. It stood on the highest ground in the area, and was always above flood level. A chopper pad was set up there, and the kids would take the helicopter to Udorn Air Force base in Thailand—about sixty kilometers south of Vientiane. There, they would switch to an Air America C46 or C47 for the trip to Bangkok, then catch their plane to Zurich.

Each one had their priorities on what needed to be taken back to school. Becky always opted for Crest toothpaste, peanut butter, and soft toilet tissue, all of which were difficult to obtain in Switzerland. Ray took up most of his baggage allowance with the rocks he'd collected during the summer. Many years later he got his Ph.D in geophysics from Cal Tech, and still carries around a bag of rocks. Walter's treasures ran to snakes, lizards, and other reptiles he'd captured and preserved in formalin. These were often hard to get through customs and security checks, but he always persevered. He ended up as a mechanical engineer and not a herpetologist.

One Christmas, when Ray and Walter were about 13 and 11, we gave them a boat. It was built at Ban Houi Sai, some 400 kilometers up the Mekong from Vientiane, and with a length of 15 meters, a width of slightly over one meter, and a very shallow draft, it was a typical river boat adapted to slipping through the rapids at low water. There was a nice little cabin on the stern, and a roof that ran the length of the boat to protect the passengers from the sun and rain. A small 15-horsepower Wisconsin engine pushed it along at about twenty kilometers per hour, and although it was quite stable when loaded, the heavy roof gave it a high center of gravity when empty, and it turned over easily.

In order to bring the boat to Vientiane from Ban Houi Sai, it would be necessary to pass through several areas controlled by the Pathet Lao. The trip would take five days if there were no problems. I agreed to pay the boat builder 400 dollars for the vessel, plus ninety dollars to recruit a reliable boatman who knew how to get by the Pathet Lao checkpoints. He was to deliver it to our house on the river in Vientiane. The boatman would return to Ban Houi Sai by bus through Thailand.

Since it was to be a Christmas present, I told him that the boat must arrive on or before Christmas Eve. Late in the afternoon on Christmas Eve there was still no sign, and I was beginning to regret my choice of present for the boys. Tony Caterucci, the USAID area co-ordinator in Ban Houi Sai, knew the boat builder, so I called Tony on the radio and asked him if the boat had left. Tony said he'd seen the boat builder two days before, and he told Tony that the boat was on its way and should arrive on schedule.

Our house had a terrace out over the river, and just at dark—as Pat and I sat sipping a cocktail and enjoying the sunset—a long, narrow river boat pulled up to the bank. There were two people in the boat—an attractive, nicely-dressed Lao lady, and a boy about ten years old who was at the helm.

The lady called up to us and asked if this was the house of Dr. Weldon. I told her, yes it was so, and that I was the good doctor himself. It turned out that the boat builder's wife and ten-year-old son had made the five-day trip down the Mekong through the Pathet Lao checkpoints by themselves. Apparently, the ten-year-old was the reliable boatman recruited with the ninety dollars.

For reasons that I've forgotten, the boys christened the boat the "Queen Mary." She took us on many pleasant picnics, fishing trips, and sightseeing voyages, but her only problem was a tendency to overturn when empty. If the boys didn't secure her to the bank properly, the wave from a large cargo or patrol boat would turn her over. It would take twenty men to pull her up and right her. The men in the village were always happy to help, but after the boat was floating again, it took at least two cases of beer and a carton of cigarettes to properly express our gratitude for their help.

For some very suspicious reason, the Queen Mary always seemed to turn flipside on a hot Sunday afternoon when all the men were sitting around doing nothing. Nevertheless, everyone had a good time righting the Queen and drying her out—including Ray, Walter, and myself.

Down But Not Out in Hong Non

Ambassador Unger and his successor, Ambassador Sullivan, had adhered to the constraints of the 1962 Geneva Accords with reference to military advisers, particularly in the Northern region of Laos where Tony Poe and Vint Lawrence—the two CIA operations officers who acted as advisers to VP, but weren't permitted to go north of the PDJ and into Sam Neua—were restricted in their movements. Officially they weren't even in the country.

Pop and I were the only two Americans whose movements had not been restricted in Xieng Khoung and Sam Neua, because of our low civilian profiles. The communists couldn't gain much political advantage from capturing an old Indiana farmer or a grey-haired country doctor.

However, in early 1966, we received intelligence that the Vietnamese were planning a major effort to take Hong Non and the surrounding Meo enclave. This area was important to the defense of Sam Neua as it anchored the northern flank of the thin line of government forces extending from just west of Sam Neua City to the Plain of Jars.

Vietnamese pressure built up all along the line from Hong Non south to Hua Muang. An attack on Hong Non appeared imminent, and we desperately needed some professional military assistance from the CIA, such as Tony could provide.

Tony and VP began putting pressure on Bill Lair, the chief of CIA field operations for Laos, to get permission to lift the restriction. Pop and I also begged Charley Mann to intercede with Ambassador Sullivan. Much to our surprise, Bill, and Doug Blaufarb, the CIA station chief in Vientiane, prevailed on Ambassador Sullivan. He lifted the restriction on Tony.

As the enemy action increased, we began to get refugees from the more exposed villages on the periphery of the line of defense. Several hundred had fled into Hua Muang. Pop and I had been working there for several days when we received word that Tony would be coming up to Sam Neua.

He landed in the early afternoon, and Colonel Khamsao, Colonel Thong, the *chao muang* of Hua Muang, Pop, and I were all there to greet him— delighted to see the rough, unshaven character with the stained Marine campaign hat and dark glasses leap off the plane. There was something reassuring about his attitude. It seemed as if he could whip a battalion of Vietnamese single-handed.

We sat and talked for a couple of hours, enjoyed some of Mrs. Khamsao's excellent home cooking, and Thong and Khamsao briefed Tony on the military situation. Since Hong Non was of the utmost concern, it was decided that Tony would go there first, to work with Boua Chou—the Meo *chao muang* and military commander—and try to bolster the defences before the Vietnamese hit the place.

After a big glass of Mrs. Khamsao's special *ya dong*—rice whiskey aged with herbs and huge, brown centipedes—to give him strength, Tony took off for Hong Non.

Hua Muang and Hong Non were both in the Military Region 2 radio net, and could inter-communicate. That evening about nine o'clock, Hong Non reported enemy movement around their positions. At eleven o'clock they reported heavy fighting on the airstrip—which was only forty or fifty meters from the radio shack. One or two minutes later, the Hong Non radio went dead and we could no longer raise anyone. It seemed certain that the place had been overrun.

We were terribly concerned about Tony and the others at Hong Non, but there was nothing we could do until morning. The security was too poor to RON aircraft at Hua Muang, and we'd need to get both choppers and STOL planes from Long Chieng or Sam Thong to start a search and rescue (SAR) operation. We had the radio operator send a message to Long Chieng to have aircraft on the ground at Hua Muang as soon as possible after daylight in the morning.

Pop and I tried to get a little sleep, but weren't too successful. We could both imagine Tony and Boua Chou dead, captured, or wounded—and all the Hong Non people fleeing through the jungle. It seemed like an age before the sky began to lighten in the east.

Soon after daylight, Lee Mullins landed at Hua Muang in a Helio Courier. Fortunately, there was no fog that morning—and indeed, Lee had taken off in the dark to be able to land at Hua Muang as soon as he could see the strip. He told us that Bob Nunez had taken off in a chopper at the same time, and that he should be landing in about twenty minutes. Bob's

H34 wasn't certified for night flying, and he was breaking all sorts of regulations by taking off in the dark.

After Bob landed and refueled, I loaded my emergency medical gear on the chopper and we took off for Hong Non. Pop went with Lee in the Helio. We knew that Tony had a little survival radio that communicated on the international emergency frequency of 121.5mhz. Hopefully, he would hear our aircraft and come up on his radio. If Pop and Lee heard or sighted something before we did, they would guide us in to make a pickup in the chopper. In the Helio they could cover the area faster than us in the slow-flying H34.

As soon as we approached the village and airstrip, we began to pick up ground fire. There was no doubt that the enemy had occupied the place. The survivors of the attack would undoubtedly be fleeing to the west—the direction of the friendly forces at Pha Thi and Houi Khammoune. We would search to the west, but it would be almost impossible to see anything in the dense jungle below. Both Lee and Bob were monitoring and calling on the emergency frequency, but no one came up on the radio. After flying several minutes to the west with no results, we turned back east.

Hong Non sits on a high ridge that runs east-west. On the south, the land drops almost straight down for several hundred meters into a densely-forested valley. As we approached Hong Non for the second time, we saw a flashing light in the deep valley below. Someone was using a signal mirror to get our attention.

Bob spiralled the chopper down toward the light, and as we approached the spot, we saw a small opening in the jungle and three or four soldiers waving at us. They appeared friendly, and—as we descended—I recognized one of them from Hong Non. We were taking some fire from the vicinity of Hong Non, but fortunately it was too far away to be effective.

Bob eased the chopper down into the small opening with the rotor blades grazing the limbs on the trees. The ground was very rough and steeply sloped, and the best he could do was get one wheel of the main gear down on the ground to steady the bird and maintain enough power to keep it level. The old radial piston engine would quickly burn up with power on but no air movement to cool it. We couldn't stay on the ground very long.

I jumped out of the chopper and the soldiers motioned for me to come down the slope. About thirty steps away were four Meo in fatigues carrying a crude litter made from bamboo poles and rice sacks. On the litter was a big, wild-looking man with a mirror-back ERK4 survival radio in his right hand. The damn thing wouldn't transmit, but it had saved Tony's life anyway.

We got him on the chopper as quickly as possible, and Bob started to lift off immediately. It was necessary to ascend vertically without any forward motion to miss the trees—but even so, the overheated engine couldn't completely clear the tops, and Bob had to go forward, dragging the chopper through the branches. We made it without damage to the rotor blades, but it was certainly a close call. Soon, the H34 began to gain altitude, and Bob got on course for Hua Muang.

Tony looked terrible, and seemed to have lost consciousness when we stretched him out on the chopper floor. I examined him quickly. A high velocity round had gone completely through his pelvis. However, his pulse was strong and his color was good. His abdomen was soft, and there didn't seem to be too much blood loss. With a little luck, he would make it.

As I worked over him, he suddenly reared up and grabbed me by the neck. Pulling me down, he shouted in my ear above the roar of the open chopper. "Where we going? Where we going?"

"I'm taking you to Hua Muang. Then we'll get a Caribou to Korat."

He was shaking me and screaming. "No! Must go back! Must go back! Turn around! Turn around!"

"I'm taking you to the hospital at Korat. Simmer down dammit. You're gonna start bleeding everywhere. Stay still."

"Doc, please. There're wounded. Have to pick up the wounded. Medic stayed with them. I told them to wait for the pickup."

I finally realized what the problem was. In spite of the seriousness of his wound—and only being semi-conscious—he was aware that we were leaving the area. His sole thought was to pick up his wounded comrades.

He dragged himself over to the door where he could see, and started pointing in the direction where he wanted to go. I took the flight mechanic's intercom headset and gave Bob directions. Tony had picked a good spot for the wounded to wait, and Bob set the chopper down without any trouble. We loaded seven badly-wounded Meo soldiers and took off again for Hua Muang. Tony laid back and lost consciousness.

I had Bob call a Caribou into Hua Muang—which landed just after us—and we transferred Tony to it. It wasn't possible to hospitalize him in Laos because he was in the country illegally—and he was just the sort of story the newspaper reporters were looking for, since the US wasn't supposed to have any military advisors in the country.

After reassuring Pop and all the Hua Muang people that Tony was going to live, we took off in the Caribou for Korat. Bob had refueled the chopper and was taking the wounded Meo soldiers to Sam Thong.

Tony was more comfortable on the Caribou, with a good stretcher and some blankets. His head was clear now, and he told me a little about the events at Hong Non.

They were hit by what he estimated to be two companies of Vietnamese. The attack came suddenly, and although they were prepared for it, they were overwhelmed by sheer numbers and greater firepower. There was heavy fighting on the airstrip and in the village within a few minutes of the first shot. Tony and Boua Chou were running around the place trying to bring some control and order to chaos, while at the same time fighting for their lives.

Boua Chou had just pulled the pin on a grenade when he was hit by rifle fire. Before he could throw it, the bullet had knocked him down and the grenade exploded in his hand. He died instantly.

A short time later, Tony took the round through the pelvis. He fell to the ground, unable to walk. With fighting going on all around him, he dragged himself to where the ground dropped off into the valley. Here, he could roll downhill and escape. He felt as if he was paralysed from the waist down, and it was a slow and difficult process. Although in great pain, he rolled for several hundred meters until he felt he was safe. Fortunately, one of the escaping medics found him. With some of the other people to help, they made the litter, and—despite their terror—carried him to safety.

The pilot had radioed ahead that we were bringing in a wounded American civilian, and when we landed, the ambulance was waiting at the strip. We rushed to the hospital where Colonel Hanard, the hospital commander, had the surgical team standing by. As soon as the doctors saw Tony, it was determined that he would need to be examined surgically.

By the time they wheeled him into the theater, he was already feeling better, joking with the doctors and nurses. With all hell breaking loose in Sam Neua, I needed to get back and help Pop.

Before leaving, I told Tony, "Listen buddy, you're going to be okay now. I have to get back upcountry and help Pop. Behave yourself. Don't give the doctors a bad time, and keep your hands off the nurses. I'll be back in two or three days to check on you."

"Okay, but you better be quick about it. I'll be out of here in two or three days myself. I gotta get back up to Sam Neua."

"Make that two or three weeks," I lied to him.

If he was getting around in three months, we'd be lucky.

"No need to hurry," I added. "If you need anything, just tell Colonel Hanard. He'll get in touch with Pat or me and we'll get it to you right away."

I started to leave but he called me back.

"What's up buddy?"

"Bend down so I can tell you something."

I bent over him. He didn't say anything but he grabbed me around the shoulders and kissed me on the cheek. Then with tears in his eyes, "I love you, you old grey-haired bastard."

Colonel Hanard and I had a cup of coffee, and I gave him the background on Tony and the circumstances of his getting wounded. He understood the security implications, and promised to keep outsiders away. Also, he would personally see that Tony had the very best care.

All the hospital personnel knew and appreciated the fact that we frequently picked up US Air Force crewmen shot down in the North, and returned them to Korat. Colonel Hanard and his staff were glad to take care of the occasional civilian we brought in to show their appreciation. Certainly the Air Force had no mandate to take care of our people, but Colonel Hanard didn't mind bending regulations.

The colonel's driver had a vehicle ready to take me out to the strip where the Caribou was waiting. We would only go as far as Vientiane, as it was too late to make it back upcountry that day—and although I wanted to get to Hua Muang as quickly as possible, it would be nice to spend the night at home. It had been two weeks since I'd seen Pat and the kids.

As we were driving out to the plane, one of the hospital vehicles whipped around us and motioned for us to stop.

The driver jumped out and ran over. "Doctor Weldon, the Colonel wants you to come back to the hospital for a few minutes. That crazy guy you brought in won't go into surgery until he talks to you."

"What!"

"Yeah. Says he has to see you and we can't do anything with him."

We turned around and drove back to the hospital.

Colonel Hanard was waiting. "I don't know what's wrong, but he says he has to talk to you before you leave. It seems important to him."

I could hear Tony yelling down the corridor, "Get my clothes! Goddammit, get my clothes!"

We hurried down to where he was lying on the stretcher. "Tony, for Christ sakes what's the matter? You can't put your clothes on."

"Doc, I don't want to put my clothes on. I need to get something out of the pocket for you."

Colonel Hanard told someone to find his clothes and bring them to him. Of course, they had already cut the filthy, bloody fatigues off Tony and thrown them away. When the rags came back, he stuck his hand in a pants pocket and pulled out what appeared to be a broken bolt.

"Doc, this is the broken swivel pin out of the tripod for the recoilless rifle at Hong Non. Soon as you get back to Long Chieng, give it to Vint and tell him to send a new one up to them right away. That's all they need to get the gun going again. Don't forget now."

"Okay Tony. We'll get it up there right away. Can you go in for your operation now?"

He was still fighting the battle in Sam Neua and couldn't conceive that the Vietnamese had his recoilless rifle.

I can't remember the exact time he stayed at Korat, but within a few weeks he was back in action—mean and raucous, and ready to go another round.

On the Run From Houi Sa An

As the Vietnamese tried to consolidate their position in Sam Neua in late 1966, they overran the village of Houi Sa An. This large enclave of displaced people was located to the southeast of Hua Muang. The enemy was trying to outflank the troops defending the Hua Muang perimeter, and thousands of terrified people were streaming along the narrow trail, fleeing westward toward the Muang Heim Valley—hopefully where they'd be able to find safety.

The enemy attacked unexpectedly and in the middle of the night. Many people were killed in the wild, chaotic shooting and panicked flight. All had lost their possessions, and some adults weren't completely clothed. Many of the children were naked and shivering in the cold damp weather. Pop and I, with two medics and some of the refugee relief workers, had set up a dispensary and a tent with food and refugee supplies by the side of the trail to Muang Heim.

As the refugees came by, we treated the sick and wounded, and gave them canned meat and what rice they could carry. If they needed clothing, we gave them lengths of cloth to wrap around their bodies and later sew into garments. We had a chopper shuttling the old people and those unable to walk any farther over to the Muang Heim Valley. The seriously wounded were put on a STOL aircraft waiting at the Muang Heim airstrip for evacuation to the Sam Thong Hospital.

There were dozens of coughing, red-eyed, rash-covered children with high fever. Not just the Vietnamese army, but also that deadly disease we had seen at Phou Nong was ravaging these miserable people. The enemy struck at the height of a measles epidemic.

I had thought the episode at Phou Nong was bad, but this situation was many times worse. Often, the mother or father would be carrying one, or even two of the sick children on their back, and another in their arms. The children they couldn't carry clung to their parents' legs and clothing for reassurance, and to keep from falling.

One poor woman stopped for me to confirm that the child she was carrying was really dead. She knew her child had gone, but she desperately wanted me to tell her that she was mistaken. There had been no time for burial, so she hurried down the trail clutching the dead child to her breast.

Another young mother wanted treatment for her one-year-old baby, her first child. The poor girl wouldn't believe me when I told her the baby had already died. She thought it had fallen asleep. When she finally realized her baby was dead, she collapsed on the ground clutching the child, silent sobs shaking her exhausted body. Her husband was one of the village militia killed by the Vietnamese. Throughout the day she lay there, completely unresponsive. Late in the afternoon, we picked her up from the ground and put her on the chopper to take her and the dead baby to Muang Heim.

All day long, the sad, miserable procession filed by: dead and dying children; the crippled and the wounded; the feeble old people; and the pregnant and nursing mothers—all terrorized and demoralized. I could only think what a shame it was that all the North Vietnamese sympathizers in the United States weren't there to see it.

Just before dark, the last of the refugees disappeared down the trail to the west. No more were coming up from Houi Sa An, and we estimated that only about half the people of the village and its surrounding area had passed through during the day. Apparently those remaining had stopped for the night.

Pop and I, along with the small group of medics and soldiers with us, ate a few handsfull of sticky rice, and rolled up in blankets on the ground by the trail. We would be ready to work in the morning as soon as the refugees started moving through again.

It was a beautiful, clear, starlit night. Lying there looking up at the sky, it seemed ludicrous—an absurdity—that such tragedy and suffering could befall these simple people in this remote corner of the world. Pop and I were both so depressed by the day's events that we hadn't said a word to each other for some time. Just as I was about to fall asleep, he rolled over and tapped me on the shoulder.

"You asleep, Doc?"

"Not yet, Pop. What's up?"

"No, I don't need nothin'. I was just thinkin'."

I didn't say anything, and there was a long pause. I thought he was going to sleep, but after a minute or two he said, "Doc, you ain't much on religion are you?"

"No, I guess not, Pop." His unexpected question had surprised me a little.

"I ain't neither, but times like this I kinda wish I was." He sighed. "Maybe it'd make it easier to figger out."

I couldn't reply, but I expected him to continue the conversation. However, he said nothing else, and I could only guess what thoughts were running through his mind until we both fell asleep.

The next morning, a few small groups of people straggled by, but by noon there were no more. A large section of the population at Houi Sa An had been trapped and couldn't escape. We took the chopper to Muang Heim to see what needed to be done to help those who made it to safety.

Must Try Harder

A few days after the horror at Houi Sa An, I was at my office in Vientiane actually enjoying doing nothing more stressful than going through the in box. Bea Perez, my secretary, came to the door and told me that Mrs. Johnson, the principal at the American School was on the line. The end of the school year was approaching, and she was calling to ask me to meet with her in regard to some problems that Walter was having.

Walter had never shown much interest in school, and his grades were only average at best. On the other hand, as an ex-pediatrician with some experience in psychometric testing and evaluation, I considered him intelligent and in excellent physical and mental health. As a consequence, Pat and I had little concern about his indifferent performance. He was a bright, personable kid with no hangups. He read a lot and was interested in many things. One day he would develop some interest in his schooling, and we believed he would do well.

I went out to the school and met with Mrs. Johnson, the principal.

"Doctor Weldon, I'm concerned about Walter. He's doing so poorly, I don't see how we can possibly advance him to the seventh grade. I do believe it best that he repeat the sixth."

This unexpected revelation was both startling and upsetting. The situation was obviously more serious than I'd anticipated.

"Well, Mrs. Johnson, this is certainly a surprise to me," I replied. "I know he's not done unusually well, but his grades have always been satisfactory. Why haven't we been notified before this? We could have done something."

"I'm sorry, but his teachers have just brought it to my attention. Recently, his work has been exceptionally poor. He's inattentive in class, and is a very disrupting influence to the other pupils. Do you and Doctor McCreedy help him with his homework, or see that he does it?"

"No, I don't suppose we do. It never occurred to us that it was necessary."

"All of the testing we've done on him shows that he's a very intelligent child. Also, he has such a charming personality that we all adore him."

"Mrs. Johnson, if Walter's an intelligent, likeable, well-adjusted child, and he's failing in school, doesn't it suggest that possibly his teachers may not be doing the best job possible."

Mrs. Johnson was a very pleasant, even-tempered lady, but we were both getting a bit irritated. She was turning red in the face, so before she could reply, I quickly suggested that I should talk to Walter, and she should talk to his teachers. We parted with tension in the air.

That evening I sat down with Walter and told him about my meeting with Mrs. Johnson.

"She says that if you don't shape up right now, you're going to repeat the sixth grade. That would be terribly embarrassing to mother and me."

He was aghast. "It would kill me, Dad. I don't want to embarrass Mom and you."

"No, it wouldn't kill you, but I might. Now get yourself straightened out or I'm going to bust your ass."

"Don't worry Dad. I'll make it. Everybody's going to call me a bookworm."

Neither Pat nor I had to prod him. He came straight home every afternoon for the remainder of the school term and hit the books.

Three or four days after the school term ended Mrs. Johnson called.

"Doctor Weldon, Walter completely defeats me. Do you know he made by far the best grades of any student in his class on his final tests. I don't know what to do with him. It would be foolish to keep him in the sixth grade."

"I agree, Mrs. Johnson. It would be foolish. We'll try to see that he continues the good work. Thank you for calling. I appreciate the good news and your interest."

I certainly wouldn't categorize Mrs. Johnson as an "ed'cated fool," but as Pop said, sometimes it makes you wonder.

A Double Tragedy

The moment I walked into the house, I knew that something terrible had happened. Walt was lying on the living room floor with some old pictures of himself and Mr. Kobiyashi in their white judo suits. Tears were streaming down his cheeks. Ray was sitting in a chair, staring off into space.

Between sobs they told me they'd just heard that Mr. Kobiyashi had been killed in a plane crash at Savannakhet. I had also heard about the crash, just as I was leaving the office, but didn't know exactly who was on the plane. A C46 on the milk run lost an engine on takeoff, crashed, and several people lost their lives. One of the victims, apparently, was Mr. Kobiyashi.

This kind and gentle agronomist on Japan's community development team, taught judo to the students at the International School. A powerful, athletic man in his forties, Mr. Kobiyashi loved children and spent a large part of his spare time working with the boys at the school. He used judo only as a vehicle to teach them self-confidence, sportsmanship, and good manners; that one could be tough and yet still be a gentleman.

Periodically, he and his students gave demonstrations for the parents. Mr. Kobiyashi would let the boys throw him around the mat just as if they were his equal at the sport—and he made them believe that they really were. The kids were very proud of themselves and adored their instructor. His death was a cruel blow. It was the first time my sons had suffered the death of a close friend. It was a terrible shock, and they would grieve for many weeks.

Later that evening, Pop called me on the radio and told me that the wife of Chao Saykham, the governor of Xieng Khoung province, was also a passenger on the plane—and hadn't survived the crash. This was indeed a double tragedy.

Mrs. Saykham was an official in the Ministry of Education, and she obtained—against strong opposition in the ministry—the approval for the establishment of the normal school at Sam Thong. This energetic lady personally supervised the construction, selected the faculty, and organized the classes that would produce our first accredited teachers. We were all extremely proud of the school, and considered it the most important project ever undertaken at Sam Thong. Her death was a terrible loss to us all.

The funeral ceremonies would be held in Savannakhet, Mrs. Saykham's birthplace. Pop would come down to Vientiane the next morning and we would go on to Savannakhet together and do what we could to help Chao Saykham.

It was a sad evening, with the boys crying over Mr. Kobiyashi, and Pat and I over Mrs. Chao Saykham

Search and Rescue

When I arrived in 1963, US military aircraft were flying reconnaissance missions over Laos, but there was no organized search and rescue (SAR) capability in the country for a further three years. If a plane went down in Northern Laos or adjacent areas of North Vietnam, it was out of range of all military SAR teams—and unfortunately, the enemy was shooting down our planes with alarming regularity.

Since the recon missions over Laos violated the Geneva Accords, the US denied making such flights—and since no flights were being made, no planes were being shot down. Therefore, there was no need for SAR capability.

This absurd charade was finally dropped, and the Air Force stationed the first Jolly Green Giant rescue helicopters and their specially-trained crews at General VP's headquarters at Long Chieng in mid-1966. The big, heavily-armed and armored choppers with their highly-skilled SAR teams were indeed a welcome sight.

However, during the three years before the arrival of the Jolly Greens, all SAR operations were carried out by our civilian contract aircraft and crews—Air America and Bird & Sons—assisted by the USAID employees who worked upcountry and the local military.

There was no obligation for anyone involved to participate in SAR for US military personnel, particularly in combat situations, and certainly these unarmed civilian aircraft were not suitable for such duty. In fact, the pilots were discouraged from doing so by the air contractor's management, and we—the USAID employees—were discouraged by our administrators. If a contract aircraft was damaged, or a pilot wounded or killed on SAR, this only increased the overhead to the contractor. Similarly, if any US personnel were captured, it would be politically embarrassing. Probably there were some people who would rest better if we were killed, since the problem would be obviated in that case. Nevertheless, the pilots and crews of the air contractors rescued 52 American crewmen before the US Air Force stationed the SAR teams at Long Chieng.

Between 1966 and 1975 when the communists took over the country, the civilian aircraft continued to help in SAR operations, and were responsible for saving the lives of many more crewmen. However, after 1966 most of the SAR was done by the Jolly Green crews with top cover.

Before 1966, our unwritten protocol took the following form. We would be working upcountry and a "mayday" would be heard on 121.5mhz—one of the international emergency radio frequencies which all aircraft monitor. Our aircraft would respond to the call and try to ascertain the location, the nature of the emergency, and the type of the damaged or malfunctioning aircraft. One of our STOL planes that was closest to the area of the emergency would then take command of the SAR. All other aircraft would maintain radio silence and monitor the emergency frequency.

Since there was always a high probability of need for medical care, any USAID public health officer working upcountry was alerted immediately, and he would get airborne as quickly as possible with medical equipment— preferably in a chopper. If a chopper wasn't immediately available, he would head toward the emergency area in one of the STOL planes.

At the same time, any other STOL aircraft in the vicinity would join the search under the direction of the pilot in charge of the operation. Also, any choppers in the vicinity would respond to instructions from the public health officer or the command pilot, and move to a position of readiness to make the pick-up. If at all possible, the public health officer would be on the chopper making the pick-up.

Speed was the essence of success. With our unarmed aircraft, we had to reach the downed airmen before the enemy, who of course soon realized that when a plane was down, we would be making a rescue attempt. If the crewmen had already been captured, they would be waiting in ambush by the parachutes or crash site. They would also try to decoy our search aircraft with signal mirrors and the emergency radio beepers the crewmen carried in their survival vests.

There were variations on the theme. In some emergencies, one of our choppers which happened to be at the right spot, rushed in immediately, picked up the crewmen, and was out again before the enemy could react. On at least three occasions that I can remember, our pilots were able to guide and direct damaged aircraft safely away from enemy areas, and— although there was no place to make an emergency landing—the crewmen bailed out and were picked up uninjured without danger from enemy troops.

On one such occasion, an Air America pilot guided a damaged A1E into a rough, dirt strip for a successful landing. The pilot didn't even know the strip existed—and, indeed, thought the area was held by the enemy. The plane had a bullet hole through the oil reservoir, which was quickly repaired. That afternoon, he and his crewman landed at their base in Thailand—to find their buddies mourning their demise.

When we picked up downed crewmen, we seldom found any that had been briefed about the American operations in Northern Laos. Almost all of them thought that everything north and east of the Mekong River was enemy territory. This was most unfortunate because the knowledge of where friendly enclaves were located could be life-saving information.

When we picked up airmen, we would fly them directly to Thailand. Because policy dictated that we conceal the fact that US planes were flying missions over Laos, we didn't want them seen in the country. If they were uninjured, they were taken to the Udorn air base. All the wounded and injured were evacuated to the US Air Force hospital on the Korat air base, which had the best medical capability in the area—particularly in traumatology and orthopedics.

Eventually, some of the units whose airmen we had picked up, found out the location of our headquarters for the Northern Laos operation at Sam Thong. Usually, the day after we returned one of their guys, a couple of planes would drag the little dirt strip at Sam Thong about fifty feet off the deck at around 500 knots, and do a few slow rolls. It was their way of saying thanks, and those of us involved in the SAR operations were grateful for the gesture. It was one of the few expressions of appreciation we ever received.

New Kid on the Block

From 1963 to 1966, the hospital commander at the Korat air base was Colonel Hanard—a delightful, amiable man who was cooperative and not afraid to bend regulations. Since I was delivering injured airmen to him on a fairly regular basis, we became good friends.

Periodically, when the fighting flared up, the hospital at Sam Thong would be inundated with casualties. Dr. Khammoung and Dr. Bounthan would be working 24 hours a day, and desperately need some assistance. I would call Colonel Hanard, and he'd always lend us someone from his staff to help out during the emergency period. Such assistance was completely against military regulations, of course, and the colonel could easily have been court martialed.

We would pick up the Air Force doctor at Korat with one of our project aircraft, and fly him to Sam Thong clandestinely. When he had to return, we flew him directly from Sam Thong to Korat. Military regulations, Lao immigration laws, the Geneva Accords, and American foreign policy were all violated—but this was small bother to Colonel Hanard and myself.

On one such occasion in late 1966, when Sam Thong hospital was overflowing with casualties, I called Korat. The operator answered and put me directly through.

"Hi Colonel, this is Doc Weldon up in Laos. How are things down in Korat?"

"Not much going on . . . fortunately. What can I do for you?"

"Colonel, things are really happening up here. We're up to our knees in blood and guts. Could you possibly lend us a general surgeon who likes traumatology for a while?"

"Yeah, I think so. I have a young guy who just passed his boards after finishing residency at Mount Sinai. Jessie Blumenthal. Got here a few weeks ago. Young and inexperienced but he's a real hot shot. Best I've seen in a long time.

"Could you spare him for a couple of weeks until we get caught up?"

"Sure, glad to help you guys. We'll never be able to pay you back for all you've done for us." There were a few moments of hesitation before the colonel added, "Doc . . . I have to tell you . . . Blumenthal's a bit abrasive, and he's had some friction with the nursing staff. Be warned."

"Don't worry Colonel. We'll be happy to get him. Anyway, he'll be too busy to enter any personality contests. If it's okay, I'll send a plane for him in the morning."

"I'll talk to him right now. If I don't call you back, go ahead and send the plane."

The next day, I couldn't get out of the office, so Pat went to Korat to pick up Jessie Blumenthal. They would fly directly to Sam Thong, where Pat would introduce the new doctor to Pop, Kathy Pollock (the new American nurse who replaced Diana Dick when she married Terry Quill, one of the CIA operations officers at Long Chieng.), and Dr. Khammoung, and see that he was settled in okay.

I didn't mention to Pat, Colonel Hanard's warning about Blumenthal's personality and his friction with the Korat staff. I only told her that the colonel thought he was one of the best young surgeons he'd seen in a long while. It would be better for her and the Sam Thong crew to form their own opinion.

Later that evening, I was at home sitting on the veranda, watching the sunset over the Mekong when Pat arrived. It was obvious that she'd had a long and tiring day. I fixed her a Scotch and soda, and she slumped down in a chair and took a deep, sighing breath.

"Well, how did it go?"

"Oh, okay I guess. Colonel Hanard sends his regards."

"Did you get Blumenthal up to Sam Thong?"

"Yes, but you may be sorry I did."

I tried to act surprised. "Why do you say that?"

"Well, he's certainly a sharp young guy—tough, energetic, handsome. Knows his business. But what a thorny son of a bitch."

"What do you mean?"

"Very abrupt and impatient. No matter what he says, it seems to irritate people. I'm afraid Pop's going to eat him alive. He made a real bad impression on the old man. It was hate at first sight."

"Oh Christ. Well, he'll only be there for a couple of weeks."

"There was a bright side though. Khammoung didn't know exactly what to think of him, but before I left, the two of them were already lining up cases. The ones Khammoung hadn't been able to handle by himself. It was obvious there was some sort of professional rapport right away."

"What did he think of the hospital and operating room? They must look pretty primitive to a slick young dude fresh from Mount Sinai."

"I don't think that's a problem. He gives you the impression he could do a craniotomy with a can opener if he had to."

I went to sleep that night with a vague feeling of anxiety about Dr. Blumenthal. Sam Thong was a most difficult place to work under the best of circumstances. Even with very careful selection by Pop and me, we had a fairly high attrition rate of personnel working there. The tension generated by a seven-day work week with an almost constant state of emergency was difficult to tolerate. A security situation which was always poor, and which could suddenly deteriorate made people irritable and short tempered. To survive in such an environment, a person had to be understanding and forgiving.

The following day, Vitoy and I went to Ban Houi Sai and stayed for three days. We were considering the possibility of putting an OB team there to work in the little dilapidated government hospital. The *chao kweng* had requested that we do so, even though the Dooley Foundation—a private voluntary agency (see *The Ban Houi Sai Hospital Saga*)—had a small hospital operation on the same compound.

We were taking a lot of casualties in the area, and had no way to adequately care for them. Neither the government hospital nor the Dooley facility had the personnel or budget to do so. I had wanted to give Dooley the necessary support to expand their operation. However, Verne Chaney, the Dooley director didn't want to accept overt US government assistance. Also, he disliked the idea of handling war casualties from the RLG military. The situation was sensitive from a political standpoint since neither the RLG nor the US wanted our actions to appear as if an organization like the Dooley Foundation was being pushed aside.

At the end of the three days, Vitoy and I had done a lot of talking, but hadn't been able to come up with a satisfactory plan. I felt it necessary to discuss things with Charley Mann and Ambassador Godley before we pushed ahead. We assured the *chao kweng* we'd be back in one or two weeks with a definitive plan, and took off for Vientiane.

We were in a Pilatus Porter, and I had just dozed off in the right seat next to the pilot, when he shook me awake. He gave me his headset and the microphone and said Sam Thong wanted to talk to me.

"Doc, this is Pop. How do you read? Over."

"Loud and clear, Pop. Go ahead."

"What's your present location and destination?"

"Ten minutes west of Sayaboury town, headed for Lima (Vientiane)."

"Can you divert to Sam Thong?"

"Negative. Important meeting in Vientiane this afternoon. What's the problem? Over."

"Goddamn it Doc. Can't talk over this radio. Get up here. I need you. Now!"

I was certain he was angry about something—rather than concerned about an emergency. I had completely forgotten about Dr. Blumenthal, but now I strongly suspected Pop's anger had to do with our new young surgeon from Korat.

Vitoy had to get back to his office so I had the pilot drop me off at Sam Thong and then he continued to Vientiane. As soon as we landed, my suspicions were confirmed. Pop ran out of the office to meet me before I could crawl off the plane.

The old man was really steamed up. "You gotta get that guy out of here right now," he hollered.

"Take it easy Pop. You're going to have a another coronary. Let's go in, sit down and talk about it."

We went in to the office and I sat down. "What guy are you talking about?"

Pop just stood over me and shook his finger in my face. "You know damn well what I'm talking about. You get him out of here. Right away. Now. This afternoon."

"Simmer down. Who are you talking about?"

"That guy Pat brought up here the other day. He's drivin' everybody crazy. Get him out of here."

"What's he done, Pop?"

"What's he done. He's chasin' everybody out of the hospital. Screamin' at the nurses. Throwin' stuff all over. Complainin' 'bout everythin'. He's got the little nurses scared to death. All of them's been up here day and night cryin' their eyes out sayin' they're goin' home. Kathy's so damn mad at him I'm afraid she's gonna kill him or quit. This guy's poison. He even cut on a man's head and the *nai kongs* were real mad about that. He's gotta go. Now."

"Look Pop, I understand he's a real pain in the ass, but regardless of what he's done, I'm not sending him out of here unless he wants to leave.

Colonel Hanard's been too good to us. He'd be real upset if we threw one of his guys out of here. It would be a hell of a way to show our appreciation for the way he sticks his neck out for us. You just take it easy until I talk to everyone, and then we'll decide what to do."

Pop quieted down and didn't say anything for a few minutes as he paced back and forth with a thoughtful look on his face. Finally, he sat down and said, "Yeah Doc, you're right. We can't hurt the Colonel's feelin's. I admire that man. Stuck his neck out a mile for us. There ain't too many like him round these days. Go down to the hospital and see if you can't get that asshole straightened out."

At the hospital—before looking up Dr. Blumenthal, who was off in one of the wards—I met Dr. Khammoung. When he saw me, he hurriedly took me into his office and locked the door. His face was grim, and I could see that he was deeply concerned. Immediately, I assumed the cause of his concern was Dr. Blumenthal's behavior.

Khammoung was one of the calmest, most impassive people I have ever known, and his attitude was truly surprising. As soon as we sat down, he did indeed start talking about his new colleague.

"I'm very concerned about Dr. Jessie. Pop wants to send him back to Korat because he hasn't been polite to the nurses and sometimes talks to them in a loud voice. Also, when we're very busy, maybe he'll get angry and throw things on the floor. He scolds them if they don't give him exactly what he wants as soon as he asks for it. Also Kathy's upset at him and she's complaining to Pop."

What he said next surprised me.

"But none of this is really important. He's a good man. I believe it's just his way, and he doesn't mean to be impolite. He's a fine surgeon and we need him badly. We work well together, and I can learn much from him. He knows all the new techniques. I know he has a good heart by the kind way he treats the patients and the way he worries about them.

"Please talk to Pop. Also you must talk to Kathy and tell her to be more patient with him."

I was greatly relieved, and told Khammoung, "If you want him to stay, he'll stay. I'll talk to Pop and Kathy. Don't worry about them. But how about our nurses? Pop says they're threatening to quit."

"That's no problem. I'll have a meeting with them tonight and explain why Jessie must stay. Why it's important for them to cooperate and be understanding. No one will leave."

We went out on the wards and found Jessie changing the dressings on a patient. Kathy and five or six of the student nurses assisted him. The oldest one was probably 15, and being at Sam Thong was surely the first time she had ever left her tiny village on some remote mountain top.

Kathy was translating and telling the nurses what to do. However, Jessie would speak in English directly to the girls and not through Kathy. If they didn't respond immediately, he'd become impatient and yell at them or brush them aside and do the thing himself. Obviously, he had them terrified. They could understand a few words of English, but not nearly well enough to follow his orders.

Khammoung and I walked up to the group and I introduced myself. Jessie was a handsome young man in his late twenties, medium height, trim and athletic. He radiated energy and enthusiasm.

We shook hands and he said, "Yeah, Hanard told me about you. I thought you ran the show up here, but looks like that old guy they call Pop calls the shots. Boy, he's really something. You got to give it to him though, all these peasants really respect and love him. When Khammoung and I get caught up, I want to sit down and talk to him. He told me last night he wanted to talk to me, but we were too busy.

"This is a great place. Thanks for saving me from a slow death down in Korat. We've done more surgery in three days than I've done the whole time I've been in the Air Force. I'd sure like to stay up here for a while. You and Hanard seem to be pretty good buddies—can't you get him to let me stay. Khammoung needs another pair of hands real bad, and Hanard has more people than he knows what to do with."

As Jessie talked, it became apparent that this intelligent, talented, young surgeon was also the tough kid from New York. He came on a bit too strong, and wasn't concerned about sensibilities. On the other hand, his behavior was completely spontaneous and without any malice or intent to offend. We discussed some of the more interesting cases until Chua came and told Dr. Khammoung that their next patient was being taken to the operating room.

When Khammoung and Jessie left, Kathy and I went over to her little cottage and had coffee. We talked about my conversation with Pop, and she admitted that she'd been outraged at Jessie's behavior toward the staff. Nevertheless, she felt as Khammoung did. Jessie was so good and so badly needed, that everyone should try to adjust to his callous manner.

Later, I talked to Pop again, and we decided to just let things take their course for the rest of the two weeks that Jessie would be at Sam Thong.

Surely, they could put up with him for that short period of time. We both agreed that my first inclination to sit down with Jessie and talk about the problems he was causing would be counter-productive. Kathy and the kids in the hospital could probably adjust to him easier than he could them.

That night, as usual, Pop and I sat around talking and sipping on a bottle of Meo corn whiskey. It was supposed to be some especially good stuff that Father B had brought from the village of Pha Phay—which had the reputation of making the best booze in Xieng Khoung province.

Father B had a few Catholics in Pha Phay, and he visited them regularly. However, it was difficult to reach the village by foot, and the good priest usually cajoled Pop into sending him there by chopper. To facilitate his appeals for transportation, Father B always brought back a couple of bottles of Pha Phay's finest to give his benefactor. The distiller at Pha Phay particularly recommended the bottle we were presently sampling. It had been aged for a full month, and the large, brown centipede in the bottom gave it an exceptional bouquet and delicate flavor.

Around midnight, we got down to the centipede and finally crawled into the big bamboo bed. The last thing I remember was Pop mumbling about how nice it would be if he didn't have all them "ed'cated fools" driving him crazy. Although he placed highest priority on the building of schools, at times he could be quite sceptical about the benefits of higher education.

✛

The following morning, I returned to Vientiane and placed "The Blumenthal Problem" in an inactive file in the back of my mind. It appeared that the situation wouldn't get out of hand. Pop would put Jessie on a plane at the end of the two-week period, and that would be that.

I was in the office for a few days, and then went to Savannakhet with Don Dougan. We were working on a plan to renovate the outpatient department and the maternity unit of the Savannakhet Provincial Hospital. After meeting with the *medcin chef* and his staff for a couple of days, Don and I visited the OB hospital at Kengkok, and the USAID-supported dispensaries in the area. By the time we returned to Vientiane, I'd forgotten about Jessie—assuming that Pop would put him on a plane for Korat at the designated time, and that would be the end of it. However, when I went to the office, Bea said that Pop wanted to talk to me as soon as possible.

Bea got him on the radio.

"Pop, this is Doc. Go ahead."

"Doc, have you talked to our friend at Korat about our problem here?"

"No Pop. Not necessary. The two weeks will be up tomorrow. We'll just put him on a plane and send him back. No need to contact Korat."

"Goddammit Doc, I ain't talkin' 'bout him goin' back. He's gotta stay up here. We can't do without him. We've been tryin' to get in touch with you for two days. Call the colonel and tell him we'll send Jessie back next month. He's savin' a damn site more lives up here than he could down in Korat."

I was certainly taken aback by this unexpected change in attitude, and wanted to say something sarcastic. Still, I thought it best to remain silent.

I called Colonel Hanard, and after some discussion, he agreed to let Jessie stay. We would leave the date of his return open, and when the case load dropped at Sam Thong, we'd put him on a plane. If the situation at Korat changed, and Jessie had to return, the colonel would let me know, and we'd fly Jessie back immediately.

As it turned out, Jessie stayed at Sam Thong for the remainder of his tour of duty overseas—almost a year. During this period, he taught Khammoung most of what he'd learned in a four-year surgical residency at Mount Sinai—one of the finest hospitals in the United States.

When the fighting flared up and the casualties started streaming into the hospital, they would work day and night. Someone would hand them something to eat, and occasionally one of them would sleep for two or three hours. After a cup of coffee and a cold shower they'd start again. If things were especially bad, they might not leave the hospital for several days.

It was interesting to me that Jessie never changed. The day he left, he was still screaming at the nurses and throwing things on the floor. Only now, no one paid any attention. Nurses, Khammoung, Kathy, Pop—they'd all come to love this strange man who could do such miraculous things for his patients.

When he finally got on the plane to leave, everyone in Sam Thong was at the airstrip to see him off. The little nurses who'd been so terrified of him when he arrived, were now crowding around him, trying to hold his hand or just be near him until the last moment. Everyone's eyes were filled with tears, and it was truly a sad departure.

Even as the plane taxied on to the strip, Jessie was yelling instructions to the nurses about what to do with certain patients above the roar of the aircraft. I had hopped on the plane to shake his hand and thank him for all his good work. The tailgate on the Caribou was still down, and the kicker told me to get out so he could close it. As I jumped down, I could see tears streaming down Jessie's cheeks. As Dr. Khammoung said, Jessie had a good heart.

Years later, I would walk through the hospital and still see evidence of Jessie's presence—in the way Khammoung and the nurses did things. He had left an invaluable legacy in this remote and troubled place. When things went to hell with the wounded streaming into the hospital and everyone was up to their knees in blood and guts, even Pop would get nostalgic and say, "Jesus Doc, wouldn't it be great if Jessie was here."

The Menagerie

I woke up one particular morning to realize that I wasn't living in a house—
I was living in a menagerie. Animals had gradually taken over our
Vientiane home. Pandora and Whitey, our two dogs, had litters almost
simultaneously. That made ten puppies, plus Pandora, Whitey, and Wags,
the adopted stray—which added up to thirteen yelping dogs.

There was also Rudolph the red-ass monkey; Bambi, the little barking
deer; Pete, the pangolin; a talking mynah bird; as well as five monitor lizards
the size of long, skinny crocodiles. Not to mention Walter's various snakes,
which came and went as they pleased.

It was more than any man could tolerate.

Fortunately, Calico, the miniature horse, strayed off and no one could
find him.

Calico was raised with dogs, not horses, and being the same size as a
Great Dane, he thought he was indeed a dog, not a horse. He ran and
played with Pandora and Wags, and when someone left the front door open
and the dogs ran into the house and jumped on the couch, Calico ran in
and jumped up on the couch, too.

I must confess that I paid the man next door to see that Calico strayed
off and not be found again.

When I discovered that every morning, Dao, the cook, bought two or
three dozen live crabs to feed the monitor lizards, bananas for Rudolph,
and fresh buffalo steak for the dogs, that was the final straw.

Ray was the animal lover, and largely accountable for assembling the
wildlife collection, but Becky and Walter had to assume some of the
responsibility, too. I called them together and demanded that they remove
all the animals within one week. This led to cries of anguish and accusations
of unfeeling cruelty. However, after lengthy negotiation, we agreed that
Pandora, Wags, Rudolph, and the mynah bird could stay. If all the other

animals hadn't departed within seven days, then I would personally see that every single one of them was escorted from the premises.

Shunned and ignored for two or three days and feeling like a pariah, I decided it was better to go upcountry until things simmered down a bit. Nevertheless, when I returned home a few days later, the menagerie was at a reasonable size, and the Vientiane zoo had been greatly enriched by the kids' generous donations.

A Gaudy Old Lady

Before the communist takeover in 1975, Laos was considered to have two capitals—Vientiane and Luang Prabang. Although the center of government was in Vientiane, Luang Prabang—the old capital of the kingdom of Lan Xang—continued to be the residence of King Sisavangvong and the royal family, as well as that of the supreme patriarch of the Buddhist faith.

Luang Prabang lies deep in the heart of the North, in a narrow valley between rugged karst hills on the east bank of the Mekong River. Remote and difficult to reach, it had little contact with the outside world. The road from Vientiane was seldom passable, and the river voyage slow and treacherous. The city had a good, hard-surfaced airstrip, but flights were unpredictable and often unavailable for long periods of time.

The diplomatic community resided in the administrative capital at Vientiane, but—on arrival in Laos—always traveled to Luang Prabang to present their credentials to the king. During the new year and the more important Buddhist holidays, both Lao and foreign dignitaries gathered in the royal capital to celebrate and pay their respects. But except for those occasions, Luang Prabang was a quiet, bucolic little market town, lost in its vague memories of past glory. Its colorful, old Buddhist temples and decaying, thick-walled masonry buildings left over from the colonial era gave (and still give) it a certain peaceful charm.

Three hundred kilometers downriver from the royal capital is the town of Vientiane. The name is a French corruption of the Lao, Wiang Chan. *Wiang* means town, and *Chan* is translated various ways—but probably moon is correct. When we arrived there in 1963, the population was estimated at 40,000. When we left in 1974 it had risen to over 200,000. But despite the fivefold increase, for some reason the town never seemed to get any larger, or change very much.

Vientiane was—and is—much more accessible than Luang Prabang because of its location near the northeastern terminus of the Thai rail and highway network at Nong Khai. This small Thai town, a few kilometers downriver from Vientiane, also had a vehicular ferry across the Mekong that could handle large trucks. In times of war or peace—with rightist or leftist governments—nearly all imported commodities that came into Vientiane and the northern half of the country, passed through Nong Khai. Most of the trucks originated in Bangkok, and—after clearing customs— proceeded directly to Vientiane to unload. Commodities arriving from Bangkok by rail were usually picked up in Nong Khai by trucks belonging to Lao merchants. In 1994, a bridge spanning the Mekong was completed at Nong Khai—linking Thailand and Laos for the first time. Wattay airport to the north of Vientiane had a good terminal building and an excellent, 3,000-meter concrete runway, both of which were constructed with USAID funding and technical help in the mid-sixties.

The city sprawled along the east bank of the Mekong for about twelve kilometers, in a narrow strip varying in width from one to two kilometers. It was a conglomeration of traditional wooden houses on stilts interspersed with the occasional modern dwelling, usually of two floors. These latter houses were often built by Lao entrepreneurs to rent to the foreign community.

There was one paved street that paralleled the Mekong, and another in the center of town that led away from the river. In the main business district, two or three blocks were paved, but all the other streets throughout the town were dirt. All were rough and pot-holed, and were either muddy or dusty depending on the season. Repaired in the dry season, they immediately deteriorated back to an almost impassable state with the onset of the monsoon.

Coconut palms and banana trees were everywhere, and most of the yards were filled with hibiscus and bougainvillea. The main streets were lined with huge, ancient, flamboyant trees, which were a mass of flaming orange flowers just before the monsoon. The city was lush and unkempt, but it had an appealing and friendly atmosphere.

The business district consisted of two large, open-air fresh food markets, and hundreds of small shops. The markets and shops weren't attractive, but they offered almost anything anyone wanted at reasonable prices. Good French wines and cheese were imported without duty, and were always in plentiful supply; fine tailoring of imported materials was very cheap; skilled Vietnamese goldsmiths fabricated beautiful jewellery—to their design or one of your own—the cost of which, regardless of design, was 25% above the base price of $35 per ounce of gold that it contained; and un-mounted gemstones were smuggled out of Burma, to evade the government monopoly—and were an outstanding bargain. Shopping was fun. It was also a social process—with a pleasant interaction between people, enjoyed at a leisurely pace—and bargaining was expected.

The municipality of Vientiane was made up of about twenty villages, each one with its chief and council of elders, and its houses built around a Buddhist temple or *wat*. Administratively, the village unit was self-sufficient in maintaining its *wat*, streets, drainage, and refuse disposal, as well as law and order.

The municipal government was rudimentary and inefficient. Everyone in a village donated their time and labor to carry out the necessary work under the supervision of the village chief. A water purification plant served the central business area, but most residents used wells or water from the Mekong. There was no sewage system, and waste flowed into seepage pits, or often into open ditches which eventually emptied into the Mekong. Considering such circumstances, gastro-intestinal infections were surprisingly low—probably because everyone sensibly boiled their water before consumption.

The Nam Ngum dam and electrical generating plant, located about sixty kilometers north of Vientiane, provided reliable, cheap electricity to the town and the surrounding countryside. Built with funding from the United States and other Western countries, the dam's sixty megawatt capacity far exceeded the Lao demand, and most of the electricity was (and still is) sold to Thailand.

There was very little crime in Vientiane when we lived there, and seldom did anyone lock a door. Occasionally, Thai thieves would slip across the river at night and rob a house, but excellent security was maintained by the villages. Everyone knew each other, and if strangers came into the village, they were closely watched. The few violent crimes were almost always the result of love or gambling, and never against a stranger. It was perfectly safe for anyone to walk down the darkest street through the worst neighborhood in town.

If Pat and I were both out of town, as we often were, the village chief or one of the neighbors would stop by the house and check with the children and servants to see that all was well. In fact, the only real danger in Vientiane was the chance of getting hit by a stray round during one of the frequent, and usually abortive, political coups.

The government buildings scattered through the central business district were relics of the French colonial past. Most were one-story structures painted a horrible mustard color, with wooden shuttered windows without screens. Nevertheless, they were very cool and comfortable on the inside.

The American Embassy was in the middle of the business district, housed in a small, undistinguished, white brick building. Across the street was the consulate—a newer structure and an architectural nightmare that appeared to be a cross between a Buddhist *wat* and a tribal longhouse.

Next door to the embassy compound was an old, French colonial building that, before 1975, was the headquarters and residence of the Pathet Lao. During the war years the Vientiane government was, in name at least, neutral—and representatives of the communist PL remained in residence in Vientiane throughout the hostilities.

During the Vietnam War era, Vientiane was one of the most important diplomatic posts in the world. Because of the professed neutrality of the country, both the socialist and capitalist nations had diplomatic relations with Laos. It was one of the few places in the world during the Cold War where representatives of both sides could meet on a daily and informal basis. This was particularly true of the incessant round of social affairs that *all* the diplomatic community attended. Many an issue that eventually surfaced officially in Paris, Moscow, Washington, Geneva, or the UN, had been tentatively raised over a cocktail in Vientiane. It was the only place where both the North Vietnamese and Pathet Lao could be contacted at any time one wished to do so.

As a consequence of this unique situation, the rustic little town of Vientiane had a large and cosmopolitan foreign community. Counting the embassy personnel, USAID, CIA, USIS, and the air contractors, there were over 1,200 Americans living and working there at the height of the US involvement. Many other diplomatic missions were also disproportionately large for such a small—and normally inconsequential—country.

☉

Lao cuisine is uniformly uninteresting, but a large number of restaurants specialized in foreign food, offering a wide variety of exotic and delicious choices. Chinese, Vietnamese, French, American, Korean, Thai, Indian, and Filipino restaurants were scattered throughout the town. Some were crude and lacking in décor, but made up for appearances with the excellence of the food. Owners would change, but there were always two or three supper clubs with a pleasant atmosphere for dining, friendly service, and music for dancing. Most often they were run by one of the old French centurions left over from the colonial days—who knew and appreciated good food and wine, and catered well for his customers.

One of the most popular places in Vientiane served nothing but duck soup with noodles. It was always packed, and you would have to wait with the pedicab drivers—and possibly an ambassador or two—for a place to sit. There was also the elegant little *patisserie*, La Pagode, run by a Cambodian who had studied in Paris, which had the most delicious sweets in Asia. With the first cool weather, everyone went to the Mongolian Hot Pot place. You sat at a round table with a hole in the center that contained a large pot of boiling broth. Each diner had a platter of raw meat and vegetables that they quickly cooked in a ladle immersed in the broth, then dipped in a delicious sauce—an Asian *bourguinonne*.

Sunday was the cook's day off. If I wasn't away on a field trip, Pat slept late and I cooked breakfast for the children. The menu varied very little: either waffles or hot cakes with ham, bacon, or sausage. If they were starving, as was often the case, it was waffles *and* hot cakes with ham, bacon *and* sausage.

For Sunday dinner we always went to the Than Dao Vieng—a terrible-looking place, but rightfully considered the best Chinese restaurant in town. The food was served family style, with each dish having sufficient for everyone to take a sample to taste. Becky, Ray, and Walter would each order one of their favorite dishes in rotation—until twelve or fifteen were on the table. This procedure required much long and serious discussion with Charley, the kids' favorite Chinese waiter—and by the time the first dish appeared, everyone was famished. Ray was considered the gourmet authority, and if there was a difference of opinion as to whether a particular dish would be appropriate, his decision was final.

✪

Many holidays and festivals added spice to life in Vientiane. Everyone celebrated not only the Western New Year and the Lao New Year, but also the Chinese New Year, Vietnamese New Year, and Meo New Year. Every village had its annual *boun*—a kind of fair to raise money for the *wat*—which usually lasted for a week. There was also the Rocket Festival, heralding the onset of the rainy season—with huge, home-made missiles fired from scaffolds on a sandbar in the Mekong.

But perhaps the most beautiful celebration was *Loy Katong*—a Buddhist ceremony celebrated annually in November in which one's sins are symbolically transferred to a raft of banana leaves and flowers, and floated away on the river. At the time of the full moon, the rafts—lit with candles and flares, and varying in size from a few centimeters to several meters in length—were released after sunset on both the Lao and Thai sides of the Mekong. The whole river appeared to be on fire, making for a spectacular and wonderful sight.

That Luang, a famous, old Vientiane *wat* held a week-long fair each year to commemorate its founding, and to raise funds for its preservation. The event was much like a state fair in the US, with agricultural competitions, exhibits by local and foreign organizations, food stalls, gambling games, rides for kids, and music and dancing at night. It was usually a fun occasion but was unfortunately twice marred by frustrated gamblers hurling fragmentation grenades into the crowd.

At the end of the rainy season and before the start of the rice harvest, boat races were held for several successive weekends in an elimination contest. On the final weekend, thousands of people lined the banks of the Mekong to watch and gamble on the races; picnic, sing, dance, and get drunk; jump in the river; and cheer their boat. There were other events too numerous to mention.

✪

Innumerable bars were scattered throughout the town—most of them similar in some ways to the neighborhood bar in the US. The clientele lived near the bar, and would meet there in the evening to drink and socialize. A liter of the local rice whiskey cost the equivalent of fifty cents, and was very strong—often over 100 proof.

Bars changed hands frequently, but there were always a half dozen or so that catered to the expatriates—with good imported whiskey, wine and beer; Western-style snacks; and the inevitable dart boards. One of the bars most frequented by the expatriates was called the Purple Porpoise. It was owned by a retired American pilot whose liver only lasted four years before he died of cirrhosis.

Drugs were cheap and readily available in Vientiane. Marijuana was sold openly in the market just like any other herb, and was used to season certain foods—especially soup. Highly purified heroin was so cheap that an addict could support a big habit for a dollar or two a day. However, there were few heroin addicts other than the handful of Western hippies who wandered through from time to time. Opium smoking was certainly the most prevalent addiction. Licensed opium dens in large part catered to a small, registered subculture of addicts who were almost all local people.

The foreign community that lived and worked in Laos hardly ever became involved with drugs, despite their cheap and easy availability. They all preferred to drink—and alcohol addiction was particularly high among the expatriate wives. Everyone could afford a house full of servants, so the ladies had little to do. Like expat wives throughout the ages, boredom and inactivity frequently led them to the bottle.

Recreational sex was a thriving business in Vientiane and all the other towns of Laos—as it was in the rest of Southeast Asia. However, it seemed to have a different aura than it had in the Western world. There was little, if any, moral overtone, and no great stigma on the girls who were prostitutes—or the men who frequented them.

Most of those who sold their bodies were pretty teenage girls from poor families in a society in which prostitution was an accepted—and even laudatory—way to help relieve the burden of poverty. They entered the profession voluntarily, in some instances eagerly, and seemed to enjoy their work—at least most did not seem distressed by their circumstances. Future marriage prospects were certainly not impaired, but rather seemed to be enhanced. After a few years in the business, these girls usually made a successful marriage and became good mothers and wives.

There were a few typical brothels, but most of the girls worked in the bars, entertaining the customers as well as serving the tables. Most bars had a private room, but usually a customer would take a girl off to his or her home. The cost was moderate, and seldom exceeded ten dollars for a night. Often, one of the foreigners who was single, or without his wife, would take one of the girls to live with him. During the day she performed the role of housemaid, and at night shared his bed. In general, this hypocrisy was frowned upon. Nevertheless, a few of these relationships developed into a real and lasting love.

Some establishments specialized. Lulu's, adjacent to the Natasin—the Lao School of Fine Arts—was known throughout Southeast Asia for its oral sex services. Madame Lulu, the proprietor, was a faded French lady in her fifties who had been the mistress of a long succession of French colonial administrators. She had trained her girls to a high level of erotic proficiency. Most were Vietnamese, because Lao girls—according to Madame Lulu—never seemed to get the knack of it.

Probably the most famous place in Vientiane was the White Rose, which had an erotic floor-show each night with an unforgettable climax. A pretty little naked nymph, Suzie, slowly lit a pack of cigarettes one by one as she undulated around the floor to the music. She then stuck each one into the introitus of her vagina until all twenty—through some remarkable muscular control—were giving off puffs of smoke. After she had smoked them down a little, each cigarette was presented to one of the cheering spectators.

One of the more interesting brothels was known simply as the Red Chinese Whorehouse. The girls had been specially trained in the Peoples Republic Of China, and spoke poor but understandable English. They traded sex for information of a political or military nature. Some misguided souls who thought it smart to trade these ladies fabricated stories for their sexual favors found that their misinformation could have crippling consequences on some dark night.

Most people who lived in Vientiane for any length of time fell in love with the place. But it wasn't really a place, so much as a state of mind. Vientiane in those days was like a gaudy lady past her prime—disreputable and fun-loving, but with a kind heart and charming personality—and you couldn't help but love the old gal.

At least that's the way it was before the communists took over.

Evacuation at Hua Muang

In 1966, after the enemy had taken Hong Non, where Tony Poe was wounded, pressure was again building up at our base at Hua Muang. Colonel Thong was reporting large movements of troops on Route 6 near his headquarters at Phu Kuk. Certainly, the enemy intended to wipe out the Hua Muang enclave this time round.

Thong got everyone together at Hua Muang and informed us that we should be ready to evacuate the place any time after the next two weeks. A contingency plan should be made to move the whole operation further to the southwest. Hopefully, the evacuation wouldn't be necessary. He would try to hold out at Phu Kuk as long as he was able, and possibly the enemy wouldn't press the attack to Hua Muang. However, under no circumstance could he get into a set-piece defence of the area. The casualties would be far too high.

We were much too close to Route 6—the enemy's main route of communication into this area and the Plain of Jars. Since losing the Hong Non area, Thong's left flank was exposed, and he didn't have the maneuvring room he needed for his guerilla type of operation.

Since we intended to stay at Hua Muang as long as possible, in the hope that it wouldn't fall, it would be better to have some place to the southwest, but not too far away, where the people in the whole friendly area could assemble. They could walk to the selected location, where we could get in supplies and care for them. Later, we could move everyone in an orderly fashion to a secure area more remote from Route 6.

Tony had made a good recovery from his wound, and was back in action, spending a lot of time upcountry at Hua Muang and at Phu Kuk, working with Thong and Colonel Phan, who had replaced Khamsao (who was arrested and jailed for supporting General Khamkhong after the Phoumi-Kouprasith coup).

One night we discussed the contingency plan, and particularly where the assembly point should be. It would be difficult to work from any of the small Helio strips in the area, and there were no other (longer) strips that could take our larger aircraft. Thong suggested we take a look at Na Khang (LS36), and it was decided that Pop and I would go there the next morning as soon as we had a plane.

Na Khang was a small paddy area about thirty kilometers to the southwest. The small village there had been abandoned. There was only a short, overgrown STOL strip, but there was probably enough room to build a longer one that would take our big birds. It would be tight, but it looked possible. However, to build a larger strip, we would need some heavy equipment and a big chopper to get it to Na Khang. Pop and I decided we should try it. I would go to Vientiane immediately and see what could be done.

We returned to Hua Muang, then I took a Helio to Vientiane. Fortunately, Charley Mann was in his office, and I was able to convince him of the necessity to get the strip built. Charley called Tom Cole, the head of USAID public works, and Colonel "Pappy" Pettigrew, the air attache, and asked them to come to his office. Tom said he was good to go, just let him know when, and Pappy agreed to give us a Chinook to deliver Tom's heavy machinery if the ambassador gave the okay. Charley would take up the question at the country team meeting the next morning. I tried to impress on all three of the necessity for haste. The strip would have to be finished in less than two weeks.

Ambassador Sullivan and the country team agreed to our request, with the one exception of Ted Shackley, the CIA station chief. Shackley said that if we wanted to build an airstrip at Na Khang it was okay with him, but the CIA had no interest in such a project. Ironically, Na Khang soon became the base for CIA operations in the area until it was knocked out by the Vietnamese three years later.

Twelve days after the meeting in Vientiane, Eric Shilling, a Flying Tiger veteran from China, greased a Bird & Sons C47 into the new strip at Na Khang and took off again without any trouble. If the old "gooney bird" could get in and out, our larger STOL planes would have no problem.

Unfortunately, Thong's worst-case scenario developed. Within a week he informed us that the enemy was all over the place and he would need to start a slow withdrawal from Phu Kuk and fall back on Hua Muang. Possibly, the enemy would stop after they took Phu Kuk.

Since we had several thousand refugees slowly filtering into Hua Muang and were also taking a few casualties, Pop and I were spending most of our time there. Tony had come up from Long Chieng one particular morning, and went to Phu Kuk to work with Thong. We had a chopper and a Helio shuttling between the two places, which brought out the sick and wounded from Phu Kuk, and took in supplies from Hua Muang that Thong and Tony requested.

By mid-afternoon Jack Houston, the Helio pilot, reported that all the civilians were fleeing Phu Kuk and the situation was deteriorating. Tony had told Jack to make one more trip and then he'd return to Hua Muang on the Helio with him.

A round trip to Phu Kuk took about twenty minutes at the most. Close to an hour elapsed, but Jack and Tony hadn't returned. It was getting close to sunset and we couldn't raise Jack on the radio. The chopper had been on the ground at Hua Muang for about a half hour, and the pilot said Jack was waiting for Tony when he left Phu Kuk. Pop and I had a bad feeling there was trouble.

I got in the chopper and we set out to find Tony and Jack. There was a well-marked footpath running east to Phu Kuk, and we could see people scurrying toward Hua Muang. When we got in the Phu Kuk area, the place appeared deserted and we started to draw small arms fire. The pilot turned back, and two or three minutes later, we saw the Helio pancaked against the side of a steep hill.

There was no place to sit down, so the pilot hovered over the wreck. The plane wasn't badly damaged and no one was in the area. Hopefully, the passengers weren't seriously injured and were walking toward Hua Muang. We flew up over the trail, and soon saw a crowd of people. I had the pilot find a place to land. The fleeing refugees had seen the two Americans. Neither was badly injured and they were only a short distance down the trail.

A couple of minutes later, this bear came running up with his old Marine campaign hat and filthy fatigues. He picked me up and kissed me on both cheeks. "Goddammit Doc, you sweet old fart. I knew you'd make it."

"Tony put me down, you smelly bastard. You're breaking my ribs. Where's Jack?"

"Not far behind. The people found him a horse to ride but it was too damn slow for me. I left him when I heard the chopper to go get help, but he's okay."

It was getting dark, and the old H34 wasn't supposed be flying at night. I was trying to decide what to do when we saw Jack coming up the trail. He was on a tiny mountain pony, feet dragging the ground, flailing away with a stick, scared to death we'd take off before we saw him. Suddenly, he jumped off the horse and came running up to the chopper.

Ten minutes later, we landed at Hua Muang in the dark. Pop and Colonel Phan had a couple of jars of *lao hai* ready. Tony, Jack, the chopper pilot, and I grabbed bamboo straws and sucked up the first jar in about five minutes. It was good to be home safe.

Jack told us what had happened after they took off.

"The engine checked out okay, but even considering we were a bit overloaded, it didn't accelerate well on take-off. We wobbled off the ground but couldn't gain any altitude. I thought I was going in, but I wanted to get as far away from Phu Kuk as possible. The engine got sicker and sicker. I picked that little open spot and made one of my best landings ever. Soon as we got out of the plane, those good people were there to help us."

A few weeks later, Jack was murdered by a drunken FAR officer in Vientiane. Jack had parked his car in such a way that it prevented the officer from backing out.

☻☻☻

About a week later, enemy patrols were probing Hua Muang. We made an orderly move to Na Khang and there were few casualties. Unfortunately, Thong's plan to set up an enclave for the Hua Muang partisans farther to the west, away from the enemy's lines of communication, particularly Route 6, never came about. Tony, Thong, and Phan all realized the weakness of Na Khang, but after the eventual fall of Hua Muang, Thong and Phan were killed, and Tony was transferred to Nam You in Nam Tha province.

Most of the civilians moved west over to Muang Heim, and slowly filtered south of the Plain of Jars and ended up in the Ban Son area. The troops were kept at Na Khang because of American priorities, and were trapped in exactly the situation Thong wanted to avoid—a set-piece static defense. In a very short time, these guerrilla troops suffered a terrible attrition defending a place of little tactical importance, as far as the defense of Sam Neua was concerned. They certainly didn't have the weapons or training for this type of warfare.

Nevertheless, Na Khang had become important as a support facility for the radar installations on Phu Pha Thi that controlled the US bombing of North Vietnam. Also, it was a jumping off place for SAR attempts to pick up American airmen shot down over the Ho Chi Minh trail. In addition, it tied up Vietnamese military assets that could be used in South Vietnam. It wasn't abandoned as Thong had originally intended, but was eventually knocked out by the Vietnamese after several failed, bloody assaults.

The Opium Proposal

It seemed like a good time to get out of town for a few days. Pat was in a rage. She, VP, and Vint Lawrence had been working on a project for several weeks that would have cured one of VP's many small but annoying headaches.

It was a very simple proposal: the United States government would buy the Meo opium crop each year.

Just as opium was purchased from Turkey and Mexico for legitimate medical purposes, the portion of the Meo crop that could be marketed through Long Chieng would enter the same legal channels.

VP was never involved in the Golden Triangle opium trade, or any other peripheral source of opium. His only interest was the opium grown by the Meo who were his tribal adherents. The Meo farmers had to have a mechanism to market the opium crop—a middle man. Our aerial surveys had shown that Laos was producing about 35 tons of opium each year—and approximately 25 tons of it was produced in the areas accessible through Long Chieng. Five tons were consumed locally, and about twenty tons were sold to various buyers.

At that time, the farmer received from 12–15 dollars per kilogram. To buy the whole crop would cost only 250,000–300,000 dollars. Even if there was no need for the additional opium in the US pharmaceutical industry, buying and destroying it still made sense. It should be borne in mind that the growing and sale of opium was completely legal at the time, and broke no laws of the Lao government.

Contrary to many misinformed, self-seeking authors', reporters', and politicians' impressions, VP never exploited, or had any great interest in, the opium trade. Stories and reports of heroin refineries at Long Chieng are asinine and completely false. It is true that his agents bought and sold a good part of the Meo opium crop, but this activity was more in the nature of a duty, as well as a prerogative of his role as tribal leader.

The complaints of the farmers; having to dealing with the feuding Meo hierarchy; and negotiating with the people who bought the crop were all minor but periodic hassles that he preferred not to be bothered with. There were other, more pressing matters occupying his time and mind. In addition, he was becoming increasingly concerned that the media publicity surrounding the opium trade was hurting the Meo cause politically at the Washington level.

Pat had become interested in the opium trade in Laos and the Golden Triangle area soon after our arrival in Laos. Three or four years later, purely by chance, she had been caught in the middle of a shoot-out over control of the opium crop coming out of Burma.

The Lao military, the KMT, and the Shan clashed in Nam Tha province in the Golden Triangle area, and after witnessing that bloody, little war, she researched the history and (then) current dynamics of the opium trade and became quite expert on the subject. One thing in particular she found out was that VP would be happy to get out of his part of the business.

When Pat talked to VP and Vint Lawrence about such a proposal, both were very enthusiastic. They worked out some of the details of pricing and logistics, Pat put it down on paper, and she presented it first to Norm Sweet, the USAID program officer, and then to Charley Mann. Both Norm and Charley thought it was a great idea, and—after checking it out with the ambassador—they polished the proposal and got it off to USAID Washington for consideration.

The bureaucrats in DC were horrified. Under no circumstance was the Laos USAID mission to get involved in any aspect of the opium business. Pat and Vint were mad as hell, and VP was greatly disappointed. A wonderful opportunity was lost that would have prevented many problems that arose in the future.

When the news came through, I did indeed skip town for a few days.

Escape from Khang Khay

Boun Mi was born in a remote Khamu village in the southwest part of Luang Prabang province. There were about thirty bamboo-and-thatch houses built up on stilts in his village that housed slightly more than 200 people. The Khamu raised hill rice and hunted and fished for a living. Most of their few items of clothing were made of cloth woven from jungle fibres on a primitive back strap loom, but they also liked to trade for ready-made clothes when they had the opportunity.

Like many of the tribal people, the only essential needs which they couldn't supply themselves were salt and the iron bars used for making knives, axes, hoes, and other tools. To buy these two items, the villagers gathered sticlac and bee's wax in the jungle, and once or twice a year, a few of the men went down to the Mekong and took a boat to Luang Prabang. They sold these products and bought salt and iron. If there was enough money left, they would also buy cloth and possibly ready-made clothing.

Four or five of the adult males in the village could speak a little Lao, but no one could read or write. There was no school of course, nor a Buddhist *wat* to take the place of one. The people prayed to the good spirits in the trees and the streams, and performed the proper ceremonies to appease the powerful spirits of the tiger and the bear. If the cause of an illness was in doubt, the entrails of a sacrificial chicken were consulted to reveal which spirit had been offended, and what course of action should be followed to restore the person to a good state of health. The rhythm of the annual monsoon rains dictated the cycle of planting and harvest, and even of courtship and marriage; of life itself.

Boun Mi had just reached young manhood and was thinking about getting married. Around 1960, he had gone to Luang Prabang with the older men to buy salt and iron. It was the first time he had traveled more than a few kilometers from home, and he found the town a strange, frightening, but fascinating place.

Fortunately, he had learned to speak a little Lao, and could communicate with the merchants. He bought some brightly-colored cloth for his mother, and some perfumed soap for his sisters. The only wheeled vehicle he had ever seen was the ox cart in the Lao village down in the valley close to his village. However, he was captivated by the few motor vehicles in Luang Prabang, and the daring men who controlled such awesome monsters.

After he returned home from the trip, he often had dreams in which he'd be driving a huge truck like the ones he had seen in town, and everyone would be admiring how brave and clever he was.

Not long after the trip to Luang Prabang, a small group of Pathet Lao political cadre came into the village on a recruiting mission. The PL had been there before, and usually stayed the night after holding a meeting and haranguing the people for a few hours.

The villagers had no understanding or interest in the political views of their visitors, and were always happy and relieved when they departed the next morning—despite the loss of the rice they took from them. However, on this occasion the visit had a much different purpose. The cadre were recruiting young men for the military, and they painted an exciting and attractive picture of life in the Peoples Liberation Army. The new soldiers would not only be fighting to free their country from the oppressive, feudal RLG and the neocolonialist Americans, but they would also have new uniforms, plenty of good food, and regular pay. If they worked and studied hard, they would even be taught to fly airplanes and drive motor vehicles.

Neither Boun Mi nor any of the other young Khamu men had any conception of belonging to any country; had never seen a RLG official that they recognized as such; and certainly had never heard of Americans except from the Pathet Lao. Still, life in the PLA sounded wonderful to Boun Mi. If he could become a truck driver, that would be the ultimate experience.

The communist propaganda succeeded. The next morning, Boun Mi and five others left with the PL cadre. Their families and the whole village were grief stricken. Losing six of the finest young men in their small village was indeed a tragedy to these simple people.

✛

Four years later, Boun Mi was a sergeant in the PLA, confined in a political prison at the town of Khang Khay on the Plain of Jars in Xieng Khoung province.

He was a bright young man, and through hard work and study had advanced rapidly in the army. However, none of the long political sessions he had to attend day after day made any sense to him, and he found them not only boring and a nuisance, but inappropriate for his people and village. More importantly, in spite of his repeated attempts, he'd not been able to go to drivers school. It seemed that the PL only picked the better-educated ethnic Lao for such training, and consequently—being a Khamu—he would never attain his dream.

For a long time he was able to conceal his frustration, but unfortunately, after a while, his dissension and lack of political conformity became more and more apparent. Finally, he was thrown in prison.

✪✪✪

Charles Klusmann was a young navy pilot flying off the carrier, Kitty Hawk, which was on station in the South China Sea. Although prohibited under the Geneva Accords, the US had been making secret reconnaissance flights over Laos for a long time. No aggressive action could be taken by US aircraft, but if threatened, the pilot could take defensive or suppressive measures as he deemed necessary.

On June 6th, 1964 Klusmann was flying a reconnaissance mission over the Plain of Jars. He was on a westerly course at 500 feet with a speed of 550 knots. It was the third time he had flown the same mission in the previous few days. On both of the two other missions he'd been hit by ground fire. The Vietnamese operated several 40mm AA batteries in the area, and they were quite accurate. On the last mission, Klusmann had a very sick bird, but he limped back to the Kittyhawk and made a successful landing.

However, fate would not be denied. On the third mission in the same area, possibly the same guns hit him again. In the vicinity of Ban Ban, the hills on the sides of Route 7 came alive with the flame of automatic weapons fire. This time he wasn't so fortunate. The plane started to vibrate violently, and it felt as if it would disintegrate.

Klusmann gave a "mayday" on 121.5mhz, described the area he was in, and scrambled for altitude. First, there was loss of aileron control, then—at 10,000 feet—the rudder was unresponsive. The plane started to spiral to the right and was uncontrollable. He ejected.

Klusmann hit the ground in the foothills on the east side of the Plain of Jars; the most heavily-defended enemy area in Laos. He bruised his right leg badly, but was in good condition otherwise.

At the same time, Lee Mullins was flying a Helio Courier south of the PDJ, and Pop and I were working with two choppers north of the PDJ from a refugee site called Ban Song (LS29). Lee was monitoring the emergency frequency and heard Klusmann's "mayday." He immediately called us with the news there was an American airman down on the PDJ, and the general area in which he thought the pilot was located. I told Lee to go in high and see if he could spot him from the air. Pop and I would start into the area from the north with our two choppers. If Lee could find the American, he could guide one of us in to try to make the pick-up.

As soon as we got out of the hills, we began to take a lot of ground fire—but it was all from small arms, and we were high enough to make it ineffective. About ten minutes later, we got a call from Lee saying he could see the pilot on the ground being chased by several dozen of the enemy. The area was open, rolling grassy hills with no cover. No doubt the NVA and PL had seen the parachute open, and then spotted the pilot himself before very long.

Lee told us we were about two kilometers straight north of the pilot. At the same time we saw his Helio, we also saw a De Havilland Caribou flown by Bob Letourner. Both aircraft were right on the deck making passes at ground level, as if they were spraying a cotton field. We could see a figure chased by a large group of soldiers. Lee and Bob were trying to hit the enemy soldiers with their landing gear to slow up the pursuit of the American, and possibly allow him to escape. All the aircraft were unarmed, of course, and these desperate efforts were in vain. Our chopper pilots made several attempts to get to the fleeing man, but the enemy soldiers were right on top of him, and we drew extremely heavy fire.

In a minute or two, we saw that he was captured and was being led away by one group of soldiers. All the other troops were busy firing at our planes. With mixed emotions of anguish and relief, we broke off and started out of the area. At least we knew the pilot survived and he wasn't seriously injured.

That night Charles Klusmann was put in the same prison with Boun Mi, our disenchanted Pathet Lao sergeant. Klusmann had the dubious distinction of being the first American military pilot lost over Laos.

The chopper I was in had taken several rounds of fire, but no one was injured, and the aircraft performed normally. Unfortunately, the pilot of the other chopper that Pop was in reported trouble controlling his aircraft. It vibrated very badly, and the PARU guide in the left seat had been hit in the head. The wounded man was bleeding profusely and falling on the controls. Pop and the flight mechanic, who were both in the cargo compartment, couldn't get the wounded man out of the seat and down into the cargo compartment with them—or get up into the cockpit to help him.

Both choppers were old Sikorsky H34s, which have a cockpit with two seats elevated about four feet above the cargo compartment. The opening between the cockpit and cargo area is very small and difficult to climb through, even when no one is sitting at the controls.

The damaged chopper would only make about 45 knots, and—flying alongside—we could see the pilot struggling to keep it airborne. Pop and the flight mechanic were sticking arms and hands up into the cockpit trying to press a bandage against the wounded man's head. With a lot of luck, both choppers made it to Boum Long (LS32), the nearest friendly enclave in the hills on the northern periphery of the PDJ.

Pichit, the wounded Thai PARU soldier, was unconscious and in shock. He had a long grazing wound across the top of his skull, but the bullet hadn't penetrated the brain case. I got an IV started with Dextran, and bandaged his wound. In a short time, his pulse was strong and his color was good, but he was still unconscious. I called in a Pilatus Porter that was working in the area, and took Pichit to the Thai military hospital in Udorn.

The pilot who was flying the badly damaged chopper was shaken up. He refused to fly again that day, even as a passenger, so Pop spent the night with him at Boum Long. We would send a plane for them the next morning. After considerable Meo corn whiskey and a night of sound sleep, our pilot was as good as new.

☉ ☉ ☉

VP had good intelligence as to what was happening on the Plain of Jars, and we received regular reports that Klusmann was being treated well, and that he was in good health. About three months after he was shot down, we heard that he'd escaped.

On September 1st, 1964, I was working in Xieng Khoung province, and stopped at Long Chieng to see one of VP's children. The child had been seriously ill a few days previously, and Pat had taken care of him. Since I would be in the area, Pat asked me to stop by and check to be sure her little patient was getting well. I had seen the child—who was running around playing—and was sitting chatting and drinking tea with VP on the porch of his house when one of the radio operators ran up very excited. He had just received a message from Sua Pao, the commander at Boum Long, that his soldiers had contacted the American pilot. He was with a Pathet Lao sergeant who had also been a prisoner. Sua Pao's soldiers were bringing them into Boum Long.

VP and I jumped into his Jeep and raced down to the airstrip to get a plane to collect the American. However, in the excitement, the general forgot that he had a big staff meeting that afternoon and couldn't possibly leave. Reluctantly, he told me to go alone, and I took off in a Porter for Boum Long on the north side of the Plain of Jars.

When we landed at the tiny, dirt strip high on a rugged mountain ridge, the people who ran out to meet the plane, told me that the American hadn't yet arrived. He was at the village at the bottom of the mountain. Sua Pao came up about that time, and we decided to walk down to the village and meet the escapees and their escort.

We had only gone a short distance when we saw a tall, heavily-bearded Westerner coming up the trail surrounded by a group of Meo soldiers. They were in the middle of a swarm of men, women, and children. Everyone was laughing and shouting, and the children were all crowding around to get a close look at this strange, friendly foreigner who obviously enjoyed the excitement. Boun Mi, the Pathet Lao sergeant trailed along with a smiling, yet frightened, apprehensive look on his face.

Klusmann was delighted to see an American, and I was just as happy to see him. I explained who I was, and that I would fly him out of Laos. As we talked, I was puzzled by the appearance of both Klusmann's and Boun Mi's face and hands. They were a bright, iridescent red. It transpired that, in running through the tough saw grass on the Plain of Jars, they suffered innumerable little cuts from the sharp blades of the plants. The Meo medic who was with the soldiers had painted them with red tincture of merthiolate almost from head to foot. For once I had a camera with me, and took some pictures of the happy American and his Lao buddy. Unfortunately, the film was black and white, and the pictures don't show the iridescent redness of their faces.

It was getting late in the day, and I had wanted to take Boun Mi to Sam Thong, but it would be too dark to land on the unlit, dirt strip. I asked Sua Pao, the Boum Long leader, to see that Boun Mi was well cared for, and we would send a plane for him in the morning. When we were airborne, I contacted Ambassador Sullivan in Vientiane by HF radio and told him whom we had aboard, and that he was in good shape both physically and mentally.

We had a simple voice code which changed each month for such communications. The ambassador told me I was not to land in Laos, but to proceed to Udorn. He would contact them, and have the proper authorities meet us when we landed.

The Pilatus Porter is a slow STOL plane, and the flight from Boum Long to Udorn took over two hours, allowing us some time to talk about the day he was shot down.

The young naval pilot was simply euphoric at having successfully escaped. He talked and laughed the entire trip. The hair-raising events of that afternoon three months ago were suddenly hilariously funny. We laughed until we had tears in our eyes about the NVA and PL chasing him across the plain as Lee and Bob dived around with the Helio and Caribou trying to take the heads off the enemy soldiers, and the two old H34s flopping around getting shot to pieces.

After his capture, he wasn't harmed, but he had bruised his leg badly on hitting the ground after bailing out. His captors walked him to Xieng Khoungville, and with the injured leg he was in considerable pain. From there he was put on a truck and taken to the prison at Khang Khay, where he was kept isolated in a dark hut for 53 days. However, no one ever abused him physically, and he was well fed, and even given medicine when he was ill.

During this period of isolation, he made one attempt to escape by tunnelling. After loosening the dirt and carefully replacing it night after night, he ran into stakes driven far below the surface which he couldn't possibly break through. He was terribly depressed but didn't give up hope. He exercised constantly in his tiny cell. If he had the opportunity to escape, he wanted to be in the best physical condition possible.

After this long period of solitary confinement, he was put into a compound with 36 other prisoners, and his morale improved greatly with the companionship. Most of his fellow inmates were disgruntled Pathet Lao who had foolishly spoken out against the administration, or openly disagreed with the political cadre. He was able to communicate with the Lao prisoners through an English-Lao dictionary and a bit of French. He also learned a few words of Lao.

Soon after his captors moved him into the compound, one of the prisoners approached him about trying to escape. At first Klusmann didn't trust the man and would have nothing to do with him. Nevertheless, the man was extremely persistent. He insisted that if he successfully escaped by himself, the "Phoumis" would surely kill him (Phoumi derived from General Phoumi Nosavan, i.e. Rightist). On the other hand, if he escaped with an American, the Phoumis wouldn't kill him, and might even reward him.

Finally, he convinced Klusmann of his sincerity. They would try to slip under the barbed wire barricade during the night of August 28th.

Unfortunately, the guards soon found some hoarded rice—which suggested an escape attempt—thus causing them to increase their vigilance. However, when nothing happened in the period after that discovery, the guards relaxed.

On the night of the 29th, the escapees slipped under the wire. Much to Klusmann's surprise, he was accompanied not by one, but by five of his fellow prisoners. They divided into two groups of three, with the intention of rejoining at a predetermined rendezvous. It would be more difficult for their pursuers to follow two trails than one.

Klusmann's group included the man with whom he had planned the escape, and Boun Mi. They reached the rendezvous site, but the other group didn't arrive within a reasonable time, so they continued their flight.

Toward the end of the first day, they came to a small village. In spite of Klusmann's and Boun Mi's protestations, the third man decided to go into the village to beg some rice. While they watched from a small hill some distance away, they saw PL soldiers re-capture the man almost immediately. Quickly, the PL began the search for the other two escapees, but Boun Mi and Klusmann doubled back on the trail and slipped away. Boun Mi knew exactly where to go, and they had no more difficulty. After two more wet, cold, miserable days and nights, they reached the safety of Boum Long.

✪

Just about the time Klusmann finished his story, we could see the moonlight shining on the Mekong River. We crossed into Thailand and the pilot began to descend. Suddenly Klusmann was very quiet, and he appeared serious and thoughtful. I believe it was only then that he realized his ordeal was over.

When we landed at Udorn, before the Porter stopped rolling, three or four blue US Air Force vehicles pulled up to the side of the plane. The lighting was poor on the taxiway, and as soon as Klusmann got off the plane, a group of uniformed American officers immediately stuffed him in a vehicle. When I got off a few seconds later, everyone had raced over to a building about 200 meters away and disappeared through a door. No one had said a word to me and Klusmann, and I hadn't even had a chance to shake his hand or say goodbye. For some reason I felt ill-used.

I started over to the building to find Klusmann, but then changed my mind and said to hell with it. I got back in the plane and told the pilot I was ready to leave. We were taxiing back out to take off for Vientiane when I noticed that Klusmann had left a small cloth bag on the plane. In the dark, it felt like the bag contained personal articles, and it occurred to me that he might want them as mementos of his captivity. I asked the pilot to taxi back.

When the plane stopped, I got out and tried to enter the building, but the door was locked. After banging for a minute or two, a narrow slit of light appeared and I told the eyes and nose in the light that I wanted to see Klusmann. The eyes and nose said there was no one by that name in the building, and the slit of light disappeared. Again, after considerable banging, the narrow slit of light reappeared, and this time I pushed the door open enough to stick the bag inside and yell that it was Klusmann's.

At this time the United States was still publicly proclaiming respect for the Geneva Accords and the neutrality of Laos. There were no flights over the country, and—of course—Klusmann did not exist.

The next day, we picked up Boun Mi at Boum Long and took him to Sam Thong. Pop put him to work in the warehouse helping to load and unload refugee supplies. He was a quiet, hard-working young man, very pleasant to know, and we all liked him greatly.

❂❂❂

About a year or two later, I was sitting at my desk working in Vientiane when Boun Mi walked in. There was a big smile on his face, and he was obviously delighted about something. He didn't say anything, but reached in his shirt pocket and took out a little card. With an air of great satisfaction I was presented with his Lao driver's license. This was the most memorable day of his life, as he had finally attained his dream. Pop had sent him to drivers' school in Vientiane, and his class had taken their test that day. Now he could drive and control one of those great iron monsters as well as anyone.

That night, I took him and some of his driving classmates to dinner to celebrate. I'm not sure which of us was the happiest when Boun Mi proudly drove us to the restaurant through the streets of Vientiane in my old Valiant station wagon.

Back in the USA

B y 1966, Pat and I had been in Laos for a little over three years, and the personnel office at USAID Washington was getting insistent that we take home leave, which was supposed to come at the end of the second year of an overseas tour of duty. Repatriation on a regular basis was considered important to keep one from losing American identity and perspective. For the convenience of the government, the tour can be extended or shortened by three months, but the regulations are very rigid otherwise.

Despite these regulations, we had been too busy to consider leave, and had even refused to make the necessary travel arrangements. As far as we were concerned, we were fighting a war. How in the hell could we take off when the people we loved and were trying to help were dying around us? Nevertheless, things had reached the point where Charley Mann could no longer resist Washington's demands. We had to go to the States whether we liked it or not.

Fortunately, the mission had been able to increase the American staffing in the public health division during the previous year. Particularly, Dr. Joseph Westermeyer had come on board as my deputy. Joe and his wife Rachel were an attractive young couple from Minnesota who had quickly adapted to life in Laos. Both were rapidly acquiring proficiency in the language, and had fallen in love with the country and the people as the rest of us had done. They were becoming an increasingly valuable asset to the program with each day. With Joe to take over, we could delay our departure no longer.

We would spend two weeks traveling through Europe, then proceed to Washington where there would be a USAID debriefing and meetings with the administrative people concerned with Lao affairs. As soon as we were finished in Washington, we would fly down to Mississippi and stay with Pat's parents in Biloxi. Most of our friends and relatives were in Mississippi, Louisiana, and Texas, so Biloxi would be the center of our vacation. After six weeks of relaxation and visiting friends and relatives, we would take off across the Pacific, stopping in Japan and Hong Kong on the way back to Laos.

Things went well in Athens, but Becky started running high fever in Rome; Walter in Madrid; and Ray in Lisbon. They were passing a streptococcus around. Nothing serious, but a dismal start to a vacation.

Washington was particularly depressing and upsetting. People would continually confuse Vientiane with Vietnam. No one could focus on the problems of Laos, other than in the larger context of the Vietnam War. As a distinct and significant entity, the country just didn't exist at the Washington level. In particular, no one seemed to be aware of what we were doing. Worst of all, there was little interest in finding out—even by the people who were supposed to be supporting us. We left the capital greatly disgruntled and with deflated egos.

It was wonderful to see Grandpa and Grandma McCreedy, friends, brothers, sisters, cousins, aunts, and uncles for a week or so—but six weeks of family and friends was four or five weeks too long. With a sigh of relief, we took off for the Far East.

The huge room at the Takanawa Prince in Tokyo—where all five of us slept in the one big bed on the floor, and told stories and played word games most of the night—was wonderful. Likewise, we all delighted in getting to Hong Kong and the Hilton. This was familiar turf; the kids never tired of riding the Star Ferry back and forth from Hong Kong to Kowloon, and climbing around the Tiger Balm Gardens.

Ten weeks of vacation was plenty long enough, and everyone gave a little cheer when they saw the big, muddy Mekong under the wing of the old DC3 as we approached Vientiane for the landing.

Joe Westermeyer met us at the airport. He'd held the fort—and nothing too exciting or catastrophic had happened while we were gone. The whole family was happy and relieved to be home again. Thank God vacations only came every three and a half years.

That evening, as Pat and I sat around having a drink, we reviewed the accomplishments of those three-and-a-half years.

We had developed good working relationships with our Lao counterparts from the ministerial down to the village level. The village health program now operated in every province in the country. Even in the provinces of Phong Saly, Saravane, and Attopeu—which were supposedly communist strongholds—we had active, expanding programs. There were about 150 sites that had USAID-supported medical activities. The exact number varied almost daily because of the unstable security situation in many areas, but the trend was always upward.

In the past year, there had been over three million outpatient visits to the facilities; 60,000 patients had been hospitalized; and 15,000 war casualties had been treated. Unfortunately, this trend was also upward. An efficient system for the evacuation of troops injured in combat was functioning. A soldier wounded before five o'clock in the afternoon, would be hospitalized that day. After five, he would be hospitalized by mid-morning of the next day. Evacuation of casualties had top priority on all aircraft.

The main emphasis of the medical program was support to the irregular military and the population from which they were drawn—who were doing most of the fighting to keep the country from falling to the communists. Ostensibly, we were supporting refugees, but our definition of a refugee was simple, pragmatic, and flexible. Refugees were those population groups who were willing to take defensive or aggressive action against the communist invader, whether they had been displaced from their homes or not. These were, in large part, the people who *were* being displaced from their homes by the enemy, and were in fact real refugees. Everyone wanted medical care. It was a strongly-felt need. The medical program, in addition to fulfilling a humanitarian purpose, was also an important means of introducing other programs. It was the *entrée*; the foot in the door.

After the medical program, the greatest need was for primary schools. Despite the resistance from our own people, we continued to build our bamboo-and-thatch schools—and they thrived. The education program was crude but effective, and the children had tremendous motivation.

To this day, I still wonder at the bizarre experience of sitting in a USAID staff meeting in Vientiane and hearing an American Ph.D educator rage about the "bootleg teachers and clandestine schools" Buell and Weldon were building in the hills. He had certainly forgotten his pioneering heritage, and what had made his country a great nation.

All in all we were pleased with our efforts over those first three-and-a-half years. People were being fed and rehabilitated when displaced by the enemy; they were receiving medical care—basic but effective—against 90% of their ailments; infant mortality was dropping from 200-300 per 1,000 live births, to around 60-80—not too good, but a great improvement; the wounded soldier was no longer dying out in the jungle from neglect; and the children were learning to read and write, making it easier to teach them useful skills in the future. Above all, we felt that we were helping the Lao defend their homes and their happy, peaceful way of life.

We were even naive enough to believe we were winning the war.

Metrical

A dequate nutrition was by far the most serious health problem in the refugee program. The rice ration, which all refugees received, provided sufficient calories but was lacking in protein, vitamins, and minerals. Through much experience, we found that 500 grams of rice per person per day—equivalent to 1,800 calories—maintained growth and body weight. This did not mean that each person received 1,800 calories, but rather an average of this amount was given to the total number of persons in the group. The adult male might consume 3,000 calories per day, and the small child less than 1,000. However, for logistical purposes, if we were dropping rice to 1,000 people, we could calculate 500g x 1,000 = 500,000 grams or half a metric ton per day to feed the whole group.

The 500 grams of rice provided 25 grams of utilizable protein, which was marginal in amount, and seriously lacking in certain essential amino acids, particularly glycine. Vitamins were almost totally absent, particularly thiamine. If the rice dietary wasn't supplemented, protein and vitamin deficiency quickly began to appear. The infants, young children, lactating mothers, and wounded were all severely affected. We found that as little as an additional eight grams of high quality protein in meats, legumes, or milk, along with a minimal vitamin supplement per person per day, kept the population group in good health.

Appreciable quantities of powdered milk were available through the Public Law No. 480 (PL480) program, but only on a sporadic basis. PL480 authorized the utilization of farm surpluses purchased by the US government—and the feeding of victims of war and natural disasters was a major article in the law. If foodstuffs were available under PL480, regulations required that we use them rather than buy other foodstuffs. Unfortunately, the powdered milk was packaged in paper containers which absorbed moisture, and after a short period of storage, became caked and very hard. Most often it couldn't be put into solution, and had to be eaten like a piece of hard candy. This wasn't satisfactory for small children, but we used it very effectively for the older children and nursing mothers.

There were many refugee babies whose mothers had died in childbirth, through sickness, or as a result of enemy action. Some mothers had quit breast-feeding due to malnutrition or other illness. Since we were supposed to get powdered milk through PL480, budgetary approval for canned milk purchases was almost impossible to obtain. These bureaucratic restrictions were later set aside, but in the mid-sixties we were desperate for milk. As a consequence, everyone was continually scrounging canned, evaporated milk.

Around that time, Tom Ward had dozens of infants at Sam Thong being raised by foster mothers, or by mothers who had stopped lactating because of illness or malnutrition. These women were constantly at the office door begging for milk, and Tom had given them almost all his inadequate supply. He was trying to find someone who would donate a few thousand dollars to a good cause so he could buy some canned, evaporated milk.

Mrs. Unger, the wife of the American ambassador, was very sympathetic to the work we were doing with the refugees. Occasionally, this lovely and kindly lady would fly up to visit Pop and Tom, and try to help out in some small way. Often, she had money for charitable projects that had been given to her, or that she had obtained through various fund-raising activities. Tom decided to get in touch with her and see if he might get some milk money from that source. The next time he was in Vientiane he went to see her and asked if she could possibly help him.

Mrs. Unger told Tom that she had several thousand dollars, but she intended using it to buy some equipment for the orthopedic center in Vientiane. Tom and Mrs. Unger were good friends, so he didn't hesitate to push the matter. Still, she couldn't be persuaded, and his plea seemed to be in vain. Nevertheless, he extracted a promise from her to visit Sam Thong before she made a final decision to give the money to the orthopedic center. Perhaps on his home ground he could make a stronger case.

A few days later, Mrs. Unger landed at Sam Thong. Tom met her at the plane with a Jeep—the only vehicle at the site—drove her through the village, and showed her the hospital and the new school that was being built. After a couple of hours, they returned to the office to chat with Pop.

While the three of them talked, several Meo women carrying babies on their backs gathered at the door. They were quiet and orderly and didn't enter the office, but would try to catch Tom's eye. Every now and then, Tom would go to the door and talk to one of the women. He would have the woman take her baby from her back and remove its little shirt, the child's only garment. Holding the baby in his arms, Tom would very carefully examine the infant, feeling its emaciated arms and legs and wasted body.

Without being too obvious, he made sure Mrs. Unger had a good view of the procedure. He would hand the baby back to the mother, and most often would shake his head in refusal of her request for milk. The poor mother would cry and plead, but Tom would return to the conversation as if nothing had happened. However, occasionally he would go into the warehouse and come back with a can of evaporated milk and give it to the mother whose baby he had just examined.

It was clearly apparent that the little charade was upsetting Mrs. Unger, but she said nothing about it for some time. Finally, she could contain herself no longer. "Tom, what in heavens are you doing?"

"These mothers are all begging for milk to give their babies."

"I know they're asking for milk, but why do you give it to some of them and not to others?"

"Mrs. Unger, like I was telling you the other day, I don't have near enough milk for all of them."

"But how do you decide which ones get it."

"Well, I feel the bodies of these poor, starving little things, and in my mind I divide them into three groups. Skinny, skinnier, and skinniest. I don't give the skinny ones milk because they have a chance to make it, even if they don't get any, and I can't take the chance of wasting it on them. I don't give the skinniest ones any either. Most likely they won't make it, even if I give them all of the few cans I have. I just can't take a chance of wasting it on these babies either. I only give the skinnier ones milk. If they don't get milk they're surely going to die. If they get milk, I feel pretty certain they'll make it. It's a terrible decision to have to make, but I say to myself, 'Tom, you got to do what's necessary to save the most you can.'"

Mrs. Unger's eyes filled with tears. Despite this, she knew that she'd "been had," but she still gave Tom the money anyway.

Not long after this, through circumstances I can't remember, we received a huge shipment of 100,000 cases of Metrical. This milk-based, high protein, vitamin- and mineral-enriched canned liquid was highly popular in the US for dieting at the time. On first thought, it would seem to be the last thing one would want in a refugee program. However, this high protein liquid was an excellent dietary supplement for our purposes. With Metrical, even Tom's skinniest infants began to thrive. Everyone loved Metrical. Pop was happy, I was happy, Tom was ecstatic, and we all went around singing and praising Metrical.

ooo

A couple of months after we received the Metrical, I was in my office in Vientiane trying to clear out the in box. I picked up an action copy of an airgram from USAID Washington and started to read. It was shocking. I couldn't believe my eyes. I got up from my desk and walked out the door.

Tom Cole walked out of the public works office about the same time and started a conversation. After a few minutes he said, "Doc, what in hell's wrong with you? You're not listening to a damn word I'm saying."

"Sorry Tom. I've just had some terrible news."

"It's not Pat or the kids, is it?"

"No, it's worse than that. We can't use the Metrical."

"Jesus, you are screwed up this morning. I'll see you later."

I went back in the office and picked up the airgram again. It stated that USAID Washington had just become aware that the Lao mission was using Metrical as a dietary supplement in the refugee program. The Food and Drug Administration had recently removed this product from the market in the US because the cyclamate sweetener used in it was possibly carcinogenic. The Lao mission was to destroy all Metrical immediately. If we continued to use it, the US government would be liable to political criticism. If Metrical wasn't good enough for Americans, it was hypocritical of us to use it for poor refugees.

Attached were copies of some research papers. They showed that a small percentage of female beagles—fed 3,000 times the maximum amount of usual human consumption of cyclamate—developed a higher percentage of nodules in their breasts than dogs receiving controlled dosages.

The thought of destroying the Metrical made me ill. Probably the best strategy was to bury the airgram in the bottom of my in box and hope that there'd be no follow up. This was wishful thinking.

Later in the day my secretary told me to pick up the phone. Charley Mann wanted to talk to me.

"Doc, did you see that airgram about the Metrical?"

"Yes, I saw it but I was hoping you hadn't."

"What are you doing about getting rid of it."

"Nothing."

"Look Doc, I don't want any games. Get rid of it."

"I can't. I don't have anything to use in place of it."

"I said get rid of the damn stuff."

"We're saving thousands of lives with it."

"For the last time, GET RID OF IT!" He was screaming.

"Charley, do you know that the prime minister uses cyclamate in his tea to keep his weight down? What if he heard we were destroying milk used to feed starving babies because it had cyclamate in it? He'd think we were crazy."

I could hear him gritting his teeth as he slammed the phone down. It would be useless to pursue the matter further with him.

The situation was desperate. I could never bring myself to destroy the Metrical. Something drastic had to be done.

By coincidence, Father B happened to be in town, and I sent my driver to find him and ask him to come to the office that afternoon. Then I called Madame Sunthon at the Ministry of Social Welfare. Among her many other duties, Madame Sunthon ran the orphanage and worked with indigent families and widows. I asked her to come and meet with Father B and myself that afternoon, too. The three of us were good friends, and had cooperated on many things in the past. I had given both of them some of the Metrical to use in their programs, and they were both highly pleased with it.

When the three of us got together that afternoon, I told them about our instructions to destroy the Metrical and the reasons for doing so. They were aghast at such idiocy and asked me to give it to them instead of destroying it. I told them I couldn't give it to them, but had called them to see if they would help me destroy it.

Of the original 100,000 cases, there were 20,000 at Sam Thong, but 50,000 remained in Vientiane. We had used about 30,000 cases. If they agreed to help destroy it, I would send 15,000 cases to the Ministry of Social Welfare warehouse, and 35,000 cases to the Oblate missionaries warehouse. Both Madame Sunthon and Father B solemnly promised that they would do me this small favor and destroy the poisonous substance.

The next day I sent them the Metrical as we had agreed. If Madame Sunthon hadn't destroyed it, the orphans would have had enough to last two years. Father B sent his share upcountry for destruction.

There were rumors that Tom Ward would smuggle some of it into the USAID warehouse from time to time, but I doubt that Tom would do such a thing. Madame Sunthon and I would stop by the orphanage occasionally and watch the children destroy their share.

What I didn't know was that the day I had sent the Metrical to the Ministry of Social Welfare, just by chance, Keo Viprakone, the director general, had seen it arrive. Keo called Charley Mann and innocently thanked him for it. Charley didn't suggest to Keo that anything was wrong, and he never said anything to me. Madame Sunthon found out that Keo had called Charley, but it took her a year to raise the courage to tell me that the director knew about our little plot all the time.

A Fishy Tale

In the never-ending quest for protein, we had considered the possibility of fish ponds. In theory, raising certain types of pond fish is very simple. You dig a hole in the ground, fill it with water, throw in any nitrogenous matter that may be around such as buffalo manure to start a food chain, and then add some fingerlings. A few months later, you can begin harvesting fish. Leave a few of the larger fish to breed, keep throwing waste in the pond, and you have a never-ending supply of high quality protein—and an excellent utilization of bullshit.

The agricultural division of USAID had hired a Japanese fisheries expert to do a feasibility study for the development of fish ponds in Laos. They restricted the study to the lowland ethnic Lao areas and ignored the refugees in the mountains. The chief of the agriculture division thought it was a waste of time to promote any sort of program in the refugee areas, particularly among the hilltribes. Pop and Tom had been trying to get the Japanese expert up to Sam Thong in the hope that he would be able to help them get a fish pond program started.

Finally, after a lot of resistance from the chief, the expert did get upcountry. Tom and Pop showed him around the refugee communities in Xieng Khoung, and he returned to Vientiane. Within a few days he produced a report that was completely negative. Many reasons were cited as to why it wasn't feasible to breed fish in the mountains, but we all believed that the chief of agriculture had pressured the fisheries expert to discourage any sort of activity in the refugee program.

Although refugee relief had the highest priority in the USAID mission, the agriculture division had always been uncooperative in helping us with agricultural problems in refugee areas. Their attitude was that the war and the instability in the refugee areas prevented any kind of substantive agricultural projects.

Shortly after the visit by the Japanese expert, Pop, Tom, and I were having lunch with VP at Long Chieng. VP had known about the visit, and was very interested in the prospect of a fish pond project. When we told him about the negative report, he was very upset.

According to VP, the Meo had a centuries-old tradition of pond fish culture. At the time, in the stable Meo villages of Southern China, pond fish were still extensively raised, but as the Meo migrated southward into Laos, they had been unable to transport breeding stock to the new locations. As a consequence they had been unable to start new ponds. Over a period of time, they had forgotten about fish ponds as a food source. VP was positive that fish culture would spread rapidly if suitable species were introduced into the refugee communities.

That night, Pop and some of the pilots were playing poker at Sam Thong, and Pop was sipping on a bottle of the local corn whiskey. Tom was watching but not playing. He and Pop again started talking about fish ponds and the conversation with VP at lunch that day. The longer they talked, the more enthusiastic Pop got about starting the ponds.

"Tom, I want you on a plane first thing in the morning," he said. "Get down to Bangkok and get us some fish. Damn it, I know VP's right. We can grow those damn fish up here just as well as any other place."

"Can't go tomorrow, Pop. I don't have any money. I'll go the first of next month after pay day."

"Damn it Tom, I want you on that plane tomorrow. I'll cut a dollar out of every pot tonight and that oughtta be plenty to buy fish."

"Yeah, but we've got to have ponds ready or the fish will die."

"Don't worry about that. It'll take you a couple of days to find the fish and get back up here. I'll get somebody started diggin' ponds in the morning."

The next morning Tom took off for Bangkok with a little over sixty dollars that Pop had cut out of the poker game. Two or three days later, he returned with about 100 Tilapia fingerlings in well-oxygenated plastic bags. The ponds were ready. VP had found one of the old Meo men who remembered preparing fish ponds from his childhood.

A few months later, they began distributing fish to establish other ponds. The fish were given without charge, but with the stipulation that the recipient would give his neighbors' fish to start their ponds. After the Tilapia did so well, catfish and carp were introduced, and these species also thrived.

Five years after Tom's poker-financed trip to Bangkok, one of our periodic nutrition surveys was done in the Northern refugee areas. It showed that approximately 13,000 fish ponds were producing 25% of the population's total animal protein intake.

Caravans at Nam Thoui,
Chaos at Houi Thom

I had work stacked up at the office, but when Pop called on the radio, I was happy to have an excuse to leave town. He wanted me to go with him to Nam Thoui in the Ban Houi Sai area to spend a few days with Chao Mai, the Yao leader.

This was the time of the year when the caravans of opium started coming out of Burma to sell their merchandise to the Lao, Thai, and Chinese middle men. At that time there wasn't the intense and bloody rivalry among the buyers that developed in later years. Each group had their contacts and arrangements, and the transfers were made peacefully and without incident. The Lao faction used Nam Thoui as a point of contact and transfer, and they bought their opium from Chan Sy Fu, a personable, young Shan leader who was a good friend of Chao Mai.

Chan Sy Fu later became Khun Sa, and his reputation in the Golden Triangle opium trade is well-known and well-documented. Recently, he relinquished his leadership of the Shan insurgents, was given amnesty by the Burmese government, and is now "retired."

Chan Sy Fu himself led the first Shan caravan of the year, 1968, and its arrival provided occasion for a big party, with Chao Mai as the host. The caravan usually carried about twenty tons of opium on the backs of 200 little Chinese mules. There were many other pack animals with drivers, armed guards, and small merchants wanting to buy items that were scarce or non-existent in their area of Burma. Altogether, there were several hundred people, and the whole caravan and event had a colourful and festive air. It had the aspect of a country fair, with the farmers coming to sell their agricultural products, and generally having a good time.

The affair lasted most of a week. Chao Mai personally supervised the preparation of the food, and it was indeed a gourmet delight. During the day, soccer and volleyball teams from the Shan contingent competed with the Yao teams before cheering crowds of spectators. At night there was drinking, music, and dancing. The higher-ranking guests were entertained by a Yao girl sitting by their side, who was responsible for seeing that glasses were always full, food was at hand, and the guest was comfortable in every way possible. Fortunately, the Shan language is a dialect of Lao-Tai, so we could converse with the visitors from Burma—although with some difficulty.

Most of the Shan and the other Burmese hilltribe minorities have been in revolt against the Burmese government since independence from British colonial rule at the end of World War II. All had fought with the British against the Japanese during the war—while the lowland, ethnic Burmese had collaborated with the Japanese and fought against the British. In gratitude for their cooperation, Lord Mountbatten, the British commander, had promised the Shan and the other minorities a major role in forming the government of independence, and local autonomy within the Burmese Union when the war was over.

All these promises were broken, however, when the British turned over the government to the Burmese in January of 1948. U Aung San, the leader of the Burmese, had defected from the Japanese three months before the war ended when he saw the Japanese would be defeated. The British gave no consideration to the interests of the Shan and the other minorities that had fought by their side.

Over fifty years later, the Shan, and many of the other tribal people, have still not submitted to Burmese rule—and the government is still trying to suppress the rebellion that ensued.

On one particular occasion not long before the festivities at Nam Thoui, Pop and I had just flown from Sam Thong to Long Chieng and were having lunch with VP. He was depressed and in very bad humor. His troops were heavily engaged with two Vietnamese divisions on the Plain of Jars, and he felt—with some justification—that he wasn't getting the support he deserved. He beat on the table with his fist and was almost shouting when he spoke.

"I'm going to take my people and go to Sayaboury. I'll resign my commission and be a farmer. When the communists take over the country, we'll just walk across the border into Thailand and never come back. The Americans are deserting us just like the British did the Shan. All my people are getting killed and nobody cares. The Lao sit around Vientiane going to parties while the Meo are bleeding to death to protect them. All they care about is how much money they can steal."

This went on for some time. Pop and I had heard it on several previous occasions. I called it the "Burma Syndrome."

As far as Laos was concerned, probably the two worst manifestations of the syndrome occurred in 1971 when VP found out that President Nixon was going to China, and in 1973 when all military assistance was cut off to Laos.

During these periodic outbursts by VP against the Americans, Pop and I didn't feel too uncomfortable. It was always quite clear that he didn't consider us "the Americans" but rather good friends. Unfortunately, his tirades were prophetic of what the future held for him and his people.

At the time we were at Nam Thoui, the Shan were under heavy pressure from the Burmese army. Getting the opium caravan to Laos from their home villages was a difficult and dangerous undertaking. They had run into small Burmese army patrols twice during the two-week-long trip, but fortunately had been able to avoid the larger army units. They sustained only three minor casualties in the skirmishes with the patrol units.

A few months earlier, at Chao Mai's request, we had taken seven young Shan boys into the latest medic training course, which had ended the previous week. These seven new medics would be returning to their villages with the caravan. Chan Sy Fu asked that I go back with them and spend a few weeks helping to set up a medical program in the Shan State. This was impossible, of course, but the idea was tempting and intriguing.

We saw to it that our Shan students were well supplied with simple instruments and basic medications before they departed for home, and as the long line of pack animals and people wound across the hills toward Burma, Pop and I took off in a Porter for Sam Thong. It had been an interesting and enjoyable visit, and we were appreciative of Chao Mai's gracious and generous hospitality.

Two hours later, around three o'clock in the afternoon, we landed at Sam Thong. I had intended to take a quick look at the hospital and talk to Dr. Khammoung for a few minutes, then go on to Vientiane. I needed to get back to the office for two or three days and clean out the in box. However, when we landed and went into the office, Ly Choi, the radio operator, handed me a message which he'd received the day before. It was from Colonel Phan, the commanding officer at Na Khang in Sam Neua, who had replaced Colonel Khamsao. The message said that Duangtha had completed the new dispensary at Houi Thom, and that he would like for Colonel Phan and I to come and officiate at the opening ceremony. The date and time of the ceremony was that same day and evening.

Houi Thom was the last place I wanted to go, but there was no way I could refuse Duangtha's invitation. There was time to fly up to Na Khang, meet Colonel Phan, and the two of us would fly over to Houi Thom and spend the night. The medical warehouse workers quickly filled some boxes with the medicines and supplies for the new dispensary, I told Pop about the message from Phan, and asked him to call Pat and tell her I'd be in Vientiane the next afternoon.

We threw the supplies on a Porter and took off for Sam Neua. We landed at Na Khang to pick up Phan, and about five o'clock, set down on the small strip at Houi Thom. Colonel Thong remained at Na Khang since it was felt that both he and Phan shouldn't be away at the same time.

Houi Thom was the site of a tiny village, destroyed by the enemy several months previously. There were only 250 people in the immediate area, including soldiers, their families, and a handful of refugees. It was a desolate place, sitting on a barren, windswept ridge. The site was about five kilometers to the east of Na Khang, and just west of Route 6, the main line of communication between Sam Neua City and the PDJ.

Houi Thom guarded the natural avenue of approach to the Na Khang defensive perimeter; the Muang Heim valley, and the heart of Sam Neua province. Because of its crucial location and strategic importance, Thong had put Duangtha—his best commander—in charge of its defence. If the enemy decided to attack Na Khang in force, they would have to hit Houi Thom first. Duangtha would slow them down with the few soldiers he had at Houi Thom, and buy time for Na Khang to get prepared.

The enemy had probed the area several times in the last two months, and everyone there knew that it was only a question of time before they would be hit by overwhelming force. I had visited the place two weeks before, and morale was very poor. At that time Duangtha had decided to build a new dispensary, and when it was finished we would have a little opening ceremony. This would create some diversion, and might make the people a bit less nervous and despondent. If we were building a new dispensary, it was thought, maybe things weren't too bad after all.

When we landed, the few little children and women left at Houi Thom were lined up along the path from the strip to the military headquarters building to present us with the traditional flowers. Duangtha greeted us as we stepped off the plane. We were happy to see each other, and embraced like long-lost brothers even though I'd seen him only two weeks before. The Porter took off immediately, since the area was too insecure for a plane to RON. Escorted by Duangtha, Colonel Phan and I slowly walked up the line accepting the flowers from the welcoming party.

Soon, we could hear choppers in the distance, and it became apparent they were coming into Houi Thom. A few minutes later, two Air America Sikorsky H34s landed at the strip. Duangtha, Phan, and I walked back to see what was going on. Dick Elder, one of the chopper pilots, got out of his aircraft and was talking to the other pilot. He came over and told us that the other chopper was having engine trouble and the pilot was having difficulty maintaining altitude. They were going to unload the cargo from both aircraft, the flight mechanic and two soldier guides on the sick H34 would get on Dick's chopper, and the other pilot would try to limp back to Na Khang solo with as light a load as possible. With the help of some of the local soldiers, the cargo on the two choppers was quickly unloaded and they took off for Na Khang.

The H34s had been re-supplying the various military outposts around the Na Khang perimeter, and the cargo they unloaded was all fragmentation hand grenades—about 100 cases of them. Duangtha didn't like the idea of leaving the grenades on the unguarded strip, so he ordered his men divide them into three lots and take them up to their positions.

The Houi Thom soldiers were dug in on a V-shaped ridge, with the open part of the V pointing toward the enemy on the east. Each leg of the V was about 100 meters long. The ridge was higher than the surrounding terrain, and there was good visibility in all directions. The slopes were steep and completely bare of any vegetation or other cover. It was a strong defensive position.

Duangtha had a total of only 87 men at Houi Thom, but all of them were tough, well-trained veterans with many years of combat experience. He'd divided them into three groups of about equal number, and had them build strong, sandbagged bunkers on the three points of the V. The soldiers were happy to see the grenades, as ammunition of any sort had been in short supply for several weeks. The situation with respect to small arms ammo was critical. There were barely two clips per man.

Our little party went up to the headquarters located by one of the positions. There were just two bamboo-and-thatch buildings up on the ridge: the headquarters building and the dispensary. The soldiers slept in their bunkered positions, and the civilians had built their houses at the bottom of the ridge on the west. The little dispensary was decorated with wild flowers and banana leaves, which provided a little color and brightness to a very drab scene. All the civilians and soldiers gathered for the ceremony. The sun was setting, and Duangtha wanted to get started right away so things would be completed before dark. I noticed that he was unusually quiet and serious. The characteristic big smile and ready laugh were absent.

Phan and I made the mandatory speeches, and since there wasn't a monk available, one of the elders said the prayers and blessed the little dispensary. We then cut the ribbon made from parachute cloth tied across the entrance, and officially opened the new medical facility. Within a short time the crowd dispersed. The civilians returned to the village at the base of the ridge, and except for a half dozen headquarters personnel, the soldiers went back to their positions. It was obvious that Duangtha was concerned about the security situation because there wasn't to be the usual celebration party .

When we went inside and sat down, he told us that he'd received some important information. Just before we'd landed, a pair of civilian intelligence agents had come in and reported a large enemy movement. A convoy of trucks coming from the north on Route 6 had unloaded several hundred Vietnamese troops about seven kilometers east of Houi Thom. They had moved to the west of the highway and seemed to be going into bivouac. Although he thought it unlikely, it was entirely possible for the enemy to move into position and hit Houi Thom before morning. Duangtha was having self recriminations for not putting me back on the airplane as soon as we had arrived that afternoon.

The soldiers had prepared a good meal, and after eating and downing a few shots of rice whisky, the atmosphere improved. Duangtha's big smile returned, and I felt somewhat relieved. To make it light-tight, the bamboo-and-thatch building was lined with the black plastic of the type used to shelter the refugees in emergencies. We were able to have a couple of candles burning, but otherwise the area was totally blacked out. After the meal, we sat outside under a beautiful, clear, moonless sky. The stars were so bright that we could see quite well when our eyes had adjusted to the darkness.

Duangtha joked with Colonel Phan about the trip he and I were to take when the war was over. We were going to get a big black Mercedes Benz like Prince Souvanna Phouma's, and drive coast to coast across the United States. When we got to Washington, he was going to go to the White House and personally thank President Nixon for all the help he had given the Lao people.

Phan thought this was hilarious and asked Duangtha what would he say to President Nixon when he met him. Duangtha replied that he'd already prepared his speech. He stood up, and—in the most polite and formal Lao—

presented a warm and touching speech of gratitude, thanking the President and all the people of the United States of America for their help in the struggle against the communists. Phan and the other soldiers couldn't keep from laughing, and certainly there was humour in this bizarre situation. For my part it was difficult to keep the tears from my eyes.

Around ten o'clock, Duangtha and Phan left to check the positions. When they returned, Duangtha took me into the headquarters building and showed me my sleeping mat and blankets. He told me to keep my clothes on and put my pack and boots where I could find them in the dark. This was the first indication that he was still concerned about an enemy attack that night. I slipped off my boots and got under the blankets. It had been a long and tiring day since getting up at Nam Thoui that morning. I was a little apprehensive about the possibility of trouble that night, but soon fell asleep.

Suddenly someone was shaking me by the arm and shining a flashlight in my eyes. "*Tan Maw! Tan Maw!* Wake up! Wake up!"

I was startled and disoriented, and it took a few seconds to clear my head. "What's the matter? What's happening?

"Duangtha wants you to get out of the house. There might be trouble."

I slipped my boots on, grabbed my pack, then followed the soldier outside. On the reverse slope of the ridge, below the bunkers, were several large foxholes. My guide told me I was to remain there. Several civilians were already huddled down in the holes. No one seemed to know what was going on, but everyone kept whispering, "*Satru*! *Satru*!" (Enemy! Enemy!).

Colonel Phan came up before long and told us that our listening posts were pulling back, reporting large numbers of enemy troops moving into position in front of us. We should stay down in the holes, remain silent, and not move around. I told him we should get dressings and other supplies from the dispensary and set up an aid station in our protected area.

The dispensary was completely exposed on the top of the ridge, and we wouldn't be able to use it if the enemy attacked. Someone found the medic and we brought all the battle dressings, large bandages, and IV fluids down to the largest of the holes. In the darkness, the luminous dial on my watch said it was eleven-thirty. The night was so quiet and beautiful, it was difficult to conceive that we might be on the verge of a battle. A baby's plaintive cry off toward the little village at the base of the ridge was the only sound that could be heard.

A few minutes before midnight, the silence was suddenly shattered by the rushing scream of a rocket passing overhead, followed by an explosion some distance behind us. In seconds, we were under heavy rocket and recoilless-cannon attack, but most of the rounds were passing over the ridge and bursting in the distance behind us. These flat trajectory weapons were having trouble hitting the narrow top of the ridge above them. Soon, machine gun and automatic rifle fire joined in, and we could hear shouting and screaming, all in Vietnamese. It seemed there were two separate attacks directed at the positions on the two points of the legs of the V.

The shouting and screaming was now around the bunkers. The sound of exploding grenades and the Claymore mines protecting the bunkers mixed with that of the automatic rifle fire. It sounded as if our positions were being overrun. I was trying to decide which path to take if we had to run for safety. Then, gradually, after five or six minutes the noise of the battle died down, except for sporadic small arms rounds going off.

Soon, the medic and I, with some help from the civilians with us, were working on several wounded soldiers by flashlight. Fortunately, none were badly injured, and all but two were able to go back to their positions. Unfortunately, there were three killed. Occasionally, a rocket or cannon round would come shrieking overhead, but otherwise the lull lasted for about an hour and a half.

Then there was a repetition of the first attack. First, heavy preparation with rockets and cannon, and then the assault on the positions. The fighting carried right up to the bunkers, but again the enemy was thrown back. Our men were doing a magnificent job against great odds.

Casualties started coming in again. One had a high velocity round through his right chest that was sucking air. Another had a shattered femur and was in shock. We quickly put plastic patches on the chest wounds and got the femur splinted. It was a problem to get IVs going by the flashlight, but we finally got them flowing. In a half hour or so, both of the soldiers were stable and looked like they might make it.

Seven or eight other soldiers were wounded, but none were too serious. One of them had been hit in the shoulder with shrapnel during the first assault. We had bandaged him up and he had returned to his position. Now he had a high velocity wound in his flank, but it had not penetrated the abdomen. As soon we dressed his new wound, he hurried back to his position. We had four killed this round.

Duangtha and Phan came by to see how we were doing. It was only about three o'clock and they thought it highly likely the Vietnamese would make at least one more assault before dawn. With daylight we could call in air support, and in this open country, the enemy would have to withdraw. Our big problem was small arms ammunition. All three positions were desperately low, and if the enemy sustained their next assault for any length of time, we would surely run out. Thank God for the 100 cases of fragmentation grenades that we had by the grace of the sick H34.

Around four-thirty it all started again; initial rocket and cannon fire, then the ground attack. The enemy assaulted both positions on the tips of the V just as they had done before. The last of the small arms ammunition was gone, and all that remained were the grenades, a few RPGs, and some bazooka rounds.

Suddenly, at the height of the action, an incredible thing happened. The two Vietnamese assault units started firing at each other. In the darkness and chaos they were apparently confused and lost their bearings. For three or four minutes there was a heavy fire fight between the two units. Eventually, the firing died down, and all we could hear was moaning and shouting. It soon became evident that the enemy was withdrawing. The battle was over. Duangtha and his 87 men had defeated a vastly superior Vietnamese force. It was a tremendous victory that would that would boost the morale of every soldier fighting in Northern Laos.

At dawn, we counted 156 dead Vietnamese soldiers on the ground in front of the positions. All during the morning there were reports of the enemy carrying dead and wounded from the area. From documents and other evidence found on the Vietnamese, Duangtha ascertained that two battalions formed the attack—about 1,000 men in all. Our losses were eight killed and 23 wounded. The headquarters building and the new dispensary were smoldering rubble. The dispensary hadn't lasted long enough to even see its first patient.

Duangtha was in radio contact with Na Khang, and choppers arrived to evacuate the wounded. As soon as they were on their way, Phan and I flew to Na Khang. He would see that Duangtha was re-supplied as quickly as possible, while I continued on to Vientiane and began screaming about small arms ammo loud enough so that everyone from Ambassador Godley on down heard about the problem. By that afternoon it was being flown upcountry in large quantities.

It had been a long hard night and day. I drove out to the house, showered, sat on the balcony, sipped a drink, and admired the sunset across the Mekong. Laos was indeed a unique place. There weren't too many places in the world where one could be in the middle of a battle with the Vietnamese in the morning, and relaxing with a cocktail at home in the evening. It was nice to be home.

To School in Europe

The elementary grades of the American School in Vientiane were very good, but at the high school level the staffing was inadequate. Becky entered the local high school, the Lycee Pavie. At the time it was the only high school in Laos other than the American School. The language of instruction was French. The school had about 400 students, and graduated ninety of them each year. Approximately half the students were Lao, and half Vietnamese, with a few French. Becky was the only American.

Most of the teachers were from France, and were supported by the French government as part of their foreign assistance program. At first, the transition from English was quite difficult for Becky, but her teachers were very kind and supportive of their one American student. In three or four months, she was doing well. It was wonderful for her to have new friends who were part of both the Lao and international communities. There were always exciting things to do on the weekend. The local kids were a lot more fun than the kids at the American School.

Although Becky was doing well in school, Pat and I were still not satisfied with the Lycee. After doing some research, we decided to send her to Switzerland. She entered Institut Montesano at Gstaadt the following year. This small, private girl's school taught in both English and French, and the students were truly bilingual. They came from all over the world and were an education in themselves. Gstaadt has some of the best ski slopes in the Alps, and everyone was crazy about skiing. It was a fun place, but also had an intellectual and cultural atmosphere that Becky found interesting and stimulating.

Since Montesano worked out well for Becky, the next year we decided to put Ray in Institut Montana at Zug just out of Zurich. The following year, Walter joined Ray at Montana. It was reassuring to Pat and I, and pleasant for them to be close together where they could visit each other.

217

All three fell in love with winter sports, and thought Europe was wonderful. They traveled extensively in most of the West European countries, and were getting a liberal education. Nevertheless, Laos was home, and summer vacation and Christmas in Vientiane were their favorite times of year.

One year, Pat and I decided to take a vacation during December. We rented an apartment at Emmitten in Switzerland for the month. The family would spend the holidays skiing. From our viewpoint in Laos, a vacation in the Alps seemed a great idea. From the childrens' viewpoint in Switzerland—eagerly waiting to go home for Christmas—it was a disaster.

Pat and I didn't realize what a horrible mistake we'd made until we got together at Emmitten. All three of the children were truly broken-hearted that they weren't going home for Christmas. There was little we could do other than promise not to do it again.

A Close Call at Muang Heim

Muang Heim is located in the area where Xieng Khoung, Sam Neua, and Luang Prabang provinces join. It was the last ethnic Lao village north of the Plain of Jars that hadn't been overrun by the enemy. Situated in a narrow valley running north and south and strung along the east bank of the headwaters of the Nam Khan River, it was a nondescript collection of bamboo-and-thatch houses overlooked by a circle of fortifications on a small hill. By 1969 there were only a few of the original inhabitants, most having fled to Luang Prabang and Vientiane. The remaining population was largely the 100 Lao soldiers that defended the place and their families.

In better times, the fertile valley had been a rich paddy area, but now the fields were overgrown and abandoned. However, Muang Heim still had considerable importance for several reasons. The valley was a natural avenue of approach for enemy troops moving from north to south; small boats could use the river most of the year for commerce with Luang Prabang; and it helped to protect the western approach to Na Khang, the large military outpost just to the east.

There were strong Pathet Lao units in the area, and we suspected that they might try to take Muang Heim. We were concerned that our small military garrison would simply abandon the place along with the civilians. When most of the inhabitants left two years previously, in 1967, the small government medical dispensary ceased to function, and the remaining people had been without medical care since that time.

In an attempt to boost the morale of the Muang Heim people, and help stabilize the situation, we decided to build, equip, and staff a new health facility. Hopefully, this small show of support would help to hold people in place, and save a valuable asset. We sent two medics to supervise the work on the dispensary and manage it—after the villagers completed the construction. The building was of bamboo, but we flew in corrugated iron roofing sheets to give it a more prestigious and permanent appearance. Roofing sheets were a real status symbol in this primitive area. In two or three weeks the dispensary was finished, and had been well stocked and equipped.

To gain as much psychological and political benefit out of the project as possible, we planned a big inauguration ceremony with plenty of food and rice wine—which we would furnish since there was little available locally. The *chao muang* of Muang Heim, who now lived at Sam Thong, would lead the party going to the inauguration, along with newly-promoted Major Duangtha and his wife. Mrs. Duangtha was a young, vivacious lady from the Muang Heim area, and they had only recently married. Pop, Frank Becker, Don Dougan, and I would accompany them.

Pop hadn't been feeling well, and I worried about his going with us. I tried to talk him into staying at Sam Thong, but he insisted on going and I couldn't change his mind. He had suffered a coronary occlusion about five years previously. Fortunately, he made a good recovery, and his exercise tolerance returned to its previous level. Nevertheless he still had some chest pain when under stress.

Duangtha was reluctant to let his wife go, as it was a very insecure area, but Muang Heim was her home, so it was difficult for him to refuse her. Little did we know at the time, that her presence would play a major role in preventing our capture or death.

We all met at Sam Thong and departed for the ceremony late in the afternoon. The *chao muang* had stopped at Muang Heim two days before and had agreed on a date for the occasion with the local leader, but told him to pass the word around that we would be there the day after the one planned. This was done for security reasons—if by chance the enemy got word of the affair.

I believe we all had vague feelings of apprehension, and everyone appeared a bit subdued when we landed at the dirt strip that late afternoon. As soon as we got out of the aircraft, it took off and returned to Sam Thong.

Although the people didn't expect us until the next day, a large crowd gathered very quickly to greet us. Soon, there was much talk and laughter, and a hospitable atmosphere lifted our spirits. The crowd moved over to a large, open grassy area in the center of the village where the dispensary had been built. There was also a new building close by that turned out to be a guest house.

Already the villagers were beginning to decorate the two buildings with beautiful flowers and wreaths in anticipation of the opening ceremony that evening. The dispensary had a large waiting-reception area, a room for consultation and dispensing medicines, storage for medicines and supplies, and a treatment room. There were also living quarters for the two medics. Our party inspected the facility and found it clean and neat, and well-organized and -supplied. We thanked the medics and congratulated them on doing such a good job. All the visitors then went to the new guest house next door to rest until time for the ceremony later in the evening.

Normally, we held such ceremonies in the daytime, and everyone remained in the village for two or three days. In this particularly bad security situation, however, the *chao muang* and Duangtha thought it best that we get in and out as quickly as possible. Still, we would have to spend at least one night in the village not to offend the Muang Heim people—even though our presence would soon be known by the Pathet Lao and might possibly tempt them to take some sort of action against the village.

Most of the village elders crowded into the guest house, and three large jars of *lao hai* were brought into the middle of our circle. After several rounds, the *nai ban* announced the opening ceremony. The guests and the rest of the crowd moved to the front of the dispensary. The building was decorated with flowers and greenery, and illuminated by a kerosene lamp and some resin flares. The usual ribbon had been tied across the entrance, and four Buddhist monks in their orange robes sat crosslegged waiting to chant the prayers that would bring good luck and success to our project.

The *chao muang* stood and spoke to the audience, explaining to them that this dispensary was made possible through cooperation between the Royal Lao Government and the United States of America. It was an expression of the concern and admiration of their government for the heroic struggle they were making against the Vietnamese aggressors and the traitorous Pathet Lao.

Pop spoke next and said he was happy to be back with his old Muang Heim friends, as it had been many months since he'd had the chance to visit their village. He asked them to take good care of the dispensary, and give the medics their best cooperation in carrying out their work.

I was the last speaker, and thanked the people for their hospitality, and especially for the help they'd given the medics in constructing the dispensary. I assured them that we would see their medical program was well supported and supplied with drugs and other necessities. The monks chanted the appropriate prayers, and as soon as they finished, the *chao muang* and I cut the ribbon. The little bamboo-and-tin dispensary was officially open for business.

Everyone walked through, nodding approval and remarking over the abundant supply of drugs, and congratulating the medics for their good work. We then returned to the guest house, where our hosts had laid out a sumptuous meal on mats spread over the floor. When the meal was finished, the remains were quickly cleared away, and—within a few minutes—sleeping pads and blankets were brought in and prepared for the night.

Although it was only about nine-thirty, it was obvious that the celebration was over, and all the local people soon departed. On occasions like this, one would normally expect dancing and drinking until the small hours of the morning. Something was definitely wrong. Duangtha and his wife had relatives in the village, and went to sleep with them. Also, the *chao muang* left to spend the night with friends.

Pop, Frank, Don, and I—the four foreigners—were alone. We all looked at each other, and although our apprehension was obvious, everyone seemed reluctant to say anything.

Finally, Don Dougan—the old Green Beret—spoke up. "Guys, this is a goddamn trap. We're being set up. I'm getting all sorts of bad vibes. Let's act like we're going to bed, turn the lights out, and after a while slip out and sleep with some of the people in the village."

We readily agreed with Don, and made as if we were going to bed, then turned out the lantern. However, a few minutes later—just before we were ready to leave—a whispered but urgent little voice was heard at the door.

"*Tan Pop. Tan Maw.*"

It was Duangtha's wife, Sang Tian (Candle Light). She slipped into the building and we could barely see her in the darkened room.

"We think it's very dangerous for you to sleep here. Duangtha wants you to come sleep in the houses close to us."

No one needed any convincing, and we silently followed Sang Tian through the darkness. When we got out of the open field where the guest house and dispensary were located, and into the village, Duangtha met us. He and his wife put Don and Frank in one house, and Pop and I in another adjacent to where they were staying. Just then I thought about the two medics in the dispensary, and told Duangtha we should see that they were safe—but he had already sent someone to move them. The *chao muang* was also sleeping in one of the houses nearby.

Before Duangtha left us for the house where he and Sang Tian were spending the night, I asked him why he'd moved us—not letting him know that we had already decided to do the same thing. He replied that Sang

Lt. Charles Klusmann and an anxious Boun Mi after their escape from Khang Khay.

Boun Mi at Sam Thong.

Author with Boun Mi.

Children with part of the menagerie.

Father B, Ly Tou Yia, and chopper pilot.

Author and *chao muang* of Hua Muang.

The hospital at Sam Thong, in 1963 and later.

Lao Theung refugees who had just escaped after three years under the Pathet Lao.

Lao Theung refugees.

Pop, Bleu Vu, and Norm Sweet—USAID program officer, flanked by local leaders at Sam Thong.

Air America pilot, Capt. Ed Reed (left) and Tom Ward at the Sam Thong office.

(From left) Howie Freeman, the author, Tony Poe, Pat Landry, Bill Lair, and Ted Shackly at Long Chieng the day the king presented medals and made them Knights of the Order of the Million Elephants and the White Parasol.

Jack Williamson.

Pop and VP during Meo New Year, Long Chieng.

Temporary refugee dispensary.

Old hospital, Sam Thong.

Newly-wed Meo medic couple.

Friends of the author.

Dr. Phoui, director-general of health.

Bill Young.

The *chao muang's* wife, Pop, Mrs. Khamsao, and the *tasseng's* wife at Hua Muang.

Author with visitors at Phu Si, Luang Prabang.

Ban Houi Sai.

Village on mountain ridge near Sam Thong.

Hospital at Ban Son.

Tian urged him to do it, even though she couldn't give him any good reason for being fearful of our safety. She simply had a premonition of danger that she couldn't explain. He cautioned us that no matter what happened in the night, we were not to move from the house under any circumstance. In the event of trouble, he might be occupied, but if he thought we should flee the village, Sang Tian would come and guide us to safety. She knew the countryside and all the trails leading from the village. He quietly bid us goodnight, and said he would see us in the morning.

Pop and I slipped off our boots, but left all our other clothing on. It was increasingly apparent that he wasn't feeling well. In the dim candle light that flickered in the room, I could see that he kept rubbing his chest, and would take a deep breath as if he were trying to relieve some discomfort. I asked him if he was having any chest pain and he replied that the food had given him a little indigestion but he was okay otherwise. Mentally, I was cursing myself for not insisting that he remain at Sam Thong. I looked at my watch before blowing out the little candle by the side of our palettes on the hard, dirt floor. It was ten-thirty. We both crawled under our blankets.

About an hour later I was still trying to doze off, but with no success. However, I was somewhat relieved by the sound of Pop's snoring, and hoped he'd be feeling better in the morning after a good night's rest. That wasn't to be. Suddenly all hell broke loose. Booming, ground-shaking explosions nearby shattered the quiet of the night. The unmistakable chatter of AK47s soon joined in. I floundered around for my boots, jerked them on, and went to the door.

The outpost on the hill was under heavy attack, and a smaller force had hit the area of the dispensary and guest house. Soon, there were flames leaping up, and I could see that both buildings were on fire. Pop was up and standing next to me. We stood there listening to the noise and watching the fire as we wondered what to do next. Remembering Duangtha's instructions, we anxiously waited.

Along with the noise of explosions and automatic rifle fire, we could hear shouting and crying in the village about 200 meters from where we were. Immediately around us, the people could be heard—and only vaguely seen—scurrying out of their houses and leaving the village as unobtrusively as possible.

Within two or three minutes Sang Tian appeared out of the gloom and told us to follow her. She took Pop's hand and we hurried through the village toward the river, along with a small crowd of other people headed in the same direction.

As we half walked, half ran, our little guide told us that the enemy troops were going through the houses searching for the Americans, and we must get away quickly. We left the village and waded across the river into some thick brush that hid us from the sight of anyone on the opposite bank. Fortunately, it was the dry season and the water was only about two feet deep at most. Sang Tian told us to remain where we were and stay out of sight. She would go back and get the others and rejoin us as quickly as possible.

Pop and I sat down on the ground to wait, well hidden by the brush and darkness. We could hear a fierce fire fight on the hill where the military outpost was located—mostly automatic small arms fire with an occasional grenade or rocket round exploding. There was a lot of activity in the village, with screaming and shouting and a few sporadic shots being fired. It seemed that the enemy still hoped to find us in one of the houses. People were crossing the river in numbers and hurrying away into the brush and jungle. A mini exodus was soon underway.

Before long, Sang Tian returned with Duangtha, the *chao muang*, Frank, Don, and several other people. Duangtha had tried to get over to the military outpost on the hill to help the troops there, but it proved impossible, so he decided to leave with us.

We all started down a narrow trail with Sang Tian in the lead. Just as we were moving out, she pressed a small object in my hand and whispered in my ear to put it in my pocket, putting her finger on the left upper pocket of my jacket. In the dark I couldn't see what it might be, but it felt metallic and triangular in shape. I loosened the button and dropped it into my pocket. The trail seemed to head in a southerly direction, more or less following the bank of the river. The only friendly area we could reach on foot from Muang Heim was to the south.

Within a half hour or so, we left the trail—now crowded with a mass of people fleeing the village—crossed the river again, and left the river bank. After stumbling through thick jungle for a short distance, we came upon another trail heading south down the river valley, and proceeded on it.

The *chao muang* and Duangtha believed that the Pathet Lao would soon discover that we'd escaped to the south, and would follow us—thinking we'd be with the large group of people on the main trail we had just left. After some discussion with Sang Tian, they'd decided to leave the other trail—the main route south that most of the people were using—and get on the present one, which Sang Tian remembered from her childhood. It wasn't as good, but walking might be faster as our group seemed to be the only ones on it. And—possibly—it would be safer.

As we moved along, a few rounds of small arms fire could be heard sporadically to our rear, but didn't seem to be very close. However, the shooting didn't seem to be getting any further away from us either. We now had about thirty or forty people in our group. Besides the seven of us that had come from Sam Thong for the ceremony, there were five or six men, and the rest were women and children. Duangtha and the men remained some distance to the rear of the column, spread out as a rear guard to give warning of the approach of the enemy.

We hurried down the rough jungle trail in single file. There was no moon, but the skies were clear, and enough starlight filtered through the leafy canopy to reveal a vague outline of the tree trunks and the person ahead on the trail.

We were very worried about Pop, so Don and I had him in between us in order to help him as much as possible. I would ask him how he was feeling every few minutes. Each time he would reply that he was fine, and I would beg him to tell me the truth so we could stop and let him rest if necessary. In spite of my good intentions, he began to get annoyed when I kept repeating the same question. I decided it was better to keep quiet.

A short while later, I began to hear him breathing heavily, and his pace began to slow. I had Don get word to Sang Tian at the head of the column, and Duangtha at the tail, that we must let Pop rest for a while. Everyone stopped, and though Pop grumbled about the delay, he admitted he was short of breath and having some chest pain. He sat down with his back against a tree, and one of the women who had a blanket in her pack wrapped it around him. Even in the faint starlight I could see he was glad of the break.

There was still intermittent small arms fire back in the direction we'd come from, and at times we could hear angry shouting. Duangtha came up to find out what was going on, and I explained my fears about Pop's heart condition and the danger of pushing him too hard. We talked about making a litter and carrying him, but decided that it wasn't practical on the rough, narrow trail in the darkness. Probably the stubborn old man wouldn't allow it in any case.

Duangtha was certain the enemy was following, and—best he could tell—they were on both sides of the river. However, their progress was relatively slow, and they didn't seem to know the terrain very well. Nevertheless, we needed to move as quickly as possible. He would stay some distance in the rear of the column, but would maintain contact through two or three of the men with him.

Whenever I thought Pop needed to rest, I would go ahead and stop until I thought he was well enough to move on. On the other hand, if Duangtha thought the enemy were getting too close and we had stopped, he would send word for us to move out as quickly as possible.

And so the long night wore on—Duangtha pushing us to make sure we didn't get captured or killed, and me trying to give Pop as much rest as possible to prevent the old man from having a heart attack. Thank God we were with such wonderful people, willing to risk their lives to help their friends.

About six in the morning the dawn began to break, but fog was forming, and soon it was very thick—with only a few feet of visibility. We had small VHF transceivers for ground to air communication, and knew there'd be fixed-wing aircraft in the area before long. However, to make contact, the aircraft would need to be directly overhead, as our little radios would have very limited range in this deep valley and dense jungle.

As soon as we heard a plane, we would start calling for help on the emergency frequency which everyone monitored. When contact was made, the plane could call Sam Thong and have them send a chopper for us. In the meantime, we would continue down the valley to the south.

Around eight-thirty, we heard a plane off in the distance. There were shouts and cheering, and we started calling—but the sound of the engine disappeared before there was any answer. However, before the moans and curses had died down, we could hear the plane again, and soon got through on the radio. It was impossible to make visual contact with the plane, but we told the pilot we were following the river to the south. We would continue down the Muang Heim Valley until the fog cleared and have the chopper pick us up on the river. The chopper wouldn't be able to see us in the jungle, and we couldn't possibly cut a landing pad in the heavy growth. On the river, the chopper pilot would have a point of reference to find us, and we should be able to clear a place large enough to make the pickup.

We continued down the trail, not having heard any signs of pursuit for at least two hours. The fog began to clear around ten o'clock, and the sun came out bright and warm. We began to walk at a more leisurely pace, and Pop appeared to be breathing okay and having no discomfort. Everyone was in good spirits and laughing and talking.

We left the trail, and in a few minutes were at the river. It was eleven o'clock and we'd been on the run since just before midnight. After a short search, we found a suitable spot, and hacked out a pad. Right on schedule we heard the chopper coming toward us. Don got the pilot on the radio and guided him to the pad. As soon as he touched down, we filled the aircraft with Pop and some of the women and children. We would shuttle to Phou Khum (LS50), the closest friendly enclave, 15 chopper minutes to the south.

Duangtha, Frank, the *chao muang,* Don, and I left on the last load. As soon as the chopper was airborne, Frank pulled a flask out of his pack and passed it around. We all took a big swig, Duangtha lit up with a huge grin, Frank burst out laughing, and soon all five of us were laughing almost hysterically. I don't know what was so funny, but I guess it was simply the joy of being alive and safe.

Phou Khum had a STOL strip, so we called in a Porter and flew back to Sam Thong. We had been gone for about 24 hours.

Again, one of our dispensaries had been destroyed by the enemy before we had a chance to use it. I hoped that we weren't setting a precedent.

Pha Thi

Pha Thi (LS85) is a mountain about 1,786 meters high in the northern part of Sam Neua province. It is one of the taller peaks in this rough karst area. Hong Non (LS86) is 25 kilometers to the east, and Sam Neua City is ten kilometers further. The country is so rugged that it normally takes the local people two days to walk from Pha Thi to Hong Non, and another half day to reach Sam Neua City. The reader may recall that during the cholera epidemic, it took us three days to ride horse-back from Hong Non to Pha Thi.

The lower part of the mountain is forested, but the upper slopes are bare except for a thick carpet of wild mint. A solid block of bare limestone sits on the top of the mountain, with sheer, vertical faces forty to fifty meters high. This big cap rock is about 150 meters in length and fifty meters wide, with a flat top. On the east side, the vertical cliff has crumbled in one spot, forming a steep, rubble-strewn slope that allows one to scramble up to the top—but with some difficulty. The west side drops straight down for about 600 meters.

Three or four kilometers directly north, across a deep valley, was the village of Houi Khammoune (LS111). It sat on top of another limestone peak at a slightly lower level than Pha Thi. Houi Khammoune was an old Meo village of about 250 people. However, it could be flooded with refugees when there was enemy activity around the villages to the east in the direction of Sam Neua City.

In 1967, the US built an air navigation station (TACAN) on top of Pha Thi to facilitate the bombing of North Vietnam and Laos. After the TACAN was installed, a TSQ system (radar to control tactical aircraft strikes) was added. The Air Force and CIA jointly manned and operated the installation with a team of about twenty men. Usually, one or two military attache people were also on the site. Two hundred or so of VP's Meo irregulars and village militia, under the command of Major Gia Tu, provided local security for the operation, along with a small contingent of Thai troops.

The commander of the Thai unit at that time was the colorful Major-General Chamlong Srimuang (then a captain) who later became Governor of Bangkok, a member of parliament, and who led the pro-democracy movement against the military junta of General Suchinda in Bangkok in May 1992.

By coincidence, Gia Tu had attended a communications training course in Thailand that Chamlong had taught, so they knew each other on a friendly basis. Gia Tu was happy to have his old teacher with him. Chamlong's autobiography provides the only first-hand, written account of what transpired the night Pha Thi fell, so far as I know.

The security troops and their families lived in a village at the base of the cap rock, while the US Air Force technicians lived on top of the rock in trailer-like modules that had been put in place by big choppers. One to three CIA operations officers usually stayed down the slope near the security forces. The modular units also housed the navigational and radar equipment. Around the base of the mountain were an additional 800 of VP's irregulars, who formed a defensive screen facing the Vietnamese and Pathet Lao forces—which were gradually being built up to the east of Pha Thi.

After the station on Pha Thi went into operation, aerial observation reported a road being pioneered out of Sam Neua City toward the west. As it snaked farther and farther through the rugged terrain, it became evident its destination was Pha Thi. The Vietnamese were going to try to knock out the navigation-radar station—and evidently they felt they needed heavy weapons that could only be brought in by vehicles.

Periodically, the US Air Force bombed the road and construction equipment. Nevertheless, slowly—meter by meter, week after week, seldom pausing—the road crept closer and closer to Pha Thi. It was fascinating to watch.

By February of 1968, the road reached the vicinity of the mountain ridge just east of Pha Thi—a location where accurate artillery and rocket fire could be brought to bear on the installation. Everyone expected Pha Thi to be hit at any moment, but suddenly all activity seemed to cease. Days passed and nothing happened. Tension began to relax, even though there was frequent contact with the enemy all around Pha Thi. Between 2,500-3,000 Vietnamese and PL troops were reported in a tightening semi-circle to the east of the mountain.

At this time, Ernie Kuhn, the USAID refugee relief officer assigned to the area was working with the refugees at Houi Khammoune. Most of the guys like Ernie who worked in insecure areas carried two radios. Ernie had a little VHF transceiver for ground to air and line of sight contact, and a portable HF single sideband transceiver for long range contact with Vientiane and the major field stations.

It was late at night in March of 1968. Pat and I were both in Vientiane for a change, and were sound asleep. The phone rang, we both roused up, and Pat answered it. The radio room in the USAID compound was calling with a contact for her. I could hear a very excited voice, even though I was four or five feet away from the phone.

"Pat, this is Ernie. How do you read?"

"Loud and clear, Ernie."

"I'm at 111 [Houi Khammoune] looking across the valley at 85 [Pha Thi]. The commies are blowing the shit out of it. I talked to them at 85 earlier on VHF and all were okay. Now I can't raise anyone. I've been trying to get Shackley or Tyrell on the phone but no one's home. Try to find somebody. Tell 'em to get some goddamn planes up here quick. Over."

Ted Shackley was the CIA station chief, and Bob Tyrell was the air attache in Vientiane. There were always attack bombers on station that could divert and be over the target in ten or twenty minutes—or, with luck, even less.

Pat was mumbling to herself as she searched for telephone numbers. "As usual every one of the bastards is probably at some damn cocktail party when you need them."

After several tries she got through to the right party and asked for Ted Shackley. The other half of the phone conversation was revealed later by a friend who was listening.

"Ted, this is Pat McCreedy. Pha Thi's under heavy attack. They need some air support bad. Can we get something up there right away."

"Pat, that's absurd. We've been checking with them and everything's okay. If they were having trouble they'd be screaming. Who told you this story?"

"They *are* screaming. Ernie Kuhn just called and told me."

"Well, you tell your friend Ernie he doesn't know what he's talking about. Don't worry about it."

"Listen, goddammit, let me talk to Bob Tyrell."

But Shackley had already hung up.

Pat was so outraged she could only curse and sputter. Before she could regain her composure to call back and ask for Bob Tyrell, the following short conversation took place at the party.

Shackley: "I just got a call from that crazy McCreedy woman. Some wild story about Pha Thi being under heavy attack. Some guy called Ernie told her. She wanted to talk to you, but I wouldn't bother with it."

Tyrell: "Christ, you mean Pat McCreedy and Ernie Kuhn both say Pha Thi is under heavy attack and you just brush it off!"

Shackley: "How in the hell would they know what's happening in Sam Neua at this time of night?"

Tyrell: "I don't know how they know a lot of things, but if they say something, you damn well better believe it. Have your people try to contact Pha Thi and I'll call Pat."

Just as Pat was about to pick up the phone and call Bob Tyrell, he called her.

Pat explained to him what was going on, and how she got the information. Bob said he'd try to get some aircraft over Pha Thi as quickly as possible.

Pat called Ernie and told him that planes were on their way.

Ernie was still frantic. "If they don't hurry, it'll be too late. It's unbelievable. At first it seemed to be rockets mostly, but probably some artillery too. The whole goddamn place was one big mass of fire and explosions. Now there's small arms fire and grenades going off on top where the Air Force is."

"Have you been able to get anyone on the radio."

"No one answers. I keep calling but no answer. Still no aircraft overhead."

"Okay Ernie, if you have nothing else right now, give me a call in 15 minutes. I'll be standing by."

It had been about an hour since Ernie's first radio call. Pha Thi had been under assault for about an hour and twenty minutes when he called again.

"Most of the big stuff has stopped. I still hear automatic weapons fire and small explosions . . . probably grenades. I'm sure they've made a ground assault on the installation. Can't be too much left on top of that rock. Well, shit! A plane just dropped a flare. We finally got some aircraft—but shit, they're too late."

Ernie signed off and said he'd call Pat at the office the next day. We turned off the light but didn't sleep too well.

✛

Nineteen Americans were on Pha Thi that night. Eight escaped and were picked up the next day—five were wounded, and one died on the way to Thailand; and 11 were killed in the battle—their bodies buried on the site by the Vietnamese soldiers who made the assault.

When the rocket and artillery fire started that night, the first round just happened to hit the communications building. The Vietnamese overran the place, destroyed some of the equipment, and withdrew the next day. The operation had been carried out by 26 sappers who had scaled the 600-meter, vertical southwest face of Pha Thi in the dark. The defenders were caught by complete surprise. Everyone had expected the ground assault to come from the east, over the more favorable terrain.

Two days after the fall of Pha Thi, Ernie Kuhn and Gia Tu were in a chopper searching for refugees in the Pha Thi area. They had worked together for some time and had become good friends. They were both lying on the floor of the chopper with their heads out the door looking at the ground. Gia Tu took a round between the eyes and died immediately. Poor Ernie was beside himself with shock and grief for days.

The President of the United States made a policy decision to stop the bombing of North Vietnam several days later—so the installation would have lost its significance in any event. With hindsight, the whole episode was an exercise in futility for both sides.

But that can be said about most aspects of any war.

Outstanding Woman of the Year

I'd been out in the field for two weeks, but still didn't want to walk into the house. Becky, Ray, and Walter were at school in Switzerland, and Pat was in Washington. Usually I was happy to get home, but I hated an empty house.

Pat McCreedy was having dinner with Pat Nixon.

Each year, all the departments of the federal government submit recommendations to a special committee that chooses the Outstanding Women in Government. The committee is composed of prominent women in business, science, academia, entertainment, and the media. Charley Mann had recommended Pat, and she had been chosen from the several dozens of candidates. We were all very proud of her.

The protocol called for the Outstanding Woman of 1972 to have dinner with the President. Unfortunately, Mr. Nixon was out of the country hobnobbing with the Russians, instead of being in Washington as he should have been.

In place of the President, Mrs. Nixon hosted the affair. Pat's mother was also invited, and both Mom and Grandma found Mrs. Nixon to be a warm and gracious person. It was a delightful evening and they enjoyed themselves immensely.

Becky, Ray, and Walter very proudly told all their friends about the award, and that their Mom was having dinner with President Nixon. When they found that the President hadn't made it, they weren't only terribly disappointed, they were outraged. Mom stood up by the President! What a loss of face with their friends.

They got some pictures of Mrs. Nixon presenting the award to Mom at the White House, but it wasn't the same as if it had been the President.

They swore they would never vote Republican.

So far as I know, they never have.

Love Story

In mid-1969 the Vietnamese had kept up a sustained attack on Na Khang (LS36) for over two weeks—determined to wipe out the last center of resistance in Sam Neua province. There had been fighting inside the position on two occasions. When the attack began, several hundred civilians and dependants of the soldiers were still living in the immediate vicinity. Many of the women and children were killed during the fighting. Those lucky enough to escape were straggling into Phu Khum (LS50), fifty kilometers to the southwest.

We were working in the area, and landed at Phu Khum one particular morning on the way back to Sam Thong. I wanted to check with the *chao muang*, Yua Pao, to see if he had any problems that needed my attention. After we'd discussed our business and I was getting ready to leave, he asked me to wait a few minutes. He had two small children who had lost their parents and had no one to care for them at Phu Khum. If I took them to Sam Thong, possibly we could find some relatives there—or at Long Chieng—to take them in.

Yua Pao sent a man for the children, and in a few minutes he came back with a small Meo boy about ten years old who was carrying his little three-year-old sister on his back. All the strange people and activity terrified the poor girl. She sobbed as she hid her face in her tiny hands. Her brother soothed her and gently bounced her up and down while he whispered reassurance. They had no belongings and were filthy and tattered. Their emaciated little bodies and the fear in their eyes was indeed pitiful to see. I put them on the plane and wrapped them in a blanket. They covered their heads and never moved or looked out of the plane until we landed at Sam Thong.

First we fed them and tried to allay some of their fear. After a while, when they were more comfortable, we talked to the boy and he told the following story.

234

Their village had been overrun by the Vietnamese several months before, and the family had taken refuge at Na Khang. They remained there until the last attack. During the first night of the assault, their parents were killed. For some reason the mother and father had stood up at the same time in their shallow foxhole. They both died at the same instant from a burst of automatic weapons fire. The two children, huddled down in the hole, weren't hit.

The boy and his sister hid there throughout the day and into the second night of the attack with their dead parents. In the middle of the night, during a lull in the battle, they escaped from Na Khang with a large group of other civilians.

During the next four days, as they fled toward the southwest attempting to reach Phu Khum, they ran into enemy troops several times. Many people were killed or captured, but the boy was able to escape with his sister and hide each time. On the fourth day, after a terrifying and panic-stricken encounter with the enemy, they found themselves alone.

For most of their escape the boy had carried the little girl on his back. When he became too tired, he would put her down and she would walk for a short way so he could rest a little. However, after a few days, her bare feet were so badly cut on the sharp rocks that she could no longer walk. Now, he had to carry her all the time. Every 100 meters or so, they would need to stop and rest before continuing their slow, painful journey. Nevertheless, he knew they must keep moving or they would surely die.

Desperately hungry with little sister crying for food, brother gathered bits of tender leaves and grass, and occasionally took a stick and dug up roots that he knew were edible. This helped some, but after a few days, the girl's mouth was so sore she couldn't chew the rough food. He would take the most tender parts and chew them until they were soft, then feed the pulp to his sister.

The nights were cold, and their half-naked bodies shivered as they clung to each other, trying to sleep in a crevice of the roots of some large tree. The sounds and terrors of the dark jungle were even worse than the cold. For ten days and nights they struggled through this nightmare before reaching Phu Khum.

While the boy told his story, his sister continued to grasp him tightly and hide her face. He cradled her in his arms, and rocked gently back and forth as he stroked her head. His devotion and love was indeed a touching and wonderful thing to see.

Fortunately, we were able to find a family at Long Chieng from their village who were happy to care for both children.

Good Times, Bad Times

The medical program made good progress from 1967 to 1970. We had some setbacks, but overall it was a period of steady growth and improvement. Substantive projects had been undertaken in national health development with the Ministry of Health. We had built an excellent nursing school at Mahosot, the main government hospital in Vientiane, which was graduating internationally-accredited registered nurses; thanks to family planning funding, a 200-bed addition had been made to Mahosot which was actually the central core of a modern teaching hospital; hospitals were built at Pakse, Khong Sedone, Vang Vieng, and Sayaboury; and an active, well-accepted maternal and child health, family planning program was operating in all the major towns.

In addition, OB had renovated old government medical facilities at Saravane in the South and Kengkok in the Central region, and had put medical teams in place in these locations. There were now nine OB hospitals located at Attopeu, Paksong, Saravane, and Khong Sedone in the South; Kengkok in Central Laos; Vientiane and Vang Vieng in Vientiane province; and at Sayaboury and Ban Houi Sai in the Northwest.

In the village health program there had been gradual expansion, but mainly we had tried to improve the quality of care. This had been carried out through regular retraining cycles in schools established in all the major program areas of the country. Also, we were training many more girls in basic public health and midwifery to work with the medics as a team at the village level.

The hospital at Sam Thong had been rebuilt, and now had 250 beds. A 100-bed military hospital was built at Long Chieng, which handled most of the casualties in the Northern region of the country. Since most of the soldiers' families lived at Long Chieng, a hospital there was a more convenient arrangement for them than using the hospital facilities at Sam Thong. Dr. Khammoung and Dr. Bounthan were transferred to this facility, and the two American doctors—one from my office and one from the Air Force—remained at Sam Thong. As far as possible we tried to handle the civilians at Sam Thong and the military at Long Chieng—but on many occasions one overflowed into the other.

Soon after our arrival in Laos, it became obvious that poliomyelitis was endemic, and a serious problem. In every village there were crippled individuals whose history pointed to polio in early childhood, and we were seeing acute cases in small children.

The Sabin oral polio vaccine is usually difficult to use in the developing world, as it must be kept under constant refrigeration. In countries like Laos, with no roads, it is almost impossible to carry out immunization programs. However, with our large helicopter and STOL air support, we were able to fly the vaccine into the most remote areas of Laos, and a comprehensive, country-wide immunization program was carried out.

The Sabin oral vaccine is a live attenuated virus, and lives in the gut of the immunized individual. When the immunized child defecates on the ground, the virus is passed in the faeces, and so contaminates the environment. When the un-immunized child places fingers that are soiled from playing in the dirt in his mouth, he immunizes himself. This "seeding" phenomenon was much more effective than anticipated, and in a few years polio had gradually disappeared. Certainly, for me this was one of the most rewarding experiences of working in Laos.

Although our medical programs were advancing satisfactorily, by the late sixties we were becoming increasingly pessimistic about the future. Both the political and military situations in Vietnam were deteriorating, and it was obvious that the US would pull out of Indochina and abandon its allies to the communists.

Again, Pat and I hadn't taken home leave for over three years, and USAID personnel in Washington were insisting that we do so. The medical program at this point was far too big and complex for the two of us to be gone at the same time, so we took separate leave.

Becky and Ray were in school in Switzerland, so Pat and Walter would go through Europe and pick them up before going to the US. When Pat got back to Laos, I would go on leave. Things went as planned. Pat spent the summer in the US, and came back through Europe to put Becky and Ray back in school. Walter flew on to Bangkok from Zurich by himself, and I met him at Don Muong Airport in Bangkok. The next day we would return to Vientiane and he would start school. It was 1969. Walt would soon be 13, and the next year he would leave home for high school in Switzerland with Ray.

We grabbed a taxi and started into town. I was staying at the Amarin Hotel. It was the usual hot, humid Bangkok day, and we were soon wet with sweat in the smelly taxi with no air conditioning. The traffic, heat, and exhaust fumes were terrible. Nevertheless, Walter laid back in the seat with his eyes half closed and a look of contentment on his face.

He turned to me and said, "Its great to be home, Dad."

"Well, you're not home yet, Walt."

"I know but I'm back in Southeast Asia, and I'm really glad."

"What's the matter buddy? Didn't you enjoy the States?"

"Well, yeah in a way. I was glad to see Grandma and Grandpa. We had a great time fishing in the Gulf."

"You sound like things didn't go so well. Did you have any trouble?"

"No, no trouble, but I sure wouldn't want to live back there."

"Why not?"

"Well, first of all, they don't have any stores."

"No stores! That's all there is. What do you mean, no stores?"

"You know, not the kind we have in Vientiane. Nobody wants to sell you anything, and its hard to get anyone to wait on you. When they do, they're sure not friendly. Grandma took me down to buy a pair of pants and this lady waited on us. I asked her how much the pair I liked was. She told me 14 dollars. I told her I'd give her ten and she looked at me like I was crazy. She wouldn't come down at all and got about half mad."

"Walt, that's because people don't bargain in the States. The lady wasn't used to that."

"Yeah, I know. Grandma told me that, but she could've been a little more friendly. Besides, the pants weren't really worth 14 dollars. I could've bought the material in the Sunday Market and had Mr. Ly make them for six dollars."

"Okay, so the stores aren't too good. Wasn't it fun to see all your relatives?"

"I guess so, but when we visited someone, you couldn't talk or do anything because everybody was watching TV. That's about all some of them do. They'd get upset if you interrupted their program. I'm sure glad we don't have TV."

The first thing he did when he got to Vientiane was go and have tea with his friend, Mr. Ly, the tailor and tell him about the terrible price of pants in the States.

In a few days Pat got back. A week or so later, I took off for home leave. After stopping in Switzerland to see Becky at Gstaadt and Ray at Zug, I went directly to Washington. The State Department was holding a continuous cycle of seminars on Southeast Asia which lasted three weeks. All foreign service officers above a certain rank were obligated to participate while on home leave. I wanted to get this over with before I started my vacation.

The first two weeks of the seminar were devoted to discussions with high-ranking officials in government and academia on the history, politics, and US policy in regard to Southeast Asia. There were about a dozen participants, and the sessions were extremely interesting. We talked to ambassadors, senators, generals, learned professors, the head of the CIA, and people from the Rand Corporation and other think tank organizations. However, it made no difference to whom we talked, the consensus was always the same: Vietnam and the rest of Indochina was a lost cause. Get out as quickly and gracefully as possible.

The last week of the seminar, the participants divided into groups of four. Each group would prepare and present a paper on, "What Are the Minimal Conditions for an American Withdrawal from Indochina." By the end of the week, it became apparent that I was the only participant naive enough to think in terms of autonomy and freedom for South Vietnam, Cambodia, and Laos. For everyone else, it was only a question of what was the fastest and best way to disengage and turn it over to the North Vietnamese. I was upset and disappointed—and was rapidly losing what little optimism remained. Maybe the good guys didn't always win, or— worse yet—maybe I wasn't one of the good guys.

After two or three weeks of partying with friends and relatives, I flew to Nice and relaxed on the beach. The Cote d'Azur was too cool for swimming, but there were few tourists and the weather was beautiful. I laid in the sun and listened to the local girls gossip. None of them wore their bikini tops, and everyone carried a pair of tweezers to pluck the pubic hairs that straggled over their bikini shorts.

At most places in France, the local people at best ignored tourists, and at worst could be extremely rude and hostile. In Nice, everyone was relaxed and friendly. If you spoke a little French, the guy in the bar would start a conversation and you ended up buying each other drinks and making friends.

The old farmer's market was a walking gourmet feast; stall after stall of cheese, sausage, paté, *brioche*, and wine in barrels. Just wandering around buying 100 grams of this, and 50 grams of that—snacking and sipping—made for one of the best meals in the world.

Becky flew down and met me at the end of the second week. We rented a car and drove through Northern Italy, across the Alps, and up to Zug to see Ray. We were having a great time, but Becky and Ray had to get back in school. I got on the plane in Zurich and headed for Laos.

✪

When I landed in Vientiane, Pop and Walter met me. As soon as I saw their faces, I knew something was terribly wrong. They had tragic news. Colonel Thong had just died at the Air Force hospital in Korat. Pat had gone down to get his body.

Three days before, he had guided an SAR mission deep into North Vietnam for a downed American pilot. They found the pilot, but Thong took a round in the abdomen on the pickup. Pat was upcountry at the time, and had met the chopper on its return from the rescue mission. She got Thong to Korat as quickly as possible, and he'd been taken to the operating room immediately. He survived the surgery, but the damage had been too extensive. After lapsing in and out of a coma for three days, he quietly passed away.

It was a terrible loss. We were all crushed with grief. It was difficult to rationalize Thong giving his life to save that of some unknown American. My anger was as great as my sorrow. There was no justice. Yet deep down in my heart, I knew that this good Buddhist soldier had met his preordained fate without regret. He wouldn't want us to grieve his departure.

Pat brought him back to Vientiane that afternoon. Duangtha, Phan, the *chao muang* of Hua Muang, Pop, Father B, and some of the other old Sam Neua guerrillas came down for the funeral. We all sat around for two nights and two days with Thong's body playing cards, drinking, eating, crying, and laughing.

The afternoon of the second day, we went to the *wat* and watched the cremation. It was the end of an era. We all knew that things would never be the same in Northern Laos. Pessimism was turning to despair. The situation in Sam Neua was desperate at best—without Thong, Sam Neua was lost. Without Sam Neua, Laos would be lost.

There could never be anyone to take Thong's place.

The Elephant

If the reader should ever come across a bargain elephant and be tempted to buy it—don't!

I know because I tried it.

By 1970 we had established a half dozen little bamboo-and-thatch dispensaries on the Bolovens Plateau in Southern Laos—a wild and remote area that was accessible only by air. The main village of Houi Kong had a good airstrip, and was the administrative center for all our projects on the plateau—with the main dispensary, training school, and medical warehouse which supported the satellite facilities scattered over the countryside—but there were no roads through the thick jungle that covered much of the area.

Supplying and supervising the dispensaries out from Houi Kong was a problem due to the lack of transportation. There were only about 4,400 people in the area, so it was difficult to justify the high cost of aircraft—which wasn't a problem in other, more densely-settled places.

Many wild elephants still roamed the jungles in Laos, and quite a few had been domesticated and were used as draft animals—particularly useful for logging, as they can push, pull, or lift tremendous loads over short distances. There were elephants on the Bolovens Plateau, and a villager in Houi Kong owned one of them.

Win McKeithen, a young IVS community development worker from Connecticut, was stationed at Houi Kong, and he and I made the initial survey of the plateau to determine the best spots to establish dispensaries. Win hired the elephant to carry our gear, and I'd been particularly impressed with this rather exotic mode of transportation.

Later, after the dispensaries were functioning, in an attempt to solve the transport problem, we hired the mahout and his elephant on a few occasions to distribute drugs and supplies. This arrangement seemed to work fairly well, but the pair weren't always available when we needed them. Without knowing anything about pachyderms, and not giving much thought to the matter, I decided to buy the elephant and end the transportation problem once and for all.

By this time, Win had been hired by USAID and was working in another area, so I didn't have the benefit of his consultation. After some negotiation, I paid 400,000 kip—the equivalent of 800 dollars—for the big beast. I discovered later that this was considered an exorbitant sum—and four times the going price for elephants. Since no one could handle him but his mahout, it was necessary to hire him also.

But that was only the beginning of the problem. The elephant required 100 kilograms or more of fodder each day, but couldn't be allowed to graze, as he would damage the local gardens and fields. Since the mahout was too busy handling the animal to gather food, a second person had to be hired for that purpose. I was beginning to have reservations about my purchase.

When we began to use the elephant regularly, I found there were many other things that I didn't know about this method of transportation. The elephant would only walk a maximum of four hours each day. After that, he absolutely refused to go further, despite the shouting, bribery, or beating from the mahout. Elephants move slowly. So slowly that a man walking at a leisurely pace often has to stop and let the animal catch up. They also don't like to carry too much on their backs. With the mahout, the medic supervisor, and a medic on his back, the elephant would refuse to carry any great amount of drugs and supplies.

Before long, we were beset by complaints from various villagers about damage done to their gardens and property by "*Tan Maw's* elephant." Whenever I landed at Houi Kong, there were new claims to settle. The situation soon became intolerable—and I admitted my mistake. I told Pek, our medic supervisor to sell the elephant back to the mahout—or anyone else who might want him—for any price he could get.

When I returned on the next trip, Pek still had the elephant. The market had dried up. No one was buying elephants at that time. It was a most frustrating predicament, but good sense prevailed. The only other solutions were to turn the animal loose, take it to a remote spot in the jungle and shoot it, or have the biggest barbecue ever seen on the Bolovens Plateau. Finally, after a bottle or two of whiskey, the original owner reluctantly accepted the elephant—as a gift! But I had to throw in a carton of American cigarettes also!

Eventually, we pioneered some trails from Houi Kong to the dispensary sites. A Jeep was flown in by a De Havilland Caribou, and this solution worked much better than the elephant.

This particular elephant wasn't white, but I now fully understood the meaning of the expression.

On the Hill

The last few years we were in Laos, it seemed as if Pat spent as much time in Washington as she did in Vientiane. As the resistance to US participation in the Vietnam War increased, Congress held more and more hearings on Indochina. In large part, the hearings on Laos were directed at discrediting the programs we were carrying out to help prevent the country from falling to the Vietnamese invaders.

There was no objectivity or interest in the truth—or any sympathy for the desperate plight of the Lao fighting for their homes. The sole purpose was for political propaganda in an atmosphere that promoted personal aggrandisement of the committee members, and furthered American withdrawal from Indochina.

Whenever USAID Washington had to go to the Hill to testify on Laos, Pat and Jack Williamson were usually called to Washington as resource persons. They were the two people in the mission who had the most detailed knowledge of both the administrative and political situation in Vientiane, as well as the operational situation in the field. Jack had the analytical and intellectual capability, while Pat was a walking database, with an incredible recall for the most obscure fact or figure.

Their prime nemesis was Teddy Kennedy. As chairman of the Judiciary Sub-committee on Refugees, Senator Kennedy was constantly holding hearings on the refugee programs in Vietnam and Laos.

Pat found out early in the game that the senator from Massachusetts was a gentleman, and was always reluctant to be unduly harsh with a lady. She exploited this by dressing and looking as feminine as possible for the hearings. A new, tight-fitting shift always helped the cause. She used twice as much perfume as usual, and would even forego her little Filipino cigars that she smoked constantly.

In spite of the chagrin and frustration of seeing our programs attacked and criticized unjustly (or at least in our eyes unjustly), the whole affair was exciting and challenging. She returned home cursing Kennedy, all charged up and ready to go another round. She felt she'd met the enemy on his own turf, and although she hadn't won, at least she'd held her own against a very tough opponent.

The Beginning of the End

By early 1971 it was increasingly evident that we would not be able to maintain the Sam Thong operation. The enemy was determined to wipe out the Long Chieng-Sam Thong complex. Long Chieng had to be defended at all costs, and VP simply didn't have the men to defend both places.

If Long Chieng was lost, the war was over in Northern Laos, and Vientiane would quickly fall. Although the two sites are only about five kilometers apart, if Sam Thong was included in the Long Chieng defensive perimeter, Long Chieng would be greatly weakened. Pop and I understood this basic fact of life, and never put pressure on VP to strengthen the handful of soldiers assigned to maintain security at Sam Thong. All military resources had to go into the defense of Long Chieng. Nevertheless, the local leaders—and the other Americans working at Sam Thong—bitterly complained that VP was neglecting them, and that he didn't care about the Sam Thong operation; that his only concern was his own hide and the people at Long Chieng.

At first, Pop and I tried to explain to our people why VP couldn't take soldiers away from Long Chieng to protect Sam Thong. After a while, however, we realized that almost everyone resented our explanations, and that further discussion was counter-productive. As a consequence, we tried to avoid the subject whenever possible. If it came up in discussion, we listened sympathetically but tried to avoid talking about it—and possibly ending up in a confrontation.

Bill Lair, the CIA field operations officer for Laos sent Jack Shirley, one of his most experienced men, up to Sam Thong to assist us in improving security. Jack had spent a lot of time in Xieng Khoung in previous years, and he knew the situation well. With limited resources, he initially focused on setting up a warning system of intelligence agents and patrols that would give us adequate time to make an orderly evacuation. Secondly, he increased internal security with improved surveillance at night—to prevent any small units infiltrating Sam Thong and carrying out a raid or sabotage.

In our discussions about a possible evacuation under emergency circumstances, *nai kong* Zeu Keu (Pop's Meo counterpart) told me he was concerned about people crossing the Nam Ngum river, especially at night. The Nam Ngum bordered Sam Thong on the south and west, and any escape route would certainly be in that direction. Although the river in this area was only 10 or 15 meters wide and a meter to a meter-and-a-half deep, it made a steep descent and was turbulent and swift. The approach to the river valley was also steep and treacherous. Children, or even adults, could easily be swept away.

Zeu Keu asked me to get several hundred meters of heavy rope so he could cache pieces along the steep slopes and the bank of the river to make lines to cling to during the crossing. I sent the rope up to him immediately.

Around this time I also started to look for a fall-back position to use if the enemy forced us to evacuate Sam Thong. After much aerial reconnaissance and discussion with Tom Cole, the chief of USAID public works, the best site seemed to be a place called Ban Son, located about fifty kilometers south of the Sam Thong-Long Chieng area, and approximately 100 kilometers north of Vientiane.

Ban Son was a small refugee village located on a new road Tom had just completed from Vientiane to Long Chieng. It sat in a narrow, flat valley where a long airstrip could be built to take heavy aircraft. While the road was under construction, Ban Son was also the site of the USAID public works camp. The old barracks and maintenance shops were still in good condition, and Tom could convert them into a crude, but large and adequate hospital on short notice.

The surrounding area was sparsely settled, and there was plenty of room to accommodate the people displaced from Sam Thong in the event of an evacuation. A few Pathet Lao troops were located just to the west of Ban Son, but weren't present in strong enough numbers to cause much trouble.

Tom made a final check of the site, and we agreed on its selection. The airstrip could be built in a very short time—since the road would allow public works to move heavy equipment into the area quickly. Tom knew as well as I did that Sam Thong could be hit at any time, and he would expedite things as much as possible. I told Tom that I'd have to check out the plan with Pop and VP. If they agreed, then he and I would try to get Charley Mann and Ambassador Godley's approval. If they gave the go-ahead, Tom could start immediately.

Pop didn't like the idea. He felt that if we began preparing an alternative site for the evacuation of Sam Thong, it would have a very negative effect on morale. The people would think we were abandoning them. I agreed, but insisted we should be ready to evacuate the place—and do so when it was certain that enemy attack was imminent. We would wait as long as possible, but I didn't want to face the horror of the hospital with its staff and 250 patients being overrun in the middle of the night.

Pop reluctantly agreed, and we went over to Long Chieng to see VP. The general had none of Pop's reservations about making contingency plans for evacuation. Quite the opposite, in fact. He was relieved that we were considering it. The Meo leaders at Sam Thong had been harassing him constantly to send them more troops for their defence, and of course, that was impossible. He also felt that we needed to maintain Sam Thong as long as possible, but under no circumstance should we take too great a risk and allow it to be overrun. Ban Son seemed like a good choice to him, and he urged us to get the airstrip started as soon as possible.

With Pop's and VP's okay, I jumped on a plane for Vientiane, grabbed Tom Cole at public works, and went to see Charley Mann. He and Ambassador Godley readily agreed to setting up Ban Son as the fall-back position, and that we should get the work started immediately. Charley told Tom to give the Ban Son project top priority.

Going all out as usual, Tom had men and heavy earth-moving equipment rolling up the road from Vientiane to Ban Son within the hour—and by the next day, construction on the airstrip was well underway.

By the first week of March, our scouts reported daily enemy patrols just north of Sam Thong. Occasionally, a small unit would reach the ridges a few hundred meters away that overlooked the airstrip. However, no large units were seen in the area, so we sat and waited.

Each day the tension built up, and an air of gloom and despondency sat like a dark and threatening cloud over the whole place. About that time, Charley Mann and the country team decided that no Americans were to RON at Sam Thong. That was the last straw. Morale hit rock bottom, and all hope of Sam Thong surviving was gone. After that, everyone wished that the word would soon come to abandon the place so the ordeal would end. We completed our plans for routes to follow during the evacuation, and where the people were to assemble for the move to Ban Son.

On March 17th, 1971, our scouts reported large numbers of enemy troops moving toward Sam Thong. It was time to leave. About noon, Pop,

VP, and I got together at Long Chieng and agreed to evacuate the hospital immediately. Over the next few days we would phase out the rest of the operation and move it to Ban Son.

Pat, Frank Becker, and Steve Scofield were standing by at Sam Thong with Bill Leonard, the chief of USAID air operations, to supervise the evacuation. As soon as we gave them the word, Bill had Air America start bringing in C123s and Caribous. By five o'clock in the afternoon, patients, staff, and most of the major hospital equipment had been moved to the old construction camp at Ban Son.

At eleven o'clock that evening, the enemy hit Sam Thong with a heavy rocket and mortar barrage. The first rocket blew up the main ward of the hospital. Within a few minutes the whole medical and refugee support complex was a mass of shattered rubble. The civilian population had anticipated the attack, and were prepared. They quickly and quietly slipped into the jungle and crossed the river to the southwest. The Vietnamese swept through the town, but the handful of soldiers defending the place slowed them down enough for everyone to escape. There was a surprising lack of confusion and panic, and very few casualties.

In the morning, Pop and I, with the other Americans who worked at Sam Thong, met at Ban Son. Pop was in a foul mood—not depressed or sad, but mad. He and Blaine Jensen (Blaine had taken Tom Ward's place) jumped on me immediately, blaming me for the loss of Sam Thong. If I hadn't insisted on evacuating, the enemy wouldn't have attacked. The situation was so absurd that I didn't even attempt to reason with them. I grabbed a chopper, went up to the Sam Thong area, found the fleeing refugees, and shuttled our workers and the local leaders over to Long Chieng since it was the closest secure place.

Late in the afternoon, I flew back and landed at Ban Son. Pop was there to meet me. "Where in hell have you been?" he snapped.

"I've been picking our people out of the jungle, taking them to Long Chieng. We'll pick them up in the morning and bring them here."

"Goddammit, if I wanted to pick 'em up, I'd of told you so. They oughtta be out there in the jungle with everybody else."

"Pop you know we need them here—and they expected us to go get them. They'd be real upset if some of us didn't try to help them in a situation like this."

"You run the medical business and I'll run this damn operation. I don't need you tellin' me how."

We looked at each other without saying anything, then Pop turned his back to me with his head hanging down, kicking at an imaginery rock.

Finally, he turned around and there were tears in his eyes. "I'm sorry, Doc. I knew it was gonna happen, and I knew it'd be tough—but I didn't know it'd be this bad."

The enemy withdrew from Sam Thong the next day after the attack. They had accomplished their mission, and probably knew that we wouldn't attempt to reoccupy it.

✛

Pop had established his headquarters at Sam Thong in 1961, and the operation had lasted exactly ten years. During that time, it had provided the only support for approximately 800,000 refugees displaced by the Vietnamese and Pathet Lao. It had provided primary education for more than 150,000 children in tribal groups that had never seen schools before. In later years, its normal school graduated more than 300 teachers. Over 800 medical auxiliaries were trained at Sam Thong, 100,000 patients were hospitalized, and 450,000 outpatients were treated. The medical dispensaries throughout the countryside supported from Sam Thong had more than ten million patient visits in that ten-year period.

Other people, such as myself, worked in the program, and made some contribution, but all these accomplishments in the final analysis were due to one man—Edgar "Pop" Buell, Indiana farmer and proud American who truly cared.

Trouble with Uncle Oscar

The reader may recall that we stopped in Manila on our way to Laos in 1963, and at that time I met with Oscar Orellano, the head of Operation Brotherhood. Despite a pleasant and interesting visit, I had left Manila with a vague feeling of foreboding that there might be some impending problem in our relationship.

During the first few years of my association with OB, Oscar Orellano usually made an annual visit to Laos, and spent a few days with each of the OB hospital teams. It was a time for parties, with much feasting, singing, and dancing—and everyone looked forward to these visits.

Everything went smoothly, and Uncle Oscar let his nephew, Vitoy run the Lao program pretty much as he pleased. It was a time of expansion as well, and the OB budget increased every year, as did the salaries of OB personnel. The fee paid to the OB headquarters in Manila under the contract with USAID Laos also steadily increased. It was a satisfactory arrangement for all concerned, and the Lao communities served by OB were getting good medical care at a minimal cost to the United States government.

Unfortunately, as the war in Southeast Asia wore on with no end in sight, the budget for foreign assistance ran into more and more resistance in the US Congress. By 1971, the Lao program had to take cuts along with other high-priority programs. Whether we liked it or not, the cost of the OB contract had to be reduced. Vitoy was very cooperative, and—working together—he and Pat came up with a plan that would make the necessary reductions.

In spite of these cuts, we all thought that the changes would have a minimal effect as far as reducing the amount, or quality, of services to the patients. Most of the cost savings would come from USAID furnishing certain OB maintenance, transportation, and procurement services—which OB had normally provided themselves. However, a significant element in the new budget was a reduction in support for the overhead and personnel in the Manila headquarters. We didn't feel that the services which the headquarters provided to the Lao contract justified the support costs we were paying.

We normally re-negotiated the OB contract on a yearly basis, and Vitoy sent our draft of the new budget off for Oscar Orellano's approval. When he received it, Uncle Oscar's screams of anguish could be heard all the way from Manila to Vientiane. He'd been stabbed in the pocketbook. He caught the first plane for Laos.

In previous meetings, Oscar and Charley Mann hadn't hit it off well—even under the best of circumstances. In the present, controversial situation, their first meeting quickly degenerated into a confrontation, a real dog fight. Their personal animosity toward each other caused both to lose their objectivity. Orellano accused Mann of acting like a Yankee colonialist and trying to exploit the poor Filipinos. Mann accused Orellano of having no interest in helping the Lao people, but was only concerned about making money through the contract.

The first meeting ended so badly that the two refused to meet again. Vitoy and I were caught in the middle. For days, the two of us went back and forth trying to work out some sort of compromise, but neither would budge a fraction of an inch.

The contract had expired, and OB was running out of money to feed patients and pay salaries. The USAID legal counsel was insisting that we sign some piece of paper immediately, or he'd be obligated by law to start termination proceedings under the terms of the old contract. Worst of all, the dog fight in Vientiane reached the newspapers in Manila—and the publicity was very embarrassing to both the Philippine and American governments.

Vitoy and I were besides ourselves with frustration and disgust over this stupid breakdown in relations between our respective bosses. We were terribly afraid that we were about to see an end to the OB operation in Laos. That would be a real catastrophe, especially for the refugees and war casualties that depended on the OB hospital services.

One evening, at the height of our little crisis, Vitoy called and told me that he had just been to the Philippine Embassy. The ambassador had called him over to tell him that he had received a priority message from the minister of foreign affairs. President Marcos was sending the presidential secretary, Alex Melchior to Laos to look into the dispute between OB and USAID.

Mr. Melchior was to arrive the next day. It seemed that the affair had been played up in the Manila newspapers to the point where even Marcos was concerned about it.

My first reaction to this news was a mixture of skepticism and alarm. A high-powered politico from Manila would irritate Charley Mann even more than Oscar Orellano. However, Vitoy knew Alex Melchior, and had a high opinion of him. The presidential secretary was in his mid-thirties, had graduated at the top of his class at West Point, and many considered him a brilliant political intellectual. At that time, he was probably the second most powerful man in the Philippines. Besides, Vitoy assured me, Alex was so personable he could charm anyone, even Charley Mann. I was still very dubious of Mr. Melchior's intercession, but as it turned out, Vitoy was correct.

Alex Melchior arrived in Vientiane the next afternoon. He had dinner that evening with the Philippine ambassador and Oscar Orellano. The next morning he talked to Vitoy and me, and we went over the details of the new OB contract with him. Alex understood the problems we were having with Washington, and the political turmoil the war in Indochina was causing. Vitoy's high opinion of Alex Melchior certainly seemed justified.

That afternoon, he met with Charley Mann in private, and then the two of them went over to see the American ambassador, Mac Godley. That evening, Charley had everyone over for dinner—Alex, the Philippine ambassador, Oscar, Ambassador Godley, Vitoy, and myself, plus several other guests from the international community. It was a delightful evening. All was sweetness and light.

Alex was a big, friendly, intelligent bear of a man, whom everyone immediately liked. His wit and good humor were contagious. The conversation was relaxed and pleasant, and there was no mention of the contract. Charley and Oscar seemed to be making a special effort to be friendly. Their cordiality amazed us. It seemed that Alex had done the impossible.

The next morning Vitoy called and said Oscar was ready to sign the contract. That afternoon, Alex Melchior returned to the Philippines. It was never clear exactly what he'd said or done, but it was an impressive performance.

Not long after his mission to Laos, Alex resigned his position on Marcos' staff, and eventually became director of the Asian Development Bank. Some said he had become disillusioned with Marcos and quit, while others said

Marcos dismissed him out of fear that he was becoming too powerful politically and posed a threat.

✪✪✪

After the flap over the contract, Oscar didn't return to Laos for over two years. He had developed a heart problem, and his doctor restricted his travel. Then he suddenly appeared, after giving Vitoy only two days notice before his arrival. Vitoy brought him over to my office, and after the usual small talk, I asked him what had caused his sudden and unexpected visit.

Oscar told me he had received word of a serious personnel problem regarding the OB staff, and felt it needed his personal attention as quickly as possible. This was a surprising revelation to me. I knew of no such problem, and if there was one, it was odd that Vitoy hadn't discussed it with me. Also, I couldn't conceive of any personnel matter that Vitoy couldn't handle himself without Oscar's help.

I asked Oscar to tell me about the problem, but he insisted that it was an internal matter and he preferred not to discuss it until he had sorted it out with the OB staff. Our conversation was obviously embarrassing to Oscar, so I didn't press him about it.

That evening, Vitoy called me at home and said he'd be over shortly to talk with me. When he arrived, it was evident that he was upset—and he brought unpleasant news. He had come to explain to me the reason for his uncle's visit.

Oscar had received a letter from one of the Filipino doctors in OB complaining about Dr. Vic Wycoco—and the contents of that letter had brought about Oscar's sudden visit.

Vic Wycoco was the chief of staff of OB—with responsibility for the conduct and performance of the Filipino doctors, and the organization and operation of the clinical services. Under Vitoy's administrative talent, Vic and Toots Calderon (the nursing supervisor) provided the professional leadership that made OB a first-rate medical and public health service. Dr. Wycoco insisted on a high standard of discipline and performance, and wouldn't tolerate the least laxness or negligence by any of the doctors. Some of them considered him unduly harsh and dictatorial, and would like to have seen him replaced.

Vic was a handsome, athletic man in his mid-thirties. He dominated the periodic tennis tournaments in the international community, and was a gifted dancer and singer. His artistic and intellectual interests were considerable, and he had many friends outside of OB. If any of us were having a big party, we often prevailed on Vic to help with the planning and decorations. He knew good food and drink, and if he supervised the preparations, the party was always a success.

It was generally known throughout the international community that Vic was gay. However, I never knew him to have an overt love affair, and there was never any public evidence of his sexual preference. On the other hand, he was too honest and had too much integrity to try to hide his homosexuality from his friends.

Oscar had received a letter from one of the OB doctors complaining that Vic was sexually involved with some of the men in the foreign community, and was causing considerable embarrassment to the people in OB. The letter had been sent without Vitoy's knowledge. The doctor who had written the letter wasn't performing well, and Vic had found it necessary to reprimand him on several occasions. On the last such occasion the erring doctor had been very hostile and uncooperative. As a consequence, Vic recommended to Vitoy that he terminate the doctor's contract. However, Vitoy, Vic, and Pat discussed the matter, and since the doctor in question would soon depart on home leave, they decided to wait until that time to terminate the contract, and save him some embarrassment

The letter to Oscar was a deliberate lie and a vengeful attempt to discredit and hurt Vic—who was liked and respected by the ambassador, the minister of health, the majority of the Filipino and foreign community, and was no embarrassment to anyone.

Unfortunately, when Oscar received the letter, he looked on it as a very grave matter which he needed to straighten out immediately. He should have notified Vitoy, of course, and asked him to look into things and to take whatever action that needed to be taken. Instead, in his self-righteous outrage, he swooped down on Vientiane to cleanse it of the sinful and morally dangerous presence of Dr. Wycoco. Oscar's code of ethics was something out of the Philippines' Jesuit colonial past.

Vitoy told me he'd been trying to talk some sense into Oscar, but he wasn't very successful. Oscar insisted that since Vitoy and everyone else freely admitted that Vic was homosexual—even if the disgruntled doctor's accusations were false on the other points—Vic had to go. I asked Vitoy to make arrangements for me to talk to Oscar the next morning, and I would try to persuade him to drop the matter. Vitoy said he would set up a meeting, but it was evident he wasn't very optimistic that I could sway Uncle Oscar in any way.

The next morning I was sitting in the office trying to decide on the best way to approach Oscar when the secretary told me that Vitoy was on the phone. Vic had packed his belongings during the night and left them with one of his friends. Without saying anything to anyone, he'd departed the country alone. He had written a letter of resignation for Vitoy, and apologized for leaving so suddenly without any advance notice or saying goodbye to anyone.

Vitoy, Pat, and I were heartbroken and grieved, not just for the loss of our dear friend, but for the pain he must be suffering and the darkness and bigotry in this sad world.

I never saw Oscar Orellano again. He died soon after of a heart attack.

The Ban Houi Sai Hospital Saga

As one travels upriver on the Mekong, the last river port of any importance in Laos before reaching China is called Ban Houi Sai. This nondescript little town of fewer than 3,000 people is strung out along the northeast bank for about two kilometers. Most of the dwellings and shops are built on the one rough, dusty street that parallels the river, which—at this point—passes through a rocky defile and is much narrower than usual. This causes a 15-meter difference between flood and low water, and many of the wooden, tin-roofed houses and shops cling to the steep bank and hang out over the water on tall pilings.

On a high hill overlooking the town is an old French fort—called Carnot—whose guns controlled the traffic on the river, both in and out of Burma and China, during colonial days. Nowadays, Fort Carnot's thick, red-brick walls are crumbling away, and its guns are a mass of rust.

At the time of the Vietnam War, Ban Houi Sai was the capital of Nam Tha province. When the communists took over in 1975, the province was divided into three parts: Bokeo and Nam Tha provinces, and the western half of Udomsai province. The government compound sat on a narrow ridge along the one street, shaded by huge tamarind trees, and perfumed by old, gnarled plumeria. The buildings were relics of the French colonial past, painted the usual horrible mustard color seen throughout French Indochina. The *chao kweng's* residence and office were also there, along with the other government offices and the provincial hospital.

From 1962, two of the old buildings were used by the Tom Dooley Foundation (Dr. Thomas Anthony Dooley, American physician, author, and philanthropist established the hospital just before his death of lung cancer in 1961 at age 34); one served as a residence for the expatriate staff, and the other was converted to a small hospital. The provincial hospital had no surgical capability, and the Dooley facility was supposed to provide this service.

The northern part of the province that borders on China was controlled by the Pathet Lao and Vietnamese. This communist area of control included the major towns of Muang Sing and Nam Tha—the town for which the province is named. Two hundred kilometers of rough, hilly terrain separates Ban Houi Sai from Muang Sing and Nam Tha.

Although small in number, the dominant ethnic group—from a military standpoint—in the hill area were the Yao. Recent Sinitic tribal migrants from Southern China, they resemble the Meo in many ways.

The Yao were strongly anti-communist, and were the main obstacle in the path of the Pathet Lao moving down to the Mekong and Ban Houi Sai. There were also Meo and Lao Theung tribal groups in the area who opposed the communists, but they didn't have the coherence and strong leadership of the Yao.

Under pressure from the Pathet Lao and Vietnamese, many Yao, Meo, and Lao Theung had been displaced from their villages. The US was helping these refugees to re-establish themselves in new areas through the refugee relief program, which was run by Joe Flipse in that area.

The Yao and the other partisan military forces in the area were trained and supported by the FAR. They were assisted by a CIA field operations officer and a small group of Thai military specialists. The CIA officer was William (Bill) Young, an American born in Burma, whose parents and grandparents had been Christian missionaries.

The Young's were first chased out of China by the communists, then out of Burma, and into Thailand. Bill's first language was Red Lahou, and he didn't learn to speak English until he started school. He spoke fluent Lao and Thai, as well as well as several of the tribal languages.

Bill based his operation in Chiang Khong, the small Thai town directly across the river from Ban Houi Sai. He was a handsome young man with a quiet, polite manner and a pleasant personality. In addition to working with the Lao partisan groups, he also infiltrated intelligence teams into Southern China to monitor Vietnamese communications. The Vietnamese used the regular Chinese telephone system for communications with their forces in Northwest Laos—and the intelligence teams simply tapped the phone lines and plugged in their tape recorders.

Bill and Joe liked and respected each other, and worked well together. By sharing resources in aircraft and commodities, and helping each other as much as possible, both activities were benefited. They ran a good operation that was important to the partisan effort, and contributed greatly to its success.

The center of refugee activities was located at Nam Thoui, a Yao village about fifty kilometers north of Ban Houi Sai. Chao Mai, the hereditary leader of the Yao, lived there with his younger brother, Chao La. Yao tribal affairs, inter-tribal affairs, refugee relief, and liaison with the FAR and RLG, were all handled by Chao Mai. Chao La was the military commander and led the Yao partisan troops.

Bill Taylor, a young American veterinarian, and Joe Flipse had lived at Nam Thoui with Chao Mai when they were both with the IVS. The two young Americans had helped resettle the Yao refugees, and worked on various community development projects with them. Bill Taylor had tried to start a small health care program, and had sent a few Yao and Lao Theung boys to Sam Thong for training. There had been some success, but when I arrived in 1963, the medical program was having several problems. First, the only source of drugs and medical supplies was from Sam Thong, and Pop was rapidly running out of these resources. Second, Bill and Joe had no funds for salaries and other operating expenses. Also, the sending of students to Sam Thong wasn't working out very well because of language differences and the separation from family and friends.

Late in 1963, Pop took me to Nam Thoui to meet Chao Mai and take a look at the medical program. At that time, I became aware of the problems mentioned above, and promised Chao Mai that we'd try to solve them.

Soon after this visit, Bill Taylor finished his tour with IVS and returned to the US. Joe Flipse was hired by USAID, and became the USAID operations officer for Northwestern Laos. He moved from Nam Thoui to Ban Houi Sai, and set up an office at the airstrip.

Over a period of time, we were able to develop a training school at Nam Thoui for both civilian and military medics. A medical supply warehouse was built at the strip next to Joe's office in Ban Houi Sai that served the whole Northwestern region. In addition to the training school at Nam Thoui, we also established a large dispensary hospital there. This facility was run by a Burmese refugee named Doctor Duon.

The title "Doctor" was something of an honorific. Doun had been a senior medical student in Rangoon at the time Ne Win had overthrown U Nu in 1962. He belonged to a student group which opposed Ne Win in the coup, and was arrested and thrown in jail. After several months in prison, he was able to escape and make his way to Laos. How he happened to end up at Nam Thoui was a mystery I never solved. In any event, we were able to recruit several of the young Yao girls and give them on-the-job training as practical nurses.

Chao Mai wasn't nearly so rigid in his thinking as VP, and he encouraged the girls to become nurses. With the nurses and about a half dozen of the male medics, Doctor Duon was able to run a fairly effective medical service. At least we had a place to take better care of the battle casualties than before. The seriously wounded were evacuated to the Dooley hospital, but the Nam Thoui facility enabled us to keep the evacuees down to a minimum.

By this time, I had plenty of funding to pay operating expenses and salaries. The drugs and supplies were flowing out of the Department of Defense medical depot in Okinawa into our huge, new medical warehouse in Vientiane, and the simple health delivery system we had devised was working well out in the countryside.

However, there was still the serious problem of better and more definitive care for the increasing number of battle casualties. The RLG hospital at Ban Houi Sai was very small, and was poorly equipped and supplied. More important, it had only one *medcin assistant*, Doctor Phouy, who was also the *medcin chef* (Chief provincial health officer) of Nam Tha province. Phouy had no surgical capability, and was also dependent on Dooley for surgical care.

There were two Doctor Phouy's in the Ministry of Health. One was director general of the ministry, and was known as Phouy Luang (golden) because of the yellow color of his skin. Phouy in Ban Houi Sai was distinguished by the name, Phouy Lek (iron). He was a thin, fragile little man, and the name seemed to be a joke. He also had a terrible reputation for being uncooperative, dishonest, and mean—particularly in the opinion of the Dooley people. However, we found him to be quite different. As it turned out, he was certainly a man of integrity and courage; a tireless worker, and we always had his full cooperation. The name Phouy Lek was entirely appropriate.

Dr. Tom Dooley established a small hospital in the town of Muang Sing in the late fifties. When the communists took the towns of Luang Nam Tha and Muang Sing in 1962, the hospital was moved to Ban Houi Sai. After Dr. Dooley's untimely death, the hospital continued to function with volunteer, expatriate personnel—mostly American and a few Lao medical auxiliaries, whom the expatriates trained and paid. These field activities were financed by fund-raising drives in the United States conducted by the Dooley Foundation.

Later, the Dooley Foundation set up a similar medical operation at Khong Island in Southern Laos. They also attempted to operate a mobile medical clinic on the Mekong, using a river boat. In addition, a health survey program was undertaken in Nepal for a short time in the early sixties.

All these were modest activities, but costs far exceeded the funds that reached the field from the Dooley headquarters in San Francisco. The two little Lao hospitals were always out of drugs and medical supplies, and there was no money for transportation when things did arrive in Vientiane from the US. The expatriates seldom received their living allowance, nor the Lao employees their salaries on which they and their families were dependent. I'm sure there were many times when both staff and patients went hungry.

The resident expatriate and Lao staff were hard-working and dedicated, and did the best they could under such adverse circumstances. To augment the resident staff, and to create favorable publicity, the headquarters in San Francisco had promoted a special program in which airline hostesses spent two or three weeks of their vacation at one of the Lao hospitals. Many of these girls had backgrounds in nursing or other medical fields, and potentially could be very helpful. However, under the circumstances, the "Dooley Dollies" as they were called, were more of a burden than an asset.

As American officials trying to help the Lao in their desperate struggle against the Vietnamese and Pathet Lao, Joe Flipse, Bill Young, and I wanted the Dooley Foundation to make the best effort possible. Particularly, since they were a private American organization, it was important to us that they be successful. As a consequence, we tried to give them all the support we could when we realized the serious problems they faced.

Bill and Joe helped them with local transportation and in-country air travel. They diverted food, gasoline, and other commodities from their own projects, and also helped them with maintenance. I saw that the hospitals (Ban Houi Sai and Khong Island) were stocked with drugs and medical supplies. Finally, in desperation, I put their employees on our project payrolls so they wouldn't lose them. This was all highly illegal, of course, and done without official approval, but we felt such a good cause was worthy of extreme measures.

Dr. Verne Chaney who headed the Dooley Foundation, would come out to Laos from San Francisco every several months for a few days on inspection trips. He would object most strenuously to our meddling in his private affairs, and insisted that our assistance wasn't necessary. Chaney would also forbid the Dooley people to accept our help, knowing full well that nothing would change after he left.

I had hoped to work out some arrangement with Chaney where USAID would put the necessary resources into the Ban Houi Sai hospital to take care of the mounting battle casualty problem. Unfortunately, it became increasingly clear that Chaney wouldn't accept any official or overt relationship with the US government. He was quite happy with the present arrangement, in which we were taking him off the hook without any obligation on his part.

Vitoy and I had discussed with the *chao kweng* putting an OB team into the RLG hospital at Ban Houi Sai. After that meeting, I went over the casualty problem with Charley Mann and Ambassador Whitehouse, and received approval to go ahead and put the OB team in place. We would make some repairs to the old RLG hospital, and put some new equipment into it. At some point in the future, when we could get budgetary approval from Washington, we'd build a new hospital to serve the area.

Vitoy rented a house for the OB staff, and got them up to Ban Houi Sai. Bingcam—the OB maintenance chief, and Dr. Phouy started fixing up the hospital. About this time, Joe Flipse finished his tour with USAID and decided to go back to the US permanently. Joe was replaced by Tony Caterucci. Bill Young took a civilian job in Thailand, but his replacement was killed in an aircraft accident shortly after arriving in Ban Houi Sai. The replacement was in turn replaced by Tony Poe, who'd been working with VP at Long Chieng.

It was also about this time that I left for my second home leave. The war was heating up, and we were terribly busy at the time, but reluctantly I took off for the States. Tony Caterucci, Tony Poe, and I were good friends, and had worked together in other areas of Laos. Before leaving, I briefed them on my plans about fixing up the old RLG hospital, and—at some time in the future when funds were available—building a new hospital.

The day after I returned from leave, some three months later, Vitoy was in my office in Vientiane bringing me up to date on what had happened while I was away. When we got around to discussing Ban Houi Sai, I immediately sensed something was wrong. Vitoy reluctantly told me that the two Tony's had got together with the *chao kweng,* and decided to go ahead and build a hospital. The *chao kweng* had acquired a building site, and they'd started construction about a month previously.

I couldn't believe what I was hearing. Where was the money coming from? Who did the plans? Who was doing the construction?

Vitoy said that he'd tried to stop it, or at least delay it until I got back, but had been unsuccessful.

It transpired that Bingcam had drawn up some rudimentary plans, and apparently Tony Poe had diverted some CIA money from his budget to finance the project. There had been heavy fighting in Xieng Khoung and Sam Neua while I was gone. Tens of thousands of people had been displaced, and the hospitals were filled with casualties. It was necessary that I spend some time in that area—but as soon as I could, Vitoy and I went to Ban Houi Sai.

Tony Caterucci met us at the airstrip. Tony was a tall, slightly pudgy young man in his mid-twenties, with black curly hair and a pleasant, friendly personality. Before joining USAID, he'd been in the Peace Corps and was sent to Colombia, South America. In Colombia, he'd met Rosie, a charming beauty, fallen in love, and married her. They had a little boy, Tonito, about two years old, and Rosie was pregnant again. Pat and I loved the three Caterucci's, and we spent a lot of time together. We thought of them more as part of the family than just friends.

Tony came up to the plane and greeted us warmly. "Hi Doc. Hi Vitoy. Good to see you back. How was your vacation?"

"Fine, Tony. Now, what in the hell's this about you and Tony Poe building a hospital?"

"Ah. You don't sound too happy about it. I was afraid of that. I told Tony we should wait until you got back, but you know how hard-headed he is."

"You're damn well right, I'm not too happy about it. Let's go to your office and go over the plans and cost estimates and check your funding."

"Well, there's not much at the office, Doc. Bingcam has the only set of plans on site, and Tony's putting up all the money."

"Okay, let's go see Bingcam. Have someone call Tony on the radio and tell him to get his ass down here right away. I want to talk to him, too."

Tony Poe had moved Bill Young's operation out of Chiang Khong, across the Mekong from Ban Houi Sai, to Nam You—a site next to Nam Thoui, near Chao Mai's headquarters; a set-up similar to Sam Thong-Long Chieng.

We got in Tony's jeep and drove into town where Bingcam was building the hospital. The site was just out of the main business area on the side of a small hill. There had been some levelling of the ground, but it looked as if the side of the hill would wash into the building with the first rain. Although it hadn't rained in some time, water was seeping out of the ground. They were building the damn thing on top of a spring.

Some thin brick walls were going up, but there was no real foundation, nor any columns or beams. The thing looked like a disaster to me. I asked Bingcam to see the plans, and he gave me a couple of sheets of dirty paper with some pencil sketches on them. There wasn't even a materials list.

About that time, a Pilatus Porter buzzed the site and circled twice before disappearing toward the airstrip. Before long, one of the boys that worked at the strip drove up with Tony Poe.

"Hey Doc, good to see you. How was the States? What do you think of the hospital? Good deal huh?"

"Tony says you're financing this goddamn thing. How much money do you have?"

"Well, don't act so mad. Christ, we're just trying to build you a hospital. You'd think we'd committed a crime. You know how many guys are getting shot up?"

"Tony, how much money do you have?"

"Fifteen thousand."

"Jesus, Tony, do you have any idea what it costs to build a halfway decent hospital—even here?"

" Well no, not exactly. But if we need some more, I can scrounge up another two or three thousand."

I was sick. Vitoy, Tony Caterucci, Tony Poe—three of my best buddies—doing this to me. At that moment I could have killed all three of them. We had built so many bamboo-and-thatch hospitals in the refugee areas, I guess they were thinking in the same terms.

We could get by with those in the emergency situations, but facilities in the stable areas that (it was hoped) would become part of the infrastructure of the RLG had to be of modern, permanent construction. It had to be something that we could take pride in being the donor of. Since they'd made a commitment to the *chao kweng* and the people of the community, it was almost impossible to back out of the project. If we did, we'd lose a lot of face.

Certainly we needed the hospital, but we had no funds to build it. I had planned to put such a project into that current year's budget proposal, and—

if it was approved—the funds would be available in about 18 months at the earliest. We had made some estimates for a simple, but appropriate, forty-bed hospital—and the construction costs would be about 300,000 dollars. With equipment and furnishings, the two Tony's had committed me to about 500,000 dollars we didn't have.

Equipment and furnishings weren't really a problem, as I could order such items from the Department of Defense depot in Okinawa and pay for them out of our general commodity funding. I wouldn't specifically identify the items as being for a new hospital, and they would look like routine replacement items. But where could I steal the additional 300,000 dollars?

Vitoy and I went to see the *chao kweng,* and all he could talk about was the new hospital and how badly it was needed. I had a nauseating feeling in the pit of my stomach, and couldn't raise the courage to tell him that we didn't have any money to build a hospital. After leaving the *chao kweng's* office, we visited Dr. Phouy and the OB medical team that was helping him. Again, everyone was talking about the new hospital. My morale was taking a real beating.

That evening, we went over to the Caterucci's for dinner. I was in a terrible mood, but after eating some of Rosie's good food and playing with little Tonito, I decided not to murder Tony and deprive them of a husband and father. Suddenly, as I watched the pregnant mother and her little son, a thought sprang to mind. Maternal and child health—that was where we'd get the money to build the hospital!

This was at a time when the United States first started to focus on the world population problem. Foreign assistance in family planning and population control had high priority, and large sums of money were being appropriated by Congress for this purpose.

Initially, the policy-makers in USAID Washington had tried to use the population funds in a very narrow context from a programmatic standpoint. They would provide the developing countries that wanted to start population control programs with all the contraceptive pills, condoms, IUDs, and sterilization equipment they wanted. In fact, much more than was wanted or could be used in many cases. However, there was little funding available for such important aspects of family planning as maternal and child health programs.

Finally, after several years of protest from the USAID people working in the field, Washington changed this simplistic and unreasonable policy. Funds became available to support maternal and child health programs.

Someone finally got the message that mothers wouldn't limit the number of births unless there was a good chance of their children surviving into adulthood.

At the time of the Ban Houi Sai hospital crisis, we had just received funding for the construction of three maternal and child health centers. One project would be the construction of the National Maternal and Child Health Center in Vientiane, and the other two were smaller projects in two of the provincial capitals. The planning phase of the larger, national project in Vientiane, and of one of the smaller projects at Pakse, were completed—and agreements had been signed by the Ministry of Health. However, the second small project—tentatively scheduled for Savannakhet—was still under study.

The Savannakhet provincial hospital had an old, but well-constructed building that was being used for female medicine and obstetrics and gynecology. I had been discussing with Khamphay Abhay, the minister of health, the possibility of renovating the old building, making it the maternal and child health center, and using the construction funds at some other provincial site. For political reasons Khamphay was opposed to the change. If we didn't go ahead and put up an impressive new building in Savannakhet, he would get all sorts of criticism. Nevertheless, stealing the population money from the maternal and child health program seemed to be the only way to get the Ban Houi Sai hospital built.

The first step was to get Charley Mann's approval, and that might not be easy. He would know that both the auditors from USAID Washington, and particularly the General Accounting Office (GAO), would undoubtedly give us a bad time if they saw that we'd used population money to build a general hospital. As soon as I returned to Vientiane, I talked to Charley. By making a big point of how foolish we'd look if the hospital wasn't built, and the rather desperate need for a place to take care of the casualties, he finally agreed.

As soon as Charley gave his okay, I started over to Khamphay's office, but then changed my mind. In a couple of days, Pat and I were having a party for Dr. Jim Liston from the UK—a delightful old colonial from Scotland. At that time, Jim was the administrator for all the UK's foreign medical projects. There were two British medical teams in the country under the Colombo Plan, and Jim was making his annual visit to inspect them. Most of the foreign medical community, along with Khamphay and his staff, would be at the party.

Whenever Khamphay and I got together at a party, at his house or ours, we always stayed until everyone else had left, and usually talked most of the night—getting more business done than was possible at our offices. This was especially true if both of our wives were with us. Since all four of us were doctors, there was a rather close personal relationship. After the party, when everyone had left and only the four of us remained—that would be the time to get Khamphay's agreement on the Ban Houi Sai project.

Fortunately, it all turned out as planned. When we got down to the last bottle of Mateus about three o'clock in the morning, using the Savannakhet maternal and child health funds for Ban Houi Sai sounded like a great idea.

The next day, I got together with Tom Cole and gave him the background on the Ban Houi Sai situation. Tom promised he'd get the thing straightened out and start the construction as soon as we could get some plans drawn up.

About six months later, Ambassador Whitehouse and Khamphay cut the ribbon on the finest forty-bed hospital in that part of the world. Of course, it was the only modern facility in the Golden Triangle, and its fame spread rapidly. Patients sneaking in from China, Burma, and even Northern Thailand became a problem at times. However, there were no politics once you entered the door, and Dr. Phouy and the OB team took care of anyone who showed up—including Pathet Lao from time to time.

The *chao kweng*, the two Tony's, and Vitoy received the credit and appreciation of the community, while Charley Mann and I got crucified by the GAO and the Population Office in Washington.

I suppose it did seem a bit strange to see the big sign in front of the hospital—MATERNAL AND CHILD HEALTH CENTER—when most of the beds were occupied by wounded soldiers. It did have a small section for women and children, however, and Toots Calderon, the OB public health nurse, developed a very active and successful family planning program.

Public Works Program

D on Dougan and I had been inspecting the USAID-supported medical facilities out in the countryside in Central Laos at the end of 1972. We had just finished work, and were spending the night in Savannakhet in order to catch the milk run back to Vientiane the next day. Savannakhet, although a quiet, sleepy little town of only 15,000–20,000 people, was capital of the province of the same name, and an important administrative, military, and commercial center.

After checking into the Sensabay Number 2 Hotel and getting cleaned up, we had dinner at the local Chinese restaurant. The sweet and sour pork, roasted duck, fried rice, and several other dishes had almost wiped us out, so we decided to walk down to the river to revive ourselves. Savannakhet is a typical Lao river port, strung out along the east bank of the mighty Mekong. Many other people were sitting or strolling as they chatted and enjoyed the magnificent sunset and cool air from the river.

The path beside the river was bordered by colorful flamboyant, plumeria, and bougainvillea, and the sweet scent of jasmine filled the air. It was indeed a pleasant place to relax after a long, hot day, and both Don and I were reluctant to return to the Sensabay Number 2. Lao commercial hotels were unattractive and depressing at best, and the Sensabay certainly didn't fit into that category.

There was little to do in Savannakhet in the evening, and most public places closed by eight-thirty or nine o'clock. About the only places that stayed open were a couple of bars, one of which was near the river. Don suggested we drop in the bar and have a couple of beers rather than going back to the hotel. I was too full to drink beer, and I didn't care too much for Lao bars, but it was preferable to the Sensabay at that early hour of the evening.

The small, candle-lit place was actually rather attractive. Tastefully furnished in bamboo, and very clean, it had a quiet, pleasant atmosphere.

The proprietor-bartender was a Vietnamese lady in her forties or possibly older. No doubt, in her youth, she had been very pretty, but now—poor dear—she was somewhat frayed at the edges and had seen a lot of mileage. There were several young Lao girls in their mid- to late teens who served the drinks and talked to the customers. Of course, these lovely little dolls were also available for the night if one was so inclined.

We took a table, ordered two beers, and sat talking. Every now and then, one or two of the waitresses would sit down with us and try to start a conversation. Before long they would get bored and drift off when it became evident that we weren't interested. Business was slow that evening and there were only a couple of other customers in the place.

After a while, the Vietnamese lady came from behind the bar. "How are you this evening?" she said, as she sat at our table.

"Fine, thank you. Nice place you have here."

"Thank you, I'm glad you like it."

She introduced herself as Gao, then asked us our names.

"Doc," I replied, "and this is Don."

"It's a pleasure to meet you. Where are you from? I haven't seen you in the bar before."

She had either heard us speaking English, or correctly assumed we were American. Her English was precise and clear.

"We live in Vientiane. Just passing through."

"What do you do? Are you military?"

"No, not military. We work for the American government—USAID."

"Oh yes, I know Mr. Stone, the USAID man who lives here. Where are you staying?"

"At the Sensabay Number 2."

"That's good. I have two pretty young girls if you'd like to take them to the hotel."

"Well thank you, that's very kind," I said, smiling. "Maybe Don might be interested in one of the young girls, but I prefer older women, myself. You're a very lovely lady. Wouldn't you like to spend the night with me?"

"Oh no. I couldn't do that. I'm married. I don't go out with the customers."

To my surprise and amusement the old gal had taken me seriously.

"How much does it cost to take one of the girls for the night?" I asked her.

"Only 2,500 kip [five dollars]."

I couldn't resist pushing her on a little. "Okay, if the girls get 2,500, I'll give you 5,000."

She hesitated several seconds before answering, "No, I told you, I don't go out with the customers."

Nevertheless, her voice was weak and had lost much of its conviction. I was certain that if I increased the offer another 1,000 or 2,000 kip, she'd be ready to jump into bed. It was time to drop the subject before it backfired on me

"Well, if you won't go to bed with me," I added, "let me buy you a drink."

I could see that she was mentally kicking herself for turning down the 5,000, but she'd lose face if she accepted now. We sipped our beer and made small talk.

The other customers left, and eventually all the girls joined us and we bought them drinks. The conversation shifted from English to Lao. There were five girls in the place, and two of them had just arrived in Savannakhet. These two were friends from the same small village out in the countryside. Both of them were lovely, and so sweet and innocent-looking that my curiosity was aroused as to who they were and how they had come to work in a bar.

"What's the name of your village?" I asked.

"Nong Bua Deng," one of them answered.

"Where's that?"

"About fifty kilometers from here, on the way to Pakse."

"How big is Nong Bua Deng?"

"Very big. About 150 houses [approximately 900 people]."

"Why did you come to Savannakhet and work in the bar?"

"The village council asked us to do it."

I was even more intrigued. In Laos, village councils were composed of all the heads of families. This body decided all issues of general interest to the village—whether economic, social, political, or development-related. By tradition, a consensus of the members had the force of law, even though the councils had no legal status.

Even I, as a foreigner, was surprised at that information. "That sounds strange to me," I told the girl. "I've never heard of such a thing. You mean the village council forced you to come here and work in the bar?"

"No, they didn't force us. They just asked us to do it, and we agreed."

This was extremely bizarre, and I couldn't conceive of a village council doing such a thing. However, after further questioning—and drinks—the two girls' presence in the bar was explained as follows.

Nong Bua Deng was a poor, rice paddy village about three kilometers off Route 13—the highway that follows the Mekong through Laos on its way to Saigon. The road from their village to the highway was through a low, swampy, poorly-drained area. For much of the year, it was impossible for motor vehicles to get to the village, and particularly in the rainy season, even ox carts would bog down. Communication and transportation to and from Savannakhet was vital to the economic welfare of the village, and—to a certain extent—to its security.

The villagers had tried on several occasions to get the government to build a road from the highway to Nong Bua Deng. When that failed, they had tried to build the road with their hand tools and local materials. Again, they weren't successful. If they were to have a road that would last through the rainy season, it would be necessary for trucks to bring in laterite for fill, and gravel for surfacing—and that would be very expensive. Even when the villagers had scraped together all the money they had, and had sold everything they could get their hands on, there still wasn't enough to build the road.

After much deliberation, someone in the village council had come up with the idea of sending the girls to work as prostitutes in Savannakhet. Several years before, this respected member had been in Savannakhet, and while drunk, had blown all his money—1,000 kip (two dollars)—on a few moments of bliss with an attractive young woman. When he sobered up, he was greatly impressed at the way such large sums of money could be made so quickly by a pretty girl.

After considerable discussion, the village council decided to make a proposal based on the member's experience. First, they selected the two most attractive 16-year-old girls in the village. The problem about the necessity for the road, and their inability to raise enough money to build it, was carefully explained to the girls. If they would go to work in Savannakhet and donate their earnings to the village for the road project, they could marry any of the boys in the village of their choosing. Moreover, the villagers would get together and build good houses for them, complete with the usual furnishings. There would be a big wedding party, and the villagers would provide all the food and drink.

The girls agreed to this exciting and generous proposal without hesitation.

Two of the men took the girls into town, and they talked to Gao. She agreed to take the girls into the bar. They would be well cared for, and she would teach them the tricks of the trade. Their earnings would be divided evenly with their benefactor, and the girls could keep all their tips. She would see that they saved their money and sent it to the village council each month.

It was estimated that the road project would require an additional 250,000 kip (500 dollars). If things went well, they should be able to raise the money in ten months to a year. Since the lady had a reputation for honesty and integrity, the girls were left in her care without misgiving. The representatives of the village council returned to Nong Bua Deng to report the successful accomplishment of their mission.

The next day, Don and I returned to Vientiane, and I forgot about the fascinating little public works project going on in Nong Bua Deng.

✪✪✪

About a year and a half later, I decided to drive from Vientiane to Pakse. It was at one of the few times that the security along Route 13 which connected the two towns would permit such a trip. We were driving along about fifty kilometers south of Savannakhet when I suddenly saw a side road with a neat white sign—NONG BUA DENG 3 KM. I had the driver stop and back the jeep up to where I could see down the road. A smooth ribbon of laterite and gravel stretched across the paddy fields and disappeared around a small hill.

It was obvious that the girls in the bar had raised the 250,000 kip, and the village council had completed the road. Suddenly, the question struck me: Had the council kept its promise to the two girls? Did the story have a happy ending?

I was strongly tempted to drive down the road to Nong Bua Deng to find the answer. However, it was getting late, and I decided there wasn't time.

Several months later, I was in Savannakhet again. The USAID area co-ordinator, Sandy Stone, had received a request from the local *medecin chef* for help in building a medical dispensary in Nong Bua Deng. Sandy asked me to check out the area and see if USAID should undertake the project. Finally, I would have the opportunity to find how things had turned out for the girls. I told the story to Xom, the Lao medic supervisor for the Savannakhet area who was helping me, and asked him to discreetly ask about the girls when we visited Nong Bua Deng.

USAID didn't build a dispensary at Nong Bua Deng, because a Christian missionary group moved into the area and undertook the project themselves—thus relieving us of the necessity. However, when Xom and I surveyed the village, we learned that the girls were happily married and living in their new homes. One was already a mother, and the other soon would be.

According to Xom's informant, the party to celebrate the double wedding had been a joyous and lively affair that the villagers would long remember. The village council had certainly lived up to their promise. We found the road from the main highway to the village in excellent condition, even though it was in the middle of the rainy season.

Disintegration

By mid-1971 the military and political situation began to deteriorate badly. The attempt to turn the partisan military operation in Northern Laos into a conventional fighting force was an overwhelming disaster for VP and the Meo. The policy of using Lao military assets to tie up Vietnamese units in set-piece battles to relieve pressure in South Vietnam decimated the male population.

The old guerrillas—the FAR BV26 and BV27 units—that were once the hardcore of resistance in Sam Neua now existed in name only. Most of the original officers and men were dead. They had been sacrificed defending Na Khang and Pha Thi. All of Sam Neua—the key to holding Laos—had been lost, and Boum Long was the only site remaining north of the Plain of Jars. Sam Thong had been overrun, and Long Chieng was under constant siege, making it impossible to use the hospital there.

We had anticipated the fall of Sam Thong, and so constructed a 1,000-meter, all-weather airstrip at Ban Son, fifty kilometers south of Sam Thong. Ban Son was on the new road that had been built from Vientiane to Long Chieng. The new location had the important advantage of both surface and air support. However, the loss of Sam Thong was a severe blow to the morale of both the Lao and the Americans.

There was recurrent and desperate fighting around Long Chieng. On two occasions, the enemy penetrated the town, and all the civilian population had to flee. Massive bombing by US forces only prolonged the agony. The horrible attrition suffered by VP's Meo forces reduced them to the point where they could no longer defend themselves. The place was only saved by ethnic Lao FAR troops from other military regions, and by Thai mercenaries.

All the refugee and medical operations based at Sam Thong and Long Chieng were transferred to Ban Son. Here, we converted the old public works road camp into a new, 200-bed hospital, and staffed it with the medical personnel from both the Sam Thong and Long Chieng hospitals.

All four of the OB hospitals in Southern Laos—at Attopeu, Saravane, Paksong, and Wapikhamtong—had been overrun and destroyed. We had moved the Paksong team into Pakse to operate a newly-constructed, USAID-financed hospital. This was our only remaining hospital operation in Southern Laos. At the same time, most of the dispensaries on the Bolovens Plateau, around Saravane, and in the Sedone Valley had also been lost.

In Central Laos, the OB hospital outside of Savannakhet at Kengkok had been destroyed by enemy action. The enemy had warned the OB staff of the impending attack, and they escaped unscathed. A small American missionary group that worked in the area had been captured, and three or four of them remained prisoners until the peace accord was signed. One poor woman had been tied to a post in the missionary dwelling and the building was set on fire. She was burnt alive. Even though the enemy withdrew after the Kengkok attack, we didn't try to re-establish the hospital.

The dozen or so little enclaves we controlled in Phong Saly and Northern Luang Prabang were lost, too. Lao Tha, our main site in Northern Luang Prabang, had been destroyed by a Chinese military unit who massacred a large number of the civilians that they captured. The Chinese forced the captives to dig a large trench, then shot all of them and buried them. The attack took place in the middle of the night and the Chinese were gone the next morning. It seemed that we had tried to operate too close and too actively in an area where the Chinese were working with the Pathet Lao. This was probably the only instance of Chinese troops being involved during the war. The operations in Northwest Laos remained more or less stable.

In the early seventies—I don't recall exactly when—the US mission in Vietnam requested that I go to Vietnam on temporary duty for a few days. Ambassador Robert Komer had just been put in charge of the Vietnam counter-insurgency program, and apparently William Colby, who was in charge of all CIA field operations in Southeast Asia, was favorably impressed with what we were doing in Laos.

Colby and I became acquainted over the years when he visited in Laos, and he suggested to Komer that I might be a good candidate to run the health component of the counter-insurgency program in Vietnam. Although I had no intention of leaving Laos, I agreed to go to Saigon to see what was happening—mostly out of curiosity.

I saw Komer only briefly at dinner on the night of my arrival. He was a crude, arrogant, unpleasant, unimpressive man. In my opinion, he was hardly the type to be running a counter-insurgency program in Vietnam, or any other place. He was certainly not someone I should like to work under, in any circumstance. He turned me over to some of his staff, who showed me most of the bars and brothels in Saigon.

Lunch the next day lasted from noon to three in the afternoon. The main dishes were Martinis and nude waitresses. No one seemed to know why I was in Saigon. The place was a chaotic nightmare. There was an air of doom and fatalism—so what the hell, live it up.

I got on the plane for Vientiane, shocked and depressed. What difference did it make what happened in Laos with a situation like this in Vietnam?

In October 1972, peace talks began between the Vientiane government and the Pathet Lao. In the following February, the rival factions signed a ceasefire agreement, establishing a new coalition government. At the same time, of course, events were occurring in Vietnam that would culminate in the last American troops leaving that country in March 1973.

The Pathet Lao and the Vietnamese used the repeated ceasefire agreements—which they signed, and immediately broke—to mass troops and supplies for the final assault and takeover of the governments of both Laos and Vietnam.

No such assault was ever necessary in Laos. The Pathet Lao took over by default. The people of the United States and Congress were abandoning our allies as quickly as possible—and soon cut off all military assistance to Indochina. It was only a matter of time now until the enemy finally took over.

As it became obvious in Laos that these gentle people would be conquered by their ancient enemy, it was increasingly difficult to maintain an atmosphere of enthusiasm and optimism. Every day became a grinding chore. An air of cynicism and distrust permeated the relationship between the Americans and their Lao counterparts. It was the most painful and depressing time of my life. The Great Depression; fighting the Japanese in World War II; deaths in the family—those episodes were a picnic compared to the last two years in Laos.

✪ ✪ ✪

Pop had taken medical retirement from USAID, and was running a small school for the blind in Vientiane. The old man had been completely demoralized by his beloved America turning its back on their friends. His pride in being an American was destroyed, and he would never be able to look VP and the Meo in the eye again. VP had been so right. The Americans did to the Meo just what the British did to the Shan.

As before, by 1974 Pat and I hadn't been on home leave for almost four years. This time, not only did Washington insist that we return to the States on leave, but they also told us that we would not be given another overseas assignment until we had done a tour of duty in the US.

Including Samoa, it had been almost 14 years since we had lived in our homeland.

After considerable negotiation with Washington, and help from Charley Mann, we compromised on a year at the Harvard School of Public Health, instead of assignment to an office in Washington. This would give us an opportunity to refresh ourselves professionally, and also fulfil the bureaucracy's requirement that we rediscover our American heritage. We were to depart Laos in the first week of July of 1974, and be in Boston the first week of September.

At this point, all three of the children had departed Europe and were in school in California. Becky and Ray were at Pomona, and Walter was at Webb—a private high school nearby. Pat and I had always wanted to see the game parks in Africa, so we made plans to fly directly to Nairobi, and after the game parks take a boat up the Nile to Cairo. We hadn't been on vacation together for almost eight years.

About two weeks before our scheduled departure, Pat received a call from her mother in Biloxi that she was to have surgery the next week for a cancerous lesion of the colon. Pat left immediately for the States to be with her mother. The African safari was off.

When people approached me about going away parties, I lied to them, saying that my departure date had been postponed, and we'd get together later when I knew for certain when I would leave. I couldn't bear to say goodbye to my Lao friends.

The afternoon of July 4th, 1974, I slipped out to Wattay Airport alone and took the plane to Bangkok. It was a gray and gloomy day, and the monsoon was in full force.

I'm sure my fellow passengers were wondering why this foolish man was weeping alone.

The Lao episode was over. We had lost.

Epilogue

As I write this narrative 25 years after leaving Laos, time has softened my sorrow, and hopefully increased my objectivity. The world didn't end for the Lao when the communists took over.

There were vengeful murders and the horror of the Pathet Lao "re-education camps" for tens of thousands of Lao who adhered to the old regime. A fifth of the population fled the country and scattered all over the world. Most of them sought refuge in the United States. Those partisan groups who remained, particularly the Meo, were hunted down and slaughtered like wild, dangerous animals.

The Pathet Lao leadership that came out of the limestone caves of Northern Laos to take over the government was largely uneducated—and completely incompetent to function in a nation-building capacity. The country isolated itself, not so much as a political policy or through xenophobia or fear of the outside world, but rather from simple ignorance of how to proceed on a more constructive path. They seemed to prefer doing nothing rather than run the risk of doing the wrong thing.

Fortunately, in the last three or four years, things have started to change. The old, hardcore Pathet Lao cadre, with their close Vietnamese affiliations, are rapidly dying out. A new generation is taking their place.

Slowly, a market economy is developing. Tourism is increasing rapidly as accommodations become available. Foreign investment is encouraged in a steadily improving investment environment. Lao who fled the country are being encouraged to return. If they owned property before they left, and have their documents of ownership, their property is returned quickly with a minimum of red tape. The ones who have returned find they are welcome and well treated. As a consequence, the number of returnees, though small, is increasing rapidly. Most are young, well-educated entrepreneurs—which the country desperately needs.

With its spectacular natural beauty, an abundance of as-yet unexploited natural resources, and its kind and gentle people, Laos has a bright and happy future. One could even make the circuitous rationalization that the good guys eventually won. The Lao were sacrificed for our interest in Vietnam. The South Vietnamese were sacrificed for our interest in the supporters of their North Vietnamese opponents—the Chinese—so Nixon could go to Peking. American rapport with China forced the Russians to bankrupt themselves, and the communist regime to collapse and lose the cold war. Communism was contained. Democracy and the market economy prevailed!

✪✪✪

Of some of the protagonists after the communist takeover in 1975:

Pop retired in Bangkok. On New Year's Eve of 1981 he died peacefully in his sleep at the home of our old friend Lyle Brown, in Manila. Pop and Lyle were to drive to Legaspi in Southern Luzon that day, where I was on a two-year diving vacation.

Pat McCreedy retired in Biloxi, Mississippi where her parents lived. She died after a short illness in December 1997.

Father Bouchard continues his mission in the middle of Kalimantan— a ten-day trip upriver in his little wooden skiff with a 12-horsepower Evinrude.

General Vang Pao, his staff and their families were evacuated from Long Chieng to the US in May, 1975. Originally they were taken to Montana, but most moved to Los Angeles and Merced, California.

Of the original 23 officers of BV26 and BV27 in Sam Neua, only two survived—Major Duangtha is in Los Angeles, and Colonel Khamsao is in Manchester, Connecticut.

Vitoy Naranjo returned to his home town in the Philippines—Ilo Ilo on Panay—and has been very successful in several business enterprises.

Charley Mann retired in San Diego, California soon after leaving Laos. He passed away only a few months before publication of this book.

Many of the medics and nurses that went to Pop's "bootleg schools" and who were trained in the village health program ended up in the US, and have done extremely well. They function at a high level in various programs and institutions.

Most gratifying, these days, they proudly send me news that their son or daughter has finished university; just received a masters degree or a Ph.D; or has qualified as an MD.

As I was putting the finishing touches to the book, a man in his late forties stopped by unexpectedly at my home in Chiang Rai. He had worked for me in our medical supply facility at Ban Houi Sai. He was Yao, and his only schooling was six years in a primitive bamboo-and-thatch "bootleg school" at Nam Khung, a large refugee village upriver from Ban Houi Sai. He had emigrated to the US in 1975, and was on vacation in Thailand and Laos. In perfect English, he described to me the very successful business which he owns in Rockport, Illinois. He writes software for industrial robots.

Glossary and Acronyms

Ban	Village, home.
Bansee	List (particularly a roll of people).
BV	*Battalion Volontier* (Irregular infantry battalion staffed by FAR officers).
Caribou	Large twin engine STOL aircraft (Which can carry about 30 passengers or an equivalent amount of cargo. Made by De Havilland in Canada).
Chao kweng	Governor (Prince + Province).
Chao muang	District Chief (Prince + District).
CIA	The Central Intelligence Agency.
FAN	*Force Armee Neutraliste* (Neutralist Armed Forces).
FAR	*Forces Armee du Royaume* (Royal Armed Forces [rightist]).
GAO	General Accounting Office (Agency which audits government spending to see that it conforms to the law and intent of Congress).
Helio Courier	Single-engine, piston type, STOL aircraft.
IVS	International Voluntary Service (International organization which provides community development services to third-world countries. Preceded, and was a model for, the Peace Corps).
Kha	Mon-Khmer inhabitants of Laos, also referred to as Lao Toung.
Kweng	Province.
Lima	Prefix for airports in Laos (e.g. Lima 08 [Vientiane]).
Lima Site	Prefix for small airstrips in Laos (e.g. LS20 [Sam Thong])
Mae	Mother (Also a prefix for river names).
Meo	The Lao term for the Hmong (A hilltribe people found in Southern China, Vietnam, Thailand, and Laos).
Muang	District.

MR	Military Region
Nai ban	Village Chief (Mister + Village).
OB	Operation Brotherhood (Filipino hospital organization).
PDJ	The Plain of Jars (From the French, *Plaine des Jarres*—an area in Xieng Khoung province with many huge stone jars from an unknown era).
Pilatus Porter	Single-engine, turbo-prop, STOL aircraft (Originally for glacier landings. Normally configured for six or seven passengers, but frequently carried 12 or 14 with seats removed. Could land in 100 meters with no head wind. Replaced Helio Courier. Made in Switzerland).
PL	Pathet Lao (Revolutionaries under the control of the Marxist Lao Peoples Party. Used as a general term for Lao communists).
RLG	Royal Lao Government.
RON	Remain Overnight.
SAR	Search and Rescue (Most often applied to downed air crewmen).
STOL	Short Take-off and Landing (Specially designed aircraft for operating out of shorter-than-normal airstrips).
Tan	Sir (Honorific form of address—equivalent to Mr.).
Tan Maw	Doctor (Mister + Doctor).
Tasseng	Hamlet, hamlet chief.
USAID	United States Agency for International Development.
USIS	United States Information Service (The overseas division of the US Information Agency of the Department of State).
White Star	Code name for US Special Forces military assistance teams in Laos prior to 1962 Geneva Accords

About the Author (and Family)

The author, the youngest boy of 13 children, was born in the tiny lumbering town of St. James, Louisiana in 1920. His mother died when he was nine years old, and he was raised by an older sister in San Angelo, Texas.

After high school, he attended Texas Agricultural and Mechanical College and studied petroleum chemical engineering. He spent five years in the United States Marine Corps during World War II as an infantry officer, and fought in the Pacific theater against the Japanese.

After World War II, he entered medical school in New Orleans, and graduated from Louisiana State University School of Medicine in 1951. He also has a post graduate degree in International Health from the Harvard University School of Public Health.

His medical career started in pediatrics, but after one year he went into general practice in a rural area of Southern Louisiana.

Dr. Weldon has also lived and worked in Haiti, The Philippines, Cambodia, South Vietnam, South Korea, Saudi Arabia, and Thailand.

He retired to Chiang Rai, a small provincial capital and farming center in Northern Thailand, in 1987.

Dr. McCreedy and Dr. Weldon separated in 1981. She retired in Biloxi, Mississippi, and died in 1997. Rebecca, their oldest child lives in Chiang Rai with her Thai husband, Chulaphan "Jun" Sithivong and their three children. She is currently managing a project for the Tourist Authority of Thailand to create a cultural and anthropological museum for Northern Thailand.

Ray is professor of seismology at the University of Oregon, and collaborates with his colleagues in China, Mexico, France, Thailand, Kazakhstan, and Vietnam. He hopes to do some work in Laos in the near future.

Walter is a mechanical engineer and specializes in building high-tech, automated, computerized factories. In recent years he has built two such installations in Thailand, one in Indonesia, another in Romania, and is just starting one in Turkey.

Dr. Weldon married Nipaporn "Eo" Singhustita from Ubon, Thailand in 1982. Eo worked in Laos for Thai Airways during the Vietnam War years. Eo has a daughter, Tina, from a previous marriage who recently returned to Chiang Rai after several years in Anchorage, Alaska. Tina operates a car rental agency.